CHINA

CHINA

From the Long March to Tiananmen Square

by the writers and photographers of
THE ASSOCIATED PRESS

Foreword by
HARRISON SALISBURY

AURUM PRESS

PROJECT DIRECTOR: Dan Perkes
EDITOR: Norm Goldstein
WRITERS: James Abrams, Rick Gladstone, Norm Goldstein
PHOTO RESEARCHER: Robyn Beck
AP NEWS LIBRARY STAFF (Barbara Shapiro, director)

AP reporting by James Abrams, Donna Anderson, Dan Biers, Jeff Bradley, Phil Brown, Ina Chang, Charlene Fu, Rick Gladstone, Victoria Graham, Terril Jones, John Pomfret, John Roderick, Kathy Wilhelm

DESIGN AND DEVELOPMENT: Combined Books, Inc., 26 Summit Grove Avenue, Suite 207, Bryn Mawr, PA 19010
PRODUCED BY: Wieser & Wieser, Inc., 118 East 25th Street, New York, NY 10010

First published in Great Britain in 1990 by Aurum Press, Ltd., 33 Museum Street, London WC1A 1LD.

A CIP catalogue record for this book is available from the British Library.

ISBN 1-85410-156-0

First published in the USA by Henry Holt and Company, Inc.

Printed in the United States of America.

Contents

Foreword

The history of China in the 20th century is the history of a proud, ancient nation struggling to emerge from the quagmire of a feudal past and into the ranks of modern nationhood.

The years have been marked by turmoil, war, ignorance, famine, a decadent ruling class, oppression, native warlords, foreign conquerors. Amid all the murk have come some shafts of light—hope that ultimately the goals of national unity and a more advanced economic and social order may be achieved.

At the dawn of the century, China was a decaying empire, ruled by a cruel Dowager Empress. Almost half the nation's territory—including great cities—had been lost to foreigners who lived their own lives in foreign-ruled enclaves in which Chinese had no voice, no power and were present only by the leave of alien lords. Opium addicted the nation like a plague.

The year 1900 opened with the savage outbreak of the mystical Boxers, a cult that believed its members invincible to bullets, dedicated to driving foreigners from China. The Boxer Rebellion was put down in blood by foreign troops who ravaged Beijing, drove the Dowager Empress from her capital, looted the Forbidden City and put the empire into pawn.

China had no place to go but up.

The first stirrings came in 1911 when the rotting Manchu empire was overthrown and Dr. Sun Yat-sen was installed as president of an ephemeral republic. Sun fell, but the democratic goals he preached stayed alive. Students gave the movement a boost with a historic demonstration May 4, 1919. Soon, Sun and the fledgling Chinese Communist-Party joined forces in a move to unify the country. But this broke down in 1927 when Chiang Kai-shek, the Nationalist leader, turned on his Communist allies in a savage massacre in Shanghai.

A soldier guards a Great Wall pass into Shansi Province in 1937-38 war with Japan.

Over the years, Mao Tse-tung rebuilt the Communist movmement in the countryside and, with the end of World War II, civil war broke out. Mao and the Communists won. Chiang fled to offshore Taiwan.

For forty years, the Communist struggled to move China forward into the new industrial technology of the 20th century. Internal politics and Marxist ideology proved formidable barriers. From 1966 until Mao's death in 1976, China was the scene of the violent turbulence of the Cultural Revolution and plots led by Lin Biao and Mao's wife, Jiang Qing.

On Mao's death, Jiang Qing and the so-called Gang of Four were arrested and Deng Xiaoping, released from confinement after half a dozen years, took over. He pointed China on to a radical course of reform and opening to the West, welcoming capitalist innovations-joint ventures, profit incentive systems, private enterprise.

Vast gains were made-as well as good-sized economic headaches-in ten years of Deng's rule up to June 1989, when the violent and tragic killing of student demonstrators in Tiananmen Square and of common people elsewhere in Beijing shocked the world and brought Deng's progressive program to an abrupt halt.

What went wrong? Deng had presided over enlightenment, experiment, a free flow of ideas. Why did he turn against the demonstrators in Tiananmen Square? Why did he give the fateful order to the troops to open fire?

There is no simple answer. He was growing old and more rigid. He had long displayed a testy antagonism toward young people who challenged his views. Yet, he had brought in liberal and innovative men to spark his drive to get China going. But when the going got tough, he had on several occasions put the blame on others.

His first victim had been his own hand-picked successor, Hu Yaobang, a man as energetic as Deng with a free-wheeling appetite for change. Hu fright-

5

ened many Communist Party elders and ultimately Deng himself. When students began to demonstrate in the autumn of 1987, Deng fired Hu and put Premier Zhao Ziyang in his place.

Zhao was a conventional man. He followed Deng's orders and tried his best to speed up reform and innovation. Deng wanted to put China firmly on his course before age compelled him to yield the helm.

But Zhao's fast pace began to plunge China into serious economic distortions-inflation, food shortages, zooming prices, prosperity in the countryside but short rations in the cities where fixed-wage bureaucrats couldn't afford the food bills. Unrest grew. The opening to the West had brought in corruption, bribery, back door deals in which childen and other relatives of the Party higher-ups were taking a leading role. Old-timers thought things had gone too far. They did not dare attack Deng openly, but they poured out their venom against Zhao.

The fight started in June 1988, at a Party conclave at the seashore resort of Beidehai and raged through the summer and into the autumn of 1988. It went on into the winter and was still bubbling in the spring of 1989. Zhao fought back and often had Deng's support.

The student demonstrations that began in the middle of April shifted the balance of power. Deng was told that the students' target was himself and he came to believe he was in personal danger and his government might fall. He changed his bodyguards, in fear of assassination, and he had his colleagues change theirs, too. He began to spend nights in the military anti-nuclear shelter in the western hills.

Deng's order to the troops to clear out the demonstrators by whatever means it took was the logical conclusion. He did not seem to realize that the national and international impact of the Tiananmen bloodshed would bring his great crusade to lead China into the new technological world to a halt.

The dramatic events of June 1989 left the future clouded. Within a few months, Deng had formally stepped down as China's paramount leader, turning over his last office—chairman of the Military Committee-to his new chosen successor, Jiang Zemin, former leader of the Party in Shanghai. But no one felt certain he would display sufficient political force to actually become Deng's successor.

Formidable tasks lay at every side. China's tourist trade and the exports on which it depended for foreign exchange dwindled to a trickle.

More serious, Deng's conservative enemies took advantage of his weakness to gut many of his innovative programs. The Deng drive slowed to a sluggish pace. Relations between the United States and China cooled. Europe and many Asian countries cut back on investments. Taiwan backed away from participating in China's evolution. Hong Kong became frightened of its future after being turned back to China by the British in 1997. Even Japan proceeded with caution.

The China succession also was in question. Many Chinese felt that the military would play the dominant influence in the succession. Some felt that a quarrel might break out between powerful military cliques, that China might even face, once again, the specter of regionalism and warlords.

Many Chinese intellectuals and students fled abroad—if they could—and those already abroad stayed there to wait until the dust settled at home before deciding what to do next.

Some Chinese said it would be five years before the lessons of Tiananmen were clear. Others estimated ten years. All felt that ultimately China would get back on track.

—HARRISON SALISBURY

I

The Last Emperor

For centuries, China believed itself to be the superior nation, the center of civilization, surrounded by inferior "barbarians." Its name comes from the Ch'in Dynasty that existed three centuries before Christ and it can trace its civilized history back more than four thousand years, some say seven thousand years, while man was just beginning to find the fertile shores of the Mediterranean.

China's rivers, the Yellow, the Yangtze, the Pearl, were the symbols of its timelessness; the farmer, the peasant, the soil and its harvest, the taproot of its civilization; the people mere links in an endless chain of generations. Its bronzes were as old as the pyramids; its Confucian principles older than the New Testament.

Confucius, a scholar-statesman who lived before the Greek philosophers—five hundred years before Christ—defined five basic relationships: friend to friend, brother to brother, son to father, wife to husband, and subject to ruler. The state, in essence, was an expanded family. Confucius lived during the Chou Dynasty (1122-256 B.C.), a time when rulers were soldier-statesmen, as they had been during the Shang Dynasty which preceded it, and the Hsia Dynasty before that.

The legendary first emperor was Ch'in Shih Huang-ti (Qin Shihuangdi). His rule was credited with the development of silk, a compass and a three-hundred-and-sixty-five-day calendar. It was during his reign in the third century B.C. that the various walls built to defend the borders from the "barbarians" in the north were connected and consolidated into the Great Wall, a barrier eventually

stretching and snaking some fifteen-hundred miles, from Gansu in the southwest through the rugged mountains to the southern edge of Inner Mongolia and on to southern Manchuria.

The emperor was known as the Good Emperor, for his public works—roads, granaries, irrigation systems and canals. The name China is derived from this highly successful, though short-lived, dynasty.

Perhaps the most important contribution of the Ch'in Dynasty was the unification of what had been a dozen or so warring kingdoms. China was—and

The child standing at the right is two year-old Pu Yi, just months before he was enthroned on November 14, 1908. The "Boy Emperor" of China is with his father, Prince Chun, and his younger brother, Pu Chieh.

Queues

The queue, a long braid of hair once worn by men in China, became an ingrained part of the old Western stereotype, seen in images ranging from 19th century anti-Chinese cartoons to the cook Hop Sing on television's "Bonanza."

But in China the queue became a hated vestige of imperial rule and the most visible symbol of loyalty or defiance to the dying Manchu dynasty at the turn of the century. Many men risked death by cutting off their queues, a capital offense prior to the revolution that toppled the Manchus from power.

Known in Chinese as the "bianzi," the queue was a requirement of male appearance imposed by the Manchus, a northeast tribe that overthrew the Ming Dynasty in the 17th century and established the last dynastic reign, known as the Ching.

The Manchus maintained power by retaining the traditional Chinese forms of government while exacting strict standards of conformity in appearance and behavior. They exalted Confucianism and learned the Chinese language so well that even today, their descendants speak the purest form of Mandarin.

China flourished and expanded under the Manchus during the 18th century but then foundered, humiliated and weakened by foreign invaders. Eventually, the Manchus were despised by Chinese and foreigners alike.

Members of anti-Manchu secret societies formed in the mid to late 1800s cut off their queues, wearing hats to conceal their subversive identities. As anti-Manchu emotions intensified, queue-cutting became more widespread and brazen.

Perhaps the best model of defiance was Sun Yat-sen, considered the founder of modern China, who wore his hair short. He organized an anti-Manchu revolutionary movement in 1905 that overthrew the dynasty six years later.

SOVIET UNION

MONGOLIA

HEILONGJIAN

• Harbin

JILIN

• Changchun

Sea of Japan

INNER MONGOLIA

LIAONING

N. KOREA

GANSU

BEIJING SHI
BEIJING

S. KOREA

Tianjin • TIANJIN SHI • Luda

HEBEI

INGHAI

NINGXIA

SHANDONG

Yellow Sea

SHANXI

Yellow R.

SHAANXI

HENAN

JIANGSU

ANHUI

SHANGHAI SHI
Shanghai

Nanjing •

SICHUAN

HUBEI
~Wuhan

Yangtze R.

Chongqing •

ZHEJIANG

East China Sea

JIANXI

HUNAN

GUIZHOU

Fuzhou •

FUJIAN

Kunming •

YUNNAN

GUANGXI

GUANGDONG
• Canton

TAIWAN

Macao •

BURMA

• Hong Kong

VIETNAM

LAOS

South China Sea

PEOPLE'S REPUBLIC OF

CHINA

0 100 Miles 400

HAINAN

THAILAND

9

remains—a nation of numerous minorities, including the Tibetans in the west, the Miaos in the south, the Koreans in the east, the Kurds and Mongolians in the northwest. Its people speak more than six hundred dialects; in some places, those in neighboring but isolated villages do not understand each other.

Through the dynasties—the Han, Sui, Tang, Song, Yuan and Ming—China was a huge, varied and imaginative country that invented paper, porcelain, gunpowder, the clock and moveable type—an enlightened nation of art and painting while Europe was still in the Dark Ages.

Marco Polo, among others, had come back to Europe from visits to what was then known as Cathay to stun his 13th-century listeners with visions of a utopian land of love and learning—and riches. Under the rule of the Manchus, who had come from Manchuria in the north to overthrow the Mings and establish the Qing Dynasty in 1644, the vast Chinese expanse included Manchuria, Mongolia, Tibet, Formosa, and Central Asian regions of Turkestan.

These Chinese rulers treated Western imperialists with condescension and contempt. In their eyes, the foreigners were large, meaty and repulsive—"dabizi" (big noses) and "hong guizi" (red devils).

But, at the beginning of the 20th century, this ancient and adored "Chung Kuo," this Middle Kingdom between Heaven and Earth, this center of the universe, its rulers thus the Sons of Heaven, this China was a helpless giant bleeding from a thousand foreign cuts.

Its fall from ancient Oriental grace was precipitated in part by Western nations boasting adolescent muscle and macho, mercenary merchants eager to share in China's riches of tea and porcelain and silk and cotton.

These Western seafarers seeking trade with China were joined by Christian missionaries in attempts to open the doors of the East, despite the Middle Kingdom's xenophobic attitude and official air of superiority. (Under the Manchus, foreign affairs were handled by the Court for the Governance of the Borderlands, which prescribed the amount of "tribute" to be paid to the rulers.)

In the war of Manchu against might, the Western sea powers won, easily.

By mid-19th century, Western Europe and the United States were thriving on sale of tea and silk and other "things Chinese," but trade was onesided; there was little the Chinese wanted from the West. Then the British introduced opium. Grown primarily in India, the habit-forming narcotic extracted from the poppy soon became the main cargo of the British East India Company and the American clipper trade. (One of the biggest American trading

Pu Yi, with glasses, and his brother and sisters.

companies in China at the time was Russell & Company, headed by Warren Delano, grandfather of future President Franklin Delano Roosevelt.)

Chinese merchants, considered parasites at home, grew rich on the trade, while their government pronounced it illegal. The drug, called "foreign mud" by Chinese officials, created more than two million Chinese addicts by 1835.

Even as the British forced Chinese rulers to use opium in trade, they pressed for the opening of other ports besides Canton and for the right of trade to be confirmed by treaty. But the Chinese commissioner of trade, Lin Tse-hsu, noting the growing ill effects of opium smoking among the people—and the loss of customs revenue—seized and destroyed a cargo of opium valued at $6 million belonging to the British at Canton. The British responded by attacking cities along the coast. The gunboat diplomacy won what negotiations could not. By the Treaty of Nanking, in 1842, the ports of Canton, Amoy, Fuchow, Ningpo, and Shanghai were opened to trade and the colony of Hong Kong was ceded to Britain. The British also exacted an agreement from Beijing rulers for low import tariffs.

In the decades that followed, there were a series

Pu Yi was chief executive of the Chinese republic of Manchukuo when this picture was taken with family and relatives.

of popular uprisings as well as added examples of Western imperialism, a combination of disasters that threatened the existence of the already weak Manchu Dynasty. The quasi-religious Taiping Rebellion lasted fifteen years in the 1850s and early 1860s and cost some twenty million lives before it was suppressed, with Western help. And the Middle Kingdom continued to be sliced into spheres of foreign influence: China lost Tonkin and Annam to France and north Burma to Britain, along with ten more treaty ports.

Japan, with its military muscle, took China to war over Korea and easily defeated the Manchu forces. By an 1895 treaty, the Japanese Land of the Rising Sun gained Formosa (later Taiwan), the Pescadores, a group of islands in the Taiwan Strait, and the strategic Liaotung Peninsula, the door to Manchuria. Japan also demanded—and got-recognition of the independence of Korea from China, and new commercial privileges.

The Russians, having earlier taken title to the territory on the left bank of the Amur and east of the Ussuri River on their far eastern frontier, then moved Japan out of Liaotung Peninsula—and took it for themselves, building a naval base at Port Arthur and a port and railway terminus at Dairen (Dalian).

The United States, although coming late into the Far East picture, still had brought "manifest desti-

ny" to the Western Pacific through the Spanish-American War in 1898, annexing the Philippines.

Through John Hay, President Theodore Roosevelt's Secretary of State, the United States had diplomatically stressed freedom of commerce with China and its weak dynastic rulers. The endeavor became known as the Open Door policy.

As the 20th century began, the British held areas around the Yangtze River, the French a zone in South China, the Germans part of the Shantung (Shandong) Peninsula, the Russians the peninsula of Manchuria. These encroaching elements of Western civilization occurred against a background of bad crop years, famine, unrest and banditry in China.

The country made one last attempt at national survival through inner change.

On the Chinese throne at the time was Kuang Hsu, but he was emperor in name only. He had been chosen in 1875 by his aunt, the Empress Dowager Tzu Hsi, to succeed her son, Emperor Tung Chin. It was she who reigned as regent.

Kuang Hsu tried, however. Following the advice of scholar-reformist Kang Yu-wei, for a period of one hundred days between June and September 1898, Kuang attempted to institute more than forty reform decrees. The reforms involved modernization of the bureaucracy, revisions of the educational system, and improvements in agriculture and economy.

The period ended when Tzu Hsi fought back and regained control, keeping the emperor prisoner until his death and executing six of the leading reformers. China returned to its dynastic rule, led by the cruel and cold Tzu Hsi, who despised the "barbarians" and encouraged efforts to drive the foreigners out.

She told her viceroys that the empire's enemies, with "tiger-like voracity," were competing with each other in attempts to seize Chinese territories. She called for resistance—and got it.

Pu Yi, as newly-inaugurated dictator of Manchukuo, and his wife, about to board a train to Changchun, capital of the new state.

Society of Harmonious Fists

A secret sect known as the Big Swords became active around Shantung in north China, looting missionary properties and generally promoting violence against foreigners. As the anti-foreign feeling swelled, another secret society took up the cry, "Support the Manchus, Annihilate the Foreigners." Backed by the Empress Dowager, this motley collection of peasant instigators was known as "the Society of Righteous and Harmonious Fists"—foreign journalists thus called them Boxers—who wore amulets that they believed made them invincible to injury.

On June 10, 1900, in Tienstin (Tianjin), thousands of them attacked the city's foreign compound. Among the three hundred under siege was Herbert Hoover, then a twenty-six-year-old mining engineer and consultant to the Chinese director of the Ministry of Mines, and his young wife. The future 31st

Pu Yi in 1946.

President of the United States was to describe the attack in his memoirs as "an event that was to modify their lives, and also give them something to talk about the rest of their born days." At times during the siege, he wrote, the streets were "simply canals of moving lead" as the Boxers fired thousands of shells into the compound on the Peiho River. Hoover helped with the barricades and directed food relief for the victims after rescue forces freed them in mid-July.

These illegal revolutionary societies, operating first from Japan and later from other overseas communities, made Canton their capital and directed uprisings between 1907 and 1909, when coups were attempted, but failed, in Canton, Hankow and Peking.

The Chinese emperor at the time was a three-year-old. Emperor Kuang Hsu had died on November 14, 1908, and Empress Dowager Tzu Hsi died the very next day. She provided for the succession by arranging for Pu Yi, nephew of the childless Kuang Hsu, to ascend to the Dragon Throne. Of course, he had little or nothing to do with ruling the country, except as a symbol of rule.

He was to be China's last emperor.

Revolution and Republic

The demise of the impotent Manchu Dynasty was hastened by Western powers. They forced concessions to build railways in various parts of China—and pressed loans on the government with interest rates highly profitable to the foreign lenders. One such loan, for construction of the Canton-Hankow and Hankow-Chungking lines, proved the final debasement. Chinese investors protested, workers went on strike and shops closed. Rioting spread.

With this background of turmoil, in October 1911, the revolutionaries planned another coup in Wuhan. When an explosion went off prematurely, revealing the attempt, they attacked the viceroy's headquarters earlier than planned and seized the garrison. There, revolutionary converts among the imperial regiments mutinied and the garrison commander fled to Shanghai. It was October 10, the tenth day of the tenth month, and became known as the Double Ten. Within two days, the city was in rebel hands.

The success set off a chain of rebellions and within a month, nine provinces had declared their independence of the imperial government.

The Manchu rulers mounted a counterattack led by the imperial military commander, the brilliant and shrewd, but also vain and personally ambitious Yuan Shih-kai. Hankow was recaptured at the end of October as the revolutionists marched up the Yangtze from Shanghai toward Nanking. That ancient southern capital fell to the rebels on November 27. The regent, Prince Chun, Pu Yi's father, resigned in favor of the late emperor's widow, Lung Yu. She gave Yuan full powers to negotiate a settlement with the rebels, as the Manchus started to flee north, back to Manchuria.

At about this time, mid-November, a twenty-eight-year-old U.S. Army first lieutenant with three months' accumulated leave time made his first visit to China. Joseph Stilwell, not yet known as "Vinegar Joe," came into Shanghai in the midst of the revolution. As Barbara Tuchman, in her book, *Stilwell and the American Experience in China*, described it: "The Revolution added a touch of excitement for Stilwell without seriously inconveniencing him, for like most momentous upheavals, it was less noticeable to the eyewitness that it would be to history. On a tour of the Old Chinese City he saw rebel recruiting stations under the flag of the Revolution whose twelve-pointed black sun on a red ground had replaced the Imperial yellow dragon. . . . He saw beggars thick as flies lying in rags in the gutters, vile, filthy canals clogged with refuse, a coolie taking a mountain of trunks from wharf to hotel for 30 cents, a street vendor selling oranges by the section, mourners dressed in white in a temple, 'dames of fortune lined up in the doorway under a light, gaily dressed and bejewelled but stolidly listless faces.'"

Joe Stilwell was to return to China and play a key role in its history.

On December 20, 1911, at a meeting in Shanghai, a secret agreement was reached for the departure of the Manchus and for the establishment of a republican form of government.

Sun Yat-sen, who had been in the United States, returned to China on December 25. He was elected president of the provisional republic four days later and assumed that post at Nanking on January 1, 1912. On February 12, the ruling house of China, Pu Yi, the Boy Emperor, and the Empress Dowager Lung Yu, abdicated the throne.

But Yuan still exercised great power, especially in the north. Hoping to unify the country, Sun on March 12 retired as president in his favor and Yuan

Drawing shows Marines defending the U.S. Legation in Beijing during an attack by the anti-foreigner Boxers in 1900.

re-established the government at Peking. A provisional constitution was proclaimed, providing for a cabinet form of government with a two-house parliament, headed by a president and a vice president. By early fall, the Tung Meng Hui, another of the illegal revolutionary societies set up for the overthrow of the Manchus, became the Kuomintang, or Nationalist Party, a legitimate political party.

The Republic of China was welcomed by the United States in a formal declaration of Congress, congratulating "the people of China on their assumption of the powers, duties and responsibilities of self-government." President Woodrow Wilson sent a message to Yuan, China's first official president: "I extend in the name of my government and of my people, a greeting of welcome to the new China thus entering into the family of nations."

However, by 1914, with the outbreak of World War I, it was clear that the revolution—never really an expression of mass protest—was failing, quickly.There had been no fundamental social reforms, China's huge economic problems remained—and Japan had moved deeper into Chinese territory.

As the treaty ally of Great Britain in the war against Germany, Japan promptly occupied the parts of Shantung that had been the German concession. Japan also made numerous demands that further subjected the weak new Chinese government to Japanese will, and might.

Meanwhile, Yuan tried to stall the Japanese while he campaigned for a return to monarchy and his role as emperor on the Dragon Throne. The plan ran into opposition from Yuan's rivals, and moreso from the foreign powers, Britain, Russia and France—and Japan. Finding himself increasingly isolated and becoming ill—his foes said he was "made ill by shame and anger"—he bowed to public pressure and Big Power disapproval and, in 1916, gave up his dream of imperial glory. He died four months later, on June 6, replaced by Li Yuan-hung, who had been vice president.

World War I only multiplied China's troubles.

The United States entered the war in April 1917, China in August that year. In September, Sun Yat-sen formally assumed the post of generalissimo of his own regime and declared war on Germany. Sun set up his headquarters in Canton in the south, while Yuan's successors struggled for power in Beijing (then Peking) in the north. With warfare spreading between the two camps and military men throughout China competing for national prominence, power shifted into hands of regional warlords.

The warlords, or "tuchuns," were leaders of rag-

Dr. Sun Yat-sen

tag private armies that gave them power of life and death over whole provinces. Some were illiterate, brutal and self-indulgent; others shrewd and intelligent.

Sun tried to unify the nation by marching against the warlords and sought Big Power help. He didn't get it, but the newly-established Communist regime of the Soviet Union, after the Revolution of 1917, sent its first ambassador to Beijing, Adolph Joffe. He was received in triumph by the Chinese.

After the war, the Versailles Treaty gave the Japanese not only Shantung, but also the Marshall, Caroline and Mariana islands in the Pacific, which Germany had bought earlier from Spain. This fostered an anti-Japanese sentiment that was only aggravated by the "Twenty-One Demands" made by Japan in 1915, which included control of Manchuria, important economic concessions and a role in Chinese government.

Coffin containing the body of Sun Yat-sen, "Father of the People's Party," founder of the Rebublic of China, carried by one hundred and twenty pallbearers, the same number reserved exclusively for emperors before the revolution in 1911.

Dr. and Mrs. Sun Yat-sen

Chiang Kai-shek, standing, in a formal photograph with Sun Yat-sen at the Wampoa Military Academy.

Chiang Kai-shek

On May 4, 1919—forever known as the May 4th Movement—the Chinese protested against Japan and the Shantung deal in a violent demonstration that had nationalism at its heart.

At Peking University, which had become the center of the intellectual ferment in China, students staged a mass parade to show their displeasure with the treaty-makers' decision. Shortly after noon on May 4, some three thousand students from thirteen colleges and universities began the march, despite warnings from police. With shouts of "Return Shantung" and "Boycott Japanese Goods," they paraded through the streets in a protest that spread through the night to Shanghai, Nanking, Canton and Hankow. The demonstration turned violent, with arrests as well as injuries, and began a nationwide movement of protest demonstrations, strikes, work stoppages and an anti-Japanese boycott. It forced China to refuse to sign the Paris peace treaty.

It also provided Sun Yat-sen the opportunity to channel the new energies into an alliance aginst the warlords and a campaign to achieve national unity.

The former site of of the Hubei military government, founded after the 1911 revolution led by Sun Yat-sen. His copper statue is in the foreground.

The May 4th Movement also brought several important organizations into being, including the Peking Students' Union and the Mass Education Speech Corps, and spurred student activity that would be the basis for revolutionary nationalism in China. It was the May 4th Movement that was to serve as a model for the protesting Chinese students of 1989, who felt that they, like their counterparts seventy years earlier, were revolutionaries fighting against social injustice.

In July 1921, two leading professors at Peking University, librarian Li Ta-chao and Chen Tu-hsiu, met clandestinely on a Shanghai river boat with ten other Marxists—including a young assistant librarian named Mao Tse-tung—to form the Communist Party of China.

Two years later, Sun Yat-sen met with Soviet diplomat Adolf Joffe in Shanghai and agreed to Soviet aid for his Kuomintang Party. Soon after, the Soviets sent a young man named Mihail Borodin—his real was name Mikhail Grusenberg, formerly a school principal in Chicago—to Canton to set up a military academy, oversee the delivery of Soviet arms and carry out the decisions of the Communist International (Comintern). Sun at first demurred working with the Communists, but finally agreed to accept them as individuals, reorganizing his Kuomintang Party in the south on communist organizational lines.

Then, in 1925, in the midst of preparations to

Chiang Kai-shek on his favorite white charger.

move north, Sun died. A doctor-turned-revolutionary, his ideas were often fuzzy and contradictory and he lacked boldness and resolve. But he laid down three principles of the people: nationalism, democracy and the people's livelihood—which long survived him. An effective visionary, his greatness was in his ability to stimulate others to share his dreams. He will always be known as the Father of China.

The man who succeeded Sun, Chiang Kai-shek, was a thirty-eight-year-old military officer who had been appointed president of the Whampoa Military Academy. The son of moderately well-to-do parents, he had spent two years in the Japanese army as a youth, fought for the overthrow of the imperial system and later helped end the career of Yuan Shih-kai. In Shanghai, he had become a member of the Green Society, widely reputed to be active in shady financial speculation. In 1918, he joined with Sun.

Chiang suspected, correctly, that the Communists were biding their time until they could make their own bid for power and he tried to stop them. In mid-1926, the combined National-Communist forces began their move against the warlords, taking over Shanghai virtually without a fight. But the industrialists, bankers and landlords of the city feared the radical wing of the Kuomintang, which included the Communists. In exchange for financial backing to complete the military expedition, Chiang promised them he would purge the Communists from the party.

In April 1927, Chiang turned on his Communist allies in a savage bloodbath that left thousands dead or wounded. Scattered military forces loyal to the Chinese Communist Party kept fighting to the end of the year, but were ruthlessly suppressed. The Communist Party went underground, with some factions leaving Shanghai for rural South China.

Chiang now resumed his northern expedition, allied with some of the pro-Nationalist warlords, and captured Peking. In 1928, he established the Republic of China, setting up his capital at Nanking.

But China still was far from the unified whole Chiang had dreamed of creating. Politically, he had to share power with the warlords who had helped him in the northern expedition and he had to cope with factions within the Kuomintang. The Big Powers continued to act like states within a state, retaining powers of trade and commerce.

Economically, the nation of some four hundred million people was the poorest in the world. Big cities teemed with the hungry, overworked and ill. Passersby in the early morning often saw in Shanghai what they believed to be bundles of rags; they were the poor and ill who had died the night before. A patrol made periodic rounds to pick them up.

In the countryside, the peasants worked their fields from sunup to sundown, often knee deep in the mud of rice paddies. Existence depended on the vagaries of the weather, as typhoons, floods, dought and locust plagues ravished the land. Famine periodically reduced the population by millions.

Never was a country so ready for revolution.

U.S. Marines on guard behind sandbag emplacements in Shanghai in 1937, when Japan renewed its attacks on China.

Names

Here is a guide to pronouncing the names of some of the leading figures in contemporary Chinese politics:

Deng Xiaoping—dung shah-oh ping
Jiang Zemin—jahng zuh-meen
Yang Shangkun—yahng shahng-kuhn
Zhao Ziyang—jow zi-yahng
Yang Baibing—yahng by-bing
Yang Shangkun—yahng shahng-kwun
Chi Haotian—chur how-tyan
Liu Huaqing—lyoo hwah-ching

A landing force of U.S. Marines outside U.S. offices in Shanghai in 1927.

A British outpost near the foreign enclave in 1927.

American sailors guarding the U.S. Consulate (center, backround) in Shanghai in 1923. On the right (background) is the Japanese Consulate and on the left, the German.

The Dynasties

Xia (Hsia)	2205-1766 B.C.
Shang (Shang)	1766-1122 B.C.
Zhou (Chou)	1122-770 B.C.
Spring and Autumn	770-476 B.C.
Warring States	476-221 B.C.
Qin (Chin)	221-206 B.C.
Han (Han)	206 B.C.-220 A.D.
Three Kingdoms	220-265
Jin (Tsin)	265-420
Southern and Northern Dynasties	420-589
Sui (Sui)	589-618
Tang (Tang)	618-907
Five Dynasties and Ten Kingdoms	907-960
Song (Sung)	960-1280
Yuan (Yuan)	1280-1368
Ming (Ming)	1368-1644
Qing (Ching)	1644-1911

II

The Long March

Mao Tse-tung had returned to Changsha in his native Hunan Province and there wrote a report to the Communist Party on the state of the peasant.

"Within a short time," he wrote, "hundreds of millions of peasants will rise in Central, South and North China, with the fury of a hurricane; no power, however strong, can restrain them. They will break all the shackles that bind them and rush toward the road of liberation. All imperialists, warlords, corrupt officials, and bad gentry will meet their doom at the hands of the peasants. All revolutionary parties will be judged by them. Are we to get in front of them and lead them, or criticize them behind their backs, or fight them from the opposite camp?"

While in Hunan, Mao had attempted, unsuccessfully, to lead the peasants to revolt (later called the Autumn Crop Uprising), forming the first units of an army made up solely of peasants and workers. It fought its way to the Chingkangshan, a mountain on the Hunan-Jiangxi border. There they were joined the next spring by remnants of the 20th Army under Ho Lung, Yeh Ting and Chu Teh and the Red Army came into being. Chu Teh was the Red Army's first commander in chief and Mao its political commissar. The army, often referred to as the Chu-Mao Army, depended on the peasant for support and was careful to cultivate him. Strict rules provided that soldiers must replace all doors when leaving a house (they were used to sleep on), return straw matting and borrowed articles and repair or replace damaged ones.

Mao's revolt, however, had not been approved by the Communist Central Committee, which had remained in hiding in Shanghai, and Mao's chances of success in the countryside were slim. He was

Mao Tse-tung making a report to cadres in the cave city of Yenan in 1942.

thrown out of the ruling Politburo as well as the party Front Committee, but together with Chu Teh went ahead with plans to establish a government on the Russian Soviet model. The first Soviet came into being in the Hunan-Jiangxi-Guangdong border area and gradually expanded under the protection of the Red military forces.

Mao defended the use of violence and bloodshed to accomplish his goals. "Revolution," he said, "is not a dinner party, nor a literary composition, nor painting, nor embroidery. It cannot be done so delicately, so leisurely, so gentlemanly and so 'gently, kindly, politely, plainly and modestly.' Revolution is insurrection, the violent action of one class overthrowing the power of another. An agrarian revolution is a revolution by the peasantry to overthrow the power of the feudal landlord class. If the peasants do not apply great force, the power of the landlords, consolidated over thousands of years, can never be uprooted."

Mao's military tactics stressed secrecy, surprise, speed and subtlety. ""When the enemy advances," he wrote, "we retreat; when he halts and camps, we harass him; when he seeks to avoid battle, we attack; when he retreats, we pursue."

Chiang Kai-shek was determined to drive the Communists out. He organized a series of Northern Expeditions, or "extermination" campaigns. The first, in late 1930, involved one hundred thousand men led by Generalissimo Chiang, but the Communists beat them back, as they did two more attacks in the following months. In 1932, the Communists went on the offensive, while Chiang prepared his fourth campaign against them, with a quarter of a million men. In 1934, he brought in German advisers for the fifth "bandit suppression" campaign, which used nearly a million soldiers against Communist forces of about one hundred and sixty thousand. His government forces moved a ring of fortifications progressively closer to the Communist center, forcing them into positional instead of guerrilla warfare. They then burned houses and drove people and cattle away, their aim to turn the region into a wasteland incapable of supporting the Communist troops. An estimated million people in the Soviet areas died of execution or starvation as a result of the successful Nationalist blockade. The Communist remnants, facing total defeat, broke out to the west and scattered, then set out on the Long March.

Mao Tse-tung in 1933.

Portrait of Mao described as taken "during the days of his early revolutionary activities."

The Long March, begun in mid-October 1934, was one of the great military feats of history, and an impressive example of the tenacity of faith.

The Long March, in fact, was a retreat. It was a retreat across some six thousand miles of China, from the east coast to Shanxi Province in the distant northwest. It began with one hundred thousand men; it ended a year later with just twenty thousand. Along the tortuous route, the Communists fought a skirmish, sometimes a battle, an average of once a day. They wound across a dozen provinces, seized sixty-two cities, clambered over eighteen mountain ranges and crossed twenty-four rivers. Along the way, they handed out Communist propaganda, held mass meetintgs, staged plays and carried out land reform.

The first two-and-a-half months of the trek nearly were the last. The marchers were loaded down with excess baggage; it took a transport division of five thousand men to move it. Thus encumbered, they marched in a straight line toward the northwest, a move that sent them into head-on conflict with waiting Nationalist forces. Crossing the Xiang River in north Jiangxi resulted in the loss of half the army.

At this point, Mao, who had been replaced as the party's political commissar, asserted himself. He persuaded the youthful Communist leaders—the main column was commanded by Chu Teh and the political commissar was Chou En-lai—to move by more circuitous routes to Guizhou Province, where the enemy was weaker. They were able to capture Zunyi by disguising their troops as Nationalists. At a Communist meeting there in January 1935, Mao was named Party Chairman and gained Chou En-lai as a friend and ally.

Before resuming the march, Mao divested the troops of their surplus weight and announced that the Communist objective in struggling to the northwest was to confront the Japanese invaders. The widely-published statement won sympathy for the Communists in a nation that was growing impatient with Chiang Kai-shek's single-minded pursuit of the civil war and his reluctance to turn against the Japanese armies.

For much of the remainder of the march, the Communist armies outwitted the Nationalist forces by complicated maneuvers, twists and turns and elaborate feints, eventually setting up headquarters in a cave city at Yenan,

Chou En-lai leading Communist armies in the Long March in 1934.

Red banner of the Chinese Communists.

Bodies of twelve Chinese Communist guerrillas are unloaded by Nationalist troops at Tsingpu after an unsuccessful raid early in 1936.

Mao's Early Life

The son of a Hunan peasant, Mao Tse-tung was a rebellious child and a revolutionary youth.

His parents were unschooled; his mother was illiterate. He ran away from home when he was ten.

As a young man, he pored over books, particularly the classic stories of peasant rebellion and the translated works of Jefferson, Napoleon, Voltaire and Rousseau. When the Manchus were overthrown, he cut off his pigtail as a sign of solidarity with the revolutionaries.

A real peasant rebellion in Hunan shocked him into an awareness of the present: the peasant leaders were executed and their heads displayed on poles. He was later to say that this event influenced the course of his life.

He formed a political study group at Changsha Normal School called Hsin Min Hsueh Hui— New People's Study Society—which dissected capitalist democracy (Marxism was still virtually unknown at the time). In his free time, he toughened his body and studied physical culture.

He taught school for two years and ever afterward regarded himself as a teacher. He was a believer in experience. To discover how the common soldier lived, he enlisted in the army for six months. From this experience, he decided that China could never be indpendent without its own modern citizen army.

He was twenty-eight years old and an assistant

Mao Tse-tung, 1936.

librarian when he joined in forming the Chinese Communist Party.

"Execution wall" in Kiangsi province, where Communist soldiers killed Chinese government troops in 1935.

*Youthful Chinese Communist soldiers head off to
help fight the Japanese in the north, in 1937.*

A rare photo showing Communist leaders in 1936.

After the Long March, (l. to r.) Qin Bangxia, Chou En-lai, Chu Teh and Mao Tse-tung appear in northern Shansi Province.

Survivors of the Long March formed an elite with the Chinese Communist Party which would dominate it for many years. They had suffered, fought and bled together; they had shared victories and defeats. They had survived. As their revolution dragged on, they acquired the aura of legend.

Foreigners knew virtually nothing of the Long March, or the Communists, until journalist Edgar Snow printed a series of interviews with the Communist leaders and a report of their life in the cave city of Yenan. Published in book form as *Red Star Over China*, these were the first real reports of the Chinese Communists, their beliefs and intentions, and their Long March, and came at a time when the U.S. government continued to support Chiang Kai-shek in his fight against them.

Headquarters of the Chinese Eighth Army, in nothern Shensi. The base was carved from cliffs of the area.

The Rising Sun

Chiang, despite his obsession with the Communists, had to worry as well about another foe: Japan. Under the influence of militarism, the Japan of the 1930s had sought to cure its domestic ills by expansionism. It looked toward Manchuria, the richest part of China in resources and industry.

In 1931, the Japanese army, already stationed in Manchuria "to protect the nation's interest," killed

Thousands of students rioted in December 1935, protesting Japanese aggression.

the ruling Chinese warlord and then set up Pu Yi, the last Chinese dynastic emperor, as puppet head of the new state of Manchukuo. Soon, the Japanese occupied the whole territory, one the size of the U.S. West Coast. Japanese forces also seized Shanghai, where among those killed were three Japanese soldiers who purposely blew themselves up with a land mine to penetrate the city's defensive line. The Japanese military influence was extended to Mongolia and then to North China as Chiang's government in Nanking decided it could not withstand the Japanese until it had eliminated the domestic Communists.

This Nationalist policy, later referred to as "first

pacification and then resistance," provoked anti-Japanese demonstrations by intellectuals and students once again, especially in 1935 and 1936.

Early in December 1936, Chiang Kai-shek flew to Xian to coordinate what would be his sixth campaign against the Communists. But, instead of coming away with a plan for a knockout punch of his enemies, he was kidnapped.

Marshal Chang Hsueh-liang, the warlord ruler there, had been won over to the idea of a united Chinese military front against the Japanese. He had Chiang kidnapped and demanded the halt of the civil war and a commitment to fight the Japanese in Manchuria. Chiang refused. The young officers

there, like the Young Marshal, exiles from their Manchurian homeland, wanted to kill him. The man who saved his life, ironically, was Chou En-lai.

Chou and the Communists decided that the Generalissimo was more valuable alive than dead. They recognized that he stood as a symbol to millions of Chinese. Besides, his successor would probably have been Ho Yingchin, an extremist the Communists distrusted.

Chou met personally with Chiang, their first encounter since Chiang had put a price on the young Communist's head in 1927. But Chou did not seek vengeance. He tried to persuade Chiang to accept the common front, but couldn't. Finally, with no agreements signed and no verbal promises made, Chiang left. With him went Marshal Chang, who had voluntarily made himself a prisoner in a gesture to save face for Chiang.

On July 7, 1937, Japanese and Chinese troops began shooting at each other not far from Peking, at the Marco Polo Bridge, an eight-hundred-year-old arched stone bridge adorned by marble lions and named for the Venetian explorer who visited what was then Cathay in the 13th century. Japan sent in reinforcements and the war with China began in earnest. Japanese planes bombed roads and towns and the infantry moved in behind tanks to rail centers in the northeast.

Manchurian overlord Chang Hsueh-liang met in Nanking in 1930 with Chiang Kai-shek (r.) for peace talks. They flank (1. to r.) Mme. H.H. Kung, Mme. Chang Hsueh-liang and Mme. Chiang Kai-shek.

31

Chinese defenders behind sandbag barricades on the Marco Polo Bridge, fourteen miles southwest of Beijing, in July 1937.

Chinese soldier of the 29th Army guards the Marco Polo Bridge before Japanese routed them in July 1937.

Defending the Marco Polo Bridge against Japanese attack in 1937. The bridge was named for the Venetian explorer who admired it on his journey to China in the 13th century.

Japanese infantry advance on Chinese in Beijing area in 1937. Chinese casualites outnumbered Japanese losses five-to-one.

Japanese troops advancing on Shanghai in 1937.

A bloodied, wailing infant underscores the destruction of a railroad station in Shanghai, bombed by the Japanese in their war against Chiang Kai-shek's troops in 1937.

Chinese search the debris of their homes after the Japanese invaded Beijing in July 1937.

Chapei, the native quarter of Shanghai, is left in shambles after shelling by both Chinese and Japanese in 1937.

Chiang and the Nationalists found it in their best interests then to negotiate with the Communists and form a united front against the common enemy—Japan. In the truce, the Nationalists called for an end to the civil conflict, release of all political prisoners, democratic freedoms to all and immediate steps to resist the Japanese armies. For their part, the Communists agreed to give up their policy of armed rebellion, to place their border regions in the northwest under the Nationalist government as "special regions" and to make their army part of the government's.

The united front worked for two years. But, united or not, the Chinese were no match for the better organized, better disciplined, better equipped Japanese armies.

Bu August 1937, the Japanese occupied Tientsin and Peking. In December, the Japanese marched into Nanking. There, unarmed civilians were beaten, bayonted and burned, raped and murdered, with thousands forcibly marched out of town and massacred. An estimated three hundred thousand civilians were left dead in what history sadly recalls as the infamous "rape of Nanking." The following year, Hangzhou and Canton were captured in the undeclared war, the war that the Japanese always called the "China incident" and which took a huge toll on that island nation in blood and money. In October 1938, Japenaese Emperor Hirohito attended a ceremony enshrining more than ten thousand men killed in China. They would not be the last.

Then, in December 1941, the Japanese made a fatal error. Their surprise attack on Pearl Harbor brought the United States into the war.

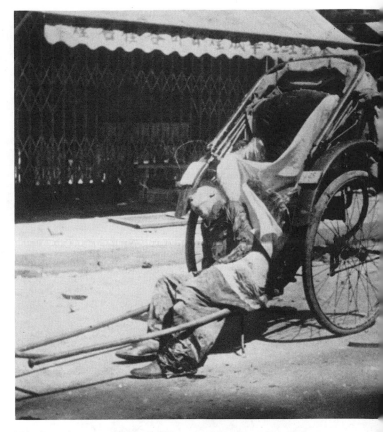

Victim of a noonday shelling on Nanking Road in Shanghai was one of about four hundred killed that September day in 1937.

Chinese woman sits amid the wreckage which once was her home in the Nantao section of Nanking after Japanese air bombing in August 1937.

Destruction of Nanking with the dead littering the streets after the city's capture by Japanese forces December 14, 1937.

Streets piled high with sandbags and littered with debris greeted Japanese forces entering Nanking December 14, 1937. Fires in the backround were set by Chinese retreating from the former capital of Nationalist China.

Japanese soldier uses the blindfolded body of a dead Chinese propped up on a pole as a bayonet dummy. The AP photo was taken near Tientsin in September 1937.

Japanese soldiers in the streets of Nanking after they invaded the city in December 1937.

Chinese Communist soldiers display equipment captured from the Japanese surprise raids along the railways in 1938.

Children watch the burial of a victim of cold and hunger in Shanghai in 1941.

With a few scant belongings at their feet, these Chinese children sit near the wreckage of what once was their home after a Japanese bombing raid on Chungking.

An estimated seven hundred people died in a Japanese bombing raid on Chungking in 1941.

Lin Biao (1.) and Mao Tse-tung during the war against Japan.

Communist Eighth Route Army drilling near Yenan in 1938.

Mao Tse-tung writing in a cave at Yenan in 1939.

World War II

Until 1941, the only major foreign aid to China had come from the Soviet Union, which had contributed $250 million in war materiel to help keep Japan away from Siberia. Madame Chiang Kai-shek had gone to President Franklin D. Roosevelt in Washington appealing for aid, but was unsuccessful. She then angered Roosevelt by taking China's case to the American public.

But by late 1943, the United States was better able to turn its attention to China, and agreed to reopen a supply route to replace the access roads cut off by Japanese conquests in Southeast Asia. China Premier T.V. Soong suggested an airlift from Assam to Kunming—over the Himalayan mountain range, the highest in the world.

The United States set up an air base and supply depot in Kunming and undertook to train thirty (later thirty-nine) Chinese divisions. The man chosen for the job was Joseph Stilwell, now Lieutenant General Stilwell, who back in 1911 had visited China while on leave from the Philippines and witnessed the overthrow of the Manchus. He had returned to China first as a language officer, then as an infantry officer and later a military attache. He spoke Chinese fluently and was familiar with Chinese history. He had earned the nickname "Vinegar Joe."

Stilwell's problems were not only military. He thought little of Chiang and called him "Peanut," once describing him as a "tricky, undependable old scoundrel." And he had to deal with General Claire Chennault, who had formed a Chinese air force for Chiang back in 1937, recruiting Americans who flew under the name of the "Flying Tigers." At one time during the war, Chennault told Washington that with a score of bombers he could wipe out the Japanese air force, reduce Japan to submission and win the war. Chiang much preferred Chennault to Stilwell.

When Stilwell arrived, Chinese ground troops were some three million poorly fed, badly trained and less than enthusiastic soldiers. Stilwell helped make them into a superior fighting force. At the same time, he pressed for an opportunity to work with the Communists, whose military ability he admired; he thought they had good organizaion and good tactics and despite their lack of arms and equipment, they were able to "scare the government to death."

Chou En-lai, Eighth Route Army general in 1938.

Lack of modern means of transportation in the China war zone forced Japanese troops to use whatever would work—including camels— in 1942.

General and Madame Chiang Kai-shek with General Joseph "Vinegar Joe" Stilwell during a 1942 conference in Burma.

Lieutenant General Joseph Stilwell (left) and Major General Claire Chennault at an airfield in China in 1943. Stilwell wears his usual campaign hat and carries his own musette bag over his shoulder.

Chu Teh (1.) and Mao Tse-tung studying military operations during the war against Japan.

Chinese students taking lessons in guerrilla warfare from Communist Eighth Route Army in anti-Japanese battles of 1938. Note the loess caves of the Yenan area in the background.

U.S. Ambassador Patrick J. Hurley in Chungking in 1945. Mao Tse-tung is at his left.

Generalissimo Chiang Kai-shek (left) confers with Supreme Allied Commander Lord Mountbatten and T.V. Soong in 1945. In backround, (l. to r.) are Captain R.V. Brookman, Lieutenant General A. Carton De Wiart and Lieutenant General Browning.

In July 1944, the United States set up the Military Liaison Mission in Yenan, headed by Colonel David Barrett. The operation was known as Dixie. Among the small group of Americans there was John Stewart Service and John Paton Davies, both young diplomats who had traveled widely and were considered shrewd and perceptive observers of the China scene. Both feared that the rivalry between Chiang and the Communists would result in the resumption of the civil war and push the Communists into the arms of Moscow. They described Chiang's government as "organically weak" and suggested the Communists be brought into a coalition government, or at least establish U.S.-Communist cooperation to influence them away from the Soviet Union.

Davies said: "The Communists are in China to stay. And China's destiny is not Chiang's but theirs."

Meanwhile, the military situation in China deteriorated badly. President Roosevelt told Chiang he was promoting Stilwell to full general and wanted him in overall command of American and Chinese forces. He sent General Patrick Hurley, a tall, mustachioed former Secretary of War who was proud of his part-Cherokee Indian origins, as his personal representative to act with Chiang on political matters. But the relationship between Stilwell and Chiang only went from bad to worse and Roosevelt, advised that Vinegar Joe and Peanut were "fundamentally incompatible," was persuaded to recall Stilwell and name Lieutenant General Albert Wedemeyer to replace him.

Hurley, meanwhile, made it his mission to bring together the Nationalist and Communist forces into a united military front to battle the Japanese. In November 1944, he went to Yenan—unannounced. The startled Communists turned out an honor guard, which Hurley reviewed. Then he drew himself up to his full height—and let out an Indian war whoop.

During his stay in Yenan, Hurley got Mao to sign an agreement calling for reorganization of the government into a coalition of anti-Japanese parties and implicitly promising the Communists a share of U.S. aid. Chiang, predictably, rejected it, offered a counterproposal which was promptly rejected by the Communists.

The bargaining went on as Hurley became the U.S. ambassador to China, replacing Clarence Gauss. In the closing days of August 1945, Hurley went to Yenan and returned to Chungking, the wartime capital, with Mao himself. Before Mao left in October, agreement was announced on the convening of a multi-party Political Consultative Council which would make recommendations for a draft constitution as well as lay plans for China's economic reconstruction. It set a date for a national congress to approve the measures. The Communists accepted a compromise of twenty on the number of military divisions they would have in the new national army of one hundred divisions.

Those main points were the basis for the long and complicated negotiations that preoccupied the Communists, the Nationalists and the United States for the next two years.

Associated Press Correspondent John Roderick talks with Mao Tse-tung at Yenan in December of 1945.

Chou En-lai signs ceasefire order for the Communists in Chungking on January 10, 1946. U.S. General George Marshall, special envoy to China (r.), and Chang Chun, representing the Nationalist government, look on.

Mao Tse-tung (c.), with Chou En-lai and Chu Teh (r.) at the Communist Chinese wartime base at Yenan.

General George C. Marshall, on a peace mission as special representative of President Truman, reviews Chinese Communist troops in Yenan in 1946.

From the left: Chou En-lai, Marshall, Chu Teh, Chang Chi-chung, Mao Tse-tung.

The Marshall Mission

On November 27, 1945, President Harry Truman appointed General George C. Marshall as his special representative, with ambassador rank, to use American influence for the "unification of China by peaceful democratic methods" and help bring about a cease-fire. Truman instructed Marshall to speak with Chiang and the other leaders and make it known they could expect no military aid or economic credits if the civil war continued to tear the nation apart.

The Communists heard the news of Marshall's appointment in Yenan and shared their pleasure with four foreign correspondents, three Americans and a Frenchman, who had arrived there the day before. They were the first to visit the blockaded and little-known Communist capital since the end of World War II. Among them was Associated Press Correspondent John Roderick, who remained in Yenan for four months and returned late in 1946 for two more months to cover the Communist aspects of the negotiations. He described the visit:

"A primitive city of fifty thousand, Yenan sits astride the camel caravan routes which lead to Inner Mongolia and North China. The sands of the nearby Gobi Desert havelaid down over the centuries the tawny loess hills which are characteristic of Northwest China. In 1938, Japanese bombers leveled the city leaving only its walls standing. Refusing to leave, the Communists dug ten thousand caves in the hills, where they lived, worked and studied.

"There were cave hospitals, universities, party schools, radio stations, printing presses, nurseries, stores and dwellings. A Tang Dynasty pagoda standing on one of the hills provided a link between old China and the Communist present. In the single city street, which the city's merchants had rebuilt within the walls, furns, bolts of cheap cloth, pots, pans, locally-made carpets, baskets, brassware and salt were on sale. In one building, a docile mule powered a crude wood-combing machine. The Communists lived a spartan life, their food rationed, their clothes faded and patches and their pleasures few.

"Horses and camels were more numerous than automobiles. The party leadership moved about in antiquated luxury in the rear of a sedan, converted into a truck, donated by a San Francisco Chinese association. There was no electricity except in the American Mission which had a gasoline generator of its own. Oil lamps and candles supplied the only light. Charcoal braziers furnished a tiny glow of heat in the chilly caves. There was, however, a perfectly functioning telephone system, captured intact from a Japanese headquarters company.

"The desert dryness and the altitude of about two thousand feet gave the air an invigorating quality and magnified the size of the stars which glowed in the clear black sky. The Communist chieftains staged performances of the Peking Opera, which Mao enjoyed, in a barn-like building open to the blasts of winter. Occasionally, they attended the movies at the U.S. Mission. Abbott and Costello were favorites."

Roderick talked with Mao about Marshall and the progress of the negotiations. Mao, he said, chain-smoked and drank hot tea as they talked, and enjoyed eating the peppery food of his native Hunan. Once, over a fish dinner that seemed rich fare for the Communists, Mao explained, with a smile: "Mr. Roderick, we are Communists but we are also Chinese, and we like good food. Also, you are a guest and nothing is too good for a guest. We don't eat like this all the time."

Chou En-lai during the Communist "People's War of Liberation" against the Nationalist troops in 1947.

Young member of the Red Army youth group holds a National flag in Yenan in 1947. Background shows the rugged loess and caves of the Communist headquarters.

Inner Mongolian troops in a drill session before going off to battle the Red Army in 1947.

The Marshall mission seemed to be going well. Both the Communists and the Nationalists had indicated they were ready for compromise. On January 10, 1946, both sides ordered a cease-fire and banned all troop movements, except those of Nationalist forces into Manchuria. But the Nationalists took that opportunity to try to seize all of Manchuria rather than solely establishing its sovereignty, to which the Communists had agreed. Clashes began again in the Manchurian countryside and this time did not stop.

The Marshall mission failed. On January 7, 1947, Marshall issued a personal statement, which said,

"the greatest obstacle to peace has been the complete, almost overwhelming suspicion with which the Chinese Communist Party and the Kuomintang [Nationalists] regard each other." He scored both the Kuomintang "reactionaries" and the "dyed-in-the-wool Communists" who "did not hesitate at the most drastic measures to gain their ends."

Wounded Nationalists of the 26th Division await evacuation after fighting with Communist troops near Shantung in early 1947. Their defeated commander committed suicide.

The civil war between Communists and Nationalists resumed in earnest.

The strength of Chiang and his armies crumbled slowly, while Communist forces gained both morale and military victories.

China's economy was now in shambles. Inflation ballooned and foreign exchange reserves had shrunk. Corruption in government was rampant; military commanders took money for nonexistent divisions. Corrupt officials squeezed money from the peasants, rich businessmen evaded taxes and soldiers and police ignored the political rights of others, throwing students in jail with no trials, no sentences.

Late in October 1948, Mukden (Shenyang) in Manchuria fell, with three hundred thousand government soldiers lost.

Youngster in the middle is one of the "Little Devils," army cooks' helpers. Most are fugitives of hunger at home.

The decapitated head of a Chinese Communist guerrilla hangs on a wall after capture and execution by Nationalist troops (1948).

On February 3, 1949, the Manchurian divisions of Lin Biao entered Beijing. On April 4, Chu Teh began massing a million troops on the north bank of the Yangtze, the final barrier between the Red Army and the southern outposts still loyal to the Nationalists. In the first week of May, Chiang fled to Taiwan (then Formosa) and a few months later announced the formation of his new government in Taipei.

In August, U.S. Secretary of State Dean Acheson issued a White Paper conceding that China had fallen into Communist hands and that there would be no more aid to Nationalist China.

Calling Chiang's regime "incompetent," Acheson added: "The unfortunate, but inescapable fact is that the result of the civil war in China was beyond the control of the government of the United States. Nothing that this country did or could have done within the limits of its capabilities [he mentioned the efforts of Stilwell, Hurley and Marshall] could have changed that result. . . . It was the product of internal Chinese forces, which this country tried to influence but could not."

A patrol truck in Peking in January 1949 carries police and military judges who had the power to execute immediately anyone violating wartime law.

A Chinese Nationalist tank rolls through the streets of Shanghai in April 1949, ready to move south for the battle against Chinese Communists.

Helmeted Communist guards herd Chinese
Nationalist troops toward prisoner of war camps
after fighting in Woosung in June 1949.

A Chinese Communist soldier stands atop a tank in Shanghai during a patrol of the business section of that city in June 1949.

A mixed brigade of soldiers of the Communist army in 1949.

Chinese in Beijing welcomed Communist forces entering the city in May 1949. In the background are portaits of the Chinese Communist leaders, with Mao Tse-tung in the middle.

Mao Tse-tung stands in a jeep to review troops moving into Beijing in 1949. After taking the city, Mao established his capital there. (The jeep is U.S.-made, captured from the Nationalist armies of Chiang Kai-shek.)

Communist troops entered Shanghai in 1949.

III

Birth of a Nation

By mid-1949, the Communists had seized Nanking (Nanjing), the Nationalist capital, and Shanghai, and were swiftly moving southward. Victory was near complete by the fall, with the southern city of Canton under seige and the main force of Chiang Kai-shek's Nationalists fleeing to Taiwan. The time had come to declare the birth of the new nation.

On September 21, Mao convened a meeting of the People's Political Consultative Conference, the forerunner to China's legislature, to adopt a Common Program that would serve as a temporary constitution.

The six hundred and sixty-two delegates chosen by the Communist Party agreed that China was to be a "people's democratic dictatorship" under the leadership of the working class. The phrasing, subtly different from the Soviet "dictatorship of the proletariat," was an indication of the party's initial desire that non-working class sectors of the society—intellectuals, small capitalists and sympathetic non-communist politicians—would cooperate in the heady task of forging the new nation. This open arms policy was reflected in the design of the new Chinese flag approved at the meeting. The flag has five yellow stars on a red background, with the big star representing the Communist Party and the four smaller ones symbolizing workers, peasants, the petty bourgeois and the national, or larger scale, bourgeois.

Mao's supremacy was reaffirmed with his election as chairman of the Central People's Government Council. He also headed the party Central Committee, the Central Secretariat of the party, and the People's Revolutionary Military Council. Chou En-lai was named premier of the State Council, China's Cabinet, and Foreign Minister.

Mao at national congress of the Communist Party in China, in 1945.

On October 1, 1949, Mao, Chou and other dignitaries such as President-to-be Liu Shaoqi, Red Army Commander in Chief Chu Teh and Chiang Kai-shek's sister-in-law Soong Ching-ling scrambled up the steep stairway of the Tiananmen Gate rostrum for ceremonies marking the founding of the People's Republic of China. At 3 p.m. Mao pushed a button to raise the national flag and proclaimed:

"A drama begins with a prologue, but the prologue is not the climax. The Chinese revolution is great, but the road after the revolution will be longer, the work greater and more arduous . . . . To win countrywide victory is only the first step in a long march . . . . Even if this step is worthy of pride, it is comparatively tiny; what will be more worthy of pride is yet to come . . . .

"The Chinese people, one quarter of humanity, have stood up . . . . From now on, no one will insult us again."

Some three hundred thousand people streamed before the rostrum, shouting, "Long Live Mao Tse-tung, Long Live the Communist Party." Mao shouted back, "Long Live the People." The crowds included soldiers riding horses, tanks and throngs of people singing revolutionary songs. One highlight was a flyover by Red Army pilots flying American-made planes captured from the Nationalists.

The communists had taken over one of the most destitute countries on earth. The peasants who comprised 80 percent of the population, exploited by landlords and helpless before frequent natural disasters, subsisted on the edge of poverty and starvation. Industry and agriculture had been destroyed by decades of warfare. Killer diseases such as plague and cholera were common, while few had access to doctors and hospitals. Eighty percent of the nation was illiterate and few peasants had the ability, or the incentive, to send their children, especially girls, to school.

Chinese Communist marchers, carrying banners and portraits of Josef Stalin and Chinese Communist leaders, parade along the Pearl River waterfront in Canton just weeks after they captured the city on October 15, 1947.

Communist troops enter Nanking.

Chairman Mao chatting with young fighters of the Eighth Route Army in Yenan in 1939.

On a tour of Beijing, Mao (center, dark coat) greeted a group of Communist army officers. General Chu Teh is at his right.

Chinese soldiers, police and civilians retreating from advancing Communist forces in 1949 jam this ferry crossing the Yangtze from Fukow to Nanking.

Mao Tse-tung (front center) attending a political conference in Beijing in June 1949.

The cities were plagued by massive unemployment, runaway inflation, opium addiction, prostitution and corruption. Government administrations were in disarray after years of war and warlord factionalism that had broken down centralized controls.

The new government sought to rectify that fragmentation by asserting adherence to "democratic centralism" that allowed for some input from lower levels in policy-making but demanded obedience to the final decisions made by the center, Beijing. Still, the leaders realized the impossibility of instantly turning a huge country of more than five hundred million people into a highly disciplined socialist state.

The state, of course, was to play the dominant role, with party cadres, or officials, fanning out across the nation to organize and control work and living units. But in the countryside, farmers were to be allowed to grow and market some of their own produce, with only a gradual shift toward collectivization. In the cities, private shopkeepers and small-scale capitalists were for the time being not to be disturbed. The party realized that their skills and business acumen were crucial in the economic rebuilding process.

Chinese intellectuals who had fled the country during the years of turmoil were encouraged to return. Thousands did, giving up comfortable lives overseas to make their patriotic contribution to "New China." The party also sanctioned the continued existence of some non-Communist but sympathetic political parties, small groups made up mainly of leftist intellectuals. The "democratic parties" were not permitted to challenge the Communist Party for power, but did serve as a handy device to show that the ruling party was willing to listen to a pluralism of opinions.

The party, however, was quick to show it would use force, and violence, in its drive to eradicate all real and perceived opponents. On March 18, 1950, the party Central Committee issued its "directive on resolute suppression of counter-revolutionaries," giving authorization to a nationwide purge of enemies of the state. Estimates of the number killed during the first five years of Chinese Communist rule have ranged up into the millions. Landlords, rich merchants, Nationalist sympathizers and criminals were dragged before mass trials for haranguing, arbitrary sentencing and quick executions. The

The hungry holding up their rice bowls for food (1955).

wave of terror reached its peak in a virulent campaign in 1951.

Those not subject to persecution faced constant political indoctrination and pressure from mass organizations, party propaganda officials and the secret police as the party moved to create the "new socialist man." Centuries of Confucian teachings that emphasized the primacy of the family, obedience to one's masters and the importance of scholarship were swept away in the interests of perpetuating revolutionary change under the new leaders—the party and the working class. People were told they must put the state ahead of their families, and were to be imbued with the "five loves"—for the fatherland, the people, labor, science and public property. Political meetings and struggle sessions were almost daily, during which people were supposed to criticize others and themselves for being faint-hearted in carrying forth the revolution.

China's communists, unlike their comrades in the Soviet Union, had their roots with the peasantry, and it was to the countryside that the new government turned in its first attempts to transform society.

On June 30, 1950, the government passed the Agrarian Reform Law designed to return the land to the people who actually worked it. Teams were dispatched throughout the country to redistribute land in favor of poor and middle-level peasants and to form associations or mutual aid groups, the forerunners of collectives.

Mass meetings were called to condemn and sometimes execute landlords who had kept the peasants in poverty and a virtual state of serfdom. By August 1952, some three hundred million peasants who previously had little or no land were assigned their own small plots.

At the same time, farmers were under pressure to transform their loosely organized mutual aid groups into agricultural producers cooperatives in which twenty to forty households actually worked common land, dividing up their labor and their returns.

The peasants, many who were farming their own land for the first time in their lives, did not take well to collectivization, and their resistance quickly brought to the surface the strains and ideological conflicts that were to become endemic to Chinese politics. Both in 1953 and 1955 the government ordered some of the new cooperatives to be dissolved and urged caution in forming new collectives. Those advocating a slower approach to agrarian reform included Chou, the pragmatic economist Chen Yun and Liu Shaoqi, then the second-ranking vice-chairman of the PRC and a member of the Politburo

Standing Committee.

Mao, however, would not tolerate what he considered to be retreats in imposing his policies. After the party formulated a cautious stance toward further collectivization in 1955, Mao stormed, "some of our comrades are tottering along like a woman with bound feet and constantly complaining, 'you're going too fast'." As he was to do so many times in the coming years, Mao used his personal influence to change the direction of the party. Instead of slowing down, the cooperative movement took off in what came to be called the High Tide movement, and by the end of 1956, 88 percent of peasant households belonged to cooperatives.

The Red Army, renamed the People's Liberation Army, marched into eastern Tibet in October 1950, consolidating Communist power over the last uncontrolled area of the mainland. The Buddhist oligarchy headed by the Dalai Lama could offer little resistance to the stronger Chinese troops, and in May 1951 agreed to what China called the "peaceful liberation" of Tibet. Troops moved into the holy city of Lhasa in September that year.

The military took on a far more dangerous enterprise with Mao's decision in October 1950 to send "volunteers" across the Yalu River to assist North Korea against U.S. and South Korean troops in the Korean War. China had stayed on the sidelines after the war started in June of that year, but Mao had moved toward involvement after U.S. President

Shengtong villagers staged an anti-American rally in 1951. Cloth banner reads: "Come on, our farming friends! Swing into action! Stand sternly against the American imperialist plan of re-arming Japan!"

Mao leading National Day celebration on the second anniversary of the founding of the People's Republic of China, October 1, 1951.

Farmers in Shengtong village in the northern outskirts of Shanghai set up boundary posts marking the land that was redistributed in 1951. "Yangko" drummers give a popular flourish to the occasion. Poster reads: "We are the farmers who finally got on top."

Harry Truman ordered the Seventh Fleet to prevent China from using the diversion in Korea as an opportunity to attack Taiwan and as U.S. troops began to drive the North Koreans toward the Chinese border. China warned that it would not tolerate a U.S.-dominated Korea, regarding it as a threat to its industrial northeast. On October 8, Mao issued orders for hundreds of thousands of troops to enter Korea to "resist the attacks of U.S. imperialism and its running dogs."

The caption from the China photo service read: "The People's Militia in northeast China prepare to defend the soil against aggression." (1951)

With Chinese assistance, the North Koreans fought their opponents to a stalemate, with a cease-fire finally called in 1953. The "victory" of the PLA over the vaunted U.S. war machine helped unite the country, elevated the status of the PLA, won the lasting gratitude of the North Korean government and, perhaps most important, proved to Stalin that the new revolutionary government in China was willing and had the ability to uphold the socialist cause in Asia.

The costs, however, were heavy. Up to nine hundred thousand Chinese, including one of Mao's sons, were killed in the war, and the military intervention was a serious setback to economic recovery plans. The war also killed any hopes some Chinese leaders had of improving relations with the United States, and eventually obtaining U.S. aid. Washington imposed a complete embargo on all trade with China and strengthened ties with the Nationalists in Taiwan.

The freeze between the two countries was to last another twenty years.

*A U.S. Marine Corps tank in Korea pauses near
what was left of a Chinese anti-tank gun.*

*U.S. Marines walking past dead Chinese soldier in
Korea in 1951.*

Mao Tse-tung at the First National People's Congress in 1954.

The Soviet Union was the first country to recognize the new government in Beijing, and became China's principal benefactor in the early 1950s, but relations were marked by distrust from the first. Stalin had long belittled Mao and his rural guerrillas, and had never given full support to their cause, pressing instead for a coalition with Chiang Kai-Shek's Nationalists. At the end of the war in 1945, the Soviets stripped industrial facilities in Manchuria and in 1949 urged the Moslem region of Xinjiang, China's westernmost province, to declare itself independent.

Mao traveled to Moscow in December 1949, but was treated coldly by Stalin and had to stay in the Soviet capital for two months before the two sides could agree on a peace treaty. The terms were not particularly generous. The Soviets provided $300 million in credit over a five-year period, but were slow to return captured property from Manchuria and retained control of Port Arthur, or Dalian, until 1955. China was forced to accept the independence of the Soviet client state of Mongolia.

Still, the Soviets sent thousands of technical advisers to aid in the operation of Chinese factories, many built with Soviet technology. China's best young students were sent to the Soviet Union, including many, such as Li Peng and Jiang Zemin, who were to become China's top leaders as the 1990s began. Mao in 1952 described the relationship with the Soviet Union as "lasting, unbreakable and invincible."

The government at the end of 1952 declared that the transitional period had been completed with resounding successes. It said agricultural and industrial output had shot up 77 percent from 1949, and that a sound economic base for further progress had been established. In 1953 the State Council under the direction of Chen Yun put into effect the nation's first five-year plan, with ambitious goals to double industrial output and increase agricultural production by one-fourth. In the end, bolstered by good weather, Soviet aid and general support for government policy, the planners exceeded targets by 17 percent. The achievements, while putting the country on a firm economic footing and helping millions escape poverty, were not without their side-effects. Mao and other revolutionaries, heady with success and certain that more socialism would spur the economy to greater heights, began to overextend themselves. The target for the second five-year plan was to increase both industrial and agricultural production by 75 percent by 1962. Instead, the country was heading toward the Great Leap Forward and disaster.

The nation's first constitution, promulgated in 1954, defined the four classes of workers, peasants and the two bourgeois and listed four types of ownership—state, cooperative, individual and capitalist. The National People's Congress was given lawmaking powers and characterized as the highest organ of the government, although in reality the NPC and all lower-level people's congresses did the bidding of the Communist Party, which in effect picked their members and decided what legislation was to be enacted.

Also in 1954 the nation held its first elections, with all citizens except landlords and counter-revolutionaries given the voting franchise. But here too it was the party that decided who would stand for office and the only direct votes were for seats in the lowest-level county and district congresses. The lower congresses then selected delegates to the provincial congresses, which in turn picked the approximately three thousand deputies to the National People's Congress.

Many Chinese today look back on the 1950s as a golden era of rapid growth, great accomplishments and high idealism. Mao, however, saw the transition of the party from fighting force to ruling power as creating new and pernicious challenges to his revolutionary goals. For Mao, constant political struggle and periodic upheaval were the only recourse to a leadership he saw slipping into complacency and self-interest and a populace that stubbornly resisted political enlightenment.

In January 1952, Mao launched his first nationwide movement, the "three antis" campaign against corruption, waste and bureaucracy. This was followed by a party Central Committee campaign against the "five evils" of bribery, tax evasion, theft of state property, cheating on government contracts and stealing economic information. Many welcomed these movements as an indication that the Communist government would not tolerate the corruption and theft that were so much a part of past Chinese regimes. But these early campaigns were to set a precedent for repeated mass movements characterized by frantic propagandizing, economic and social disruptions and vicious attacks on individuals.

The "three antis" movement, which like most others faded into oblivion as the leaders in Beijing became caught up in other concerns, also pointed out how quickly and deeply corruption took root in the

Trying out homemade skates on the ice of the Pei Hai Lake, Beijing. Nail-tipped bamboo sticks help the boys along.

fast-growing bureaucracy. Communist Party membership jumped from 4.5 million members in 1949 to 12.7 million in 1957, corresponding to the growing need for cadres to oversee the rapid collectivization in the countryside. Many of the newer members, not tempered by the hardships of Red Army service, were more susceptible to the temptations their newly won authority offered. Attacks were launched against those who ignored class struggle or engaged in side-business, and there campaigns against "commandism"—pushing people around—and "tailism"—getting ahead by mouthing the current line.

The drive to wipe out all unorthodoxy was also manifested in the 1954-55 campaign against writer Hu Feng. In 1954, Hu, a protege of the revered pre-liberation writer Lu Xun, impetuously presented a report to the Central Committee in which he said the ideological remolding of writers was leading to intellectual sterility. He claimed a "subjective struggling spirit" could bring a writer closer to communism than pat material on peasants, workers and soldiers. He was first criticized as a "deviationist," but the charges quickly escalated to "counter-revolutionary" plotting. He was stripped of all his posts and imprisoned in July 1955.

Mao's sense of being surrounded by revisionists and humanists who would undermine the revolutionary goals set down in Yenan so many years before was exacerbated by the shock of Soviet Premier Nikita Khrushchev's 1956 speech enumerating the crimes and errors of the late Josef Stalin. Despite Mao's difficult relations with Stalin, he respected the Soviet leader as a revolutionary fighter who had carried the banner of world communism. Khrushchev, however, was a mere apparatchik who was soft on ideology and preached peaceful coexistence with the capitalists. Khrushchev's speech marked the start of the rapid decline in Sino-Soviet relations. Moreover it put Mao on his guard against similar tendencies at home to accept the domestic and international status quo rather than forge ahead with bold new measures to bring about communism's ultimate triumph.

In November 1956, Mao pushed forward plans to confiscate all capitalist industrial and commercial enterprises. Almost the entire remaining private sector was incorporated into cooperatives, with former owners given positions as managers and handed bonds for their expropriated property. On January 15, 1957, some two hundred thousand people gathered on Tiananmen Square to celebrate the state takeover of all privately run industrial and commercial firms in Bejing. This, however, was only the beginning of Mao's grand designs.

IV

A Hundred Flowers

Mao, despite his experiences as a student and educator, regarded intellectuals with distrust. He considered them effete, equivocal in their thinking, divorced from the realities of China, lacking in revolutionary fervor and unable to translate ideas into action. These sentiments were shared by many in the Communist leadership, who like Mao came from peasant backgrounds and who had accomplished the liberation of China through great physical perseverance and suffering. Intellectuals were not "red"—revolutionary—enough and as Mao once put it, the more books one reads the more stupid one becomes.

But Mao was enough of a realist to understand that intellectuals—scholars, engineers, managers, scientists and even artists—could make an important contribution to the nation's development. The party was also basically correct in assuming that most intellectuals, even if not party members, supported the party's goals of removing social inequalities and transforming China into a great modern nation.

By 1956, some party leaders, buoyed by the economic successes of the first years of Communist rule, felt they could loosen the reins a bit on the open expression of personal opinion. More free speech, it was believed, would act as a safety valve allowing intellectuals to let off a little steam while carrying out their duties within the system.

On May 2, 1956, Mao proposed at a Supreme State Conference that the policy of "let a hundred flowers bloom, let a hundred schools of thought contend" should be followed in art, literature and

Young Chinese work side by side in a rice paddy in Hunan province in South China. Note the girls in the foreground have a two-pigtail hairdo, "regulation" for most young ladies in China in the late 1950s.

academic research. Party Propaganda Department chief Lu Dingyi repeated the slogan later in the month, while the party also raised the slogan "long-term coexistence and mutual supervision between party and non-Communist elements."

The initial response from intellectuals was guarded. The year, however, did produce "A New Young Man Arrives at the Organization Department," a story by young writer Wang Meng that lays bare the problem of bureaucratism.

Intellectuals might also have been forewarned by Mao's February 27, 1957, speech "on the correct handling of contradictions among the people." In this document, Mao acknowledged that non-Marxist intellectuals are needed for China's development and their opinions can help keep the party and bureaucracy on the right path. But he also stressed that in a militantly revolutionary society like China there can be only limited tolerance of public dissent. Some contradictions among the people can be handled through discussions, he said, but others are antagonistic and cannot be handled peacefully.

Two months later, at Mao's urging, the party put intellectuals to the test by issuing a directive on rectification of the party work style. The campaign was aimed at exposing "bureaucratism, sectarianism and subjectivism" within the party. Mao emphasized that criticism of the party was to be handled "like gentle breeze and fine rain."

Instead, there was a storm of complaints and criticisms of the party. Students staged protests and put up posters, writers published exposes of party wrongdoings, scholars demanded the release of imprisoned intellectuals, and some even questioned basic Communist principles of one-party rule and democratic centralism. Critics said party mottoes about "serving the people" had become a farce, and that the party was becoming a new mandarin class concerned mainly with personal gain.

The "Hundred Flowers Movement" ended abruptly on June 8, when the party Central Committee issued a directive to "muster our forces to repulse rightists' wild attacks." The Communist Party's People's Daily followed with scathing attacks on "rightists," and the "Anti-Rightist Movement," a major witchhunt against China's educated class, began in earnest. Hundreds of thousands of intellectuals and technocrats were singled out for public humiliation, imprisonment and banishment to the countryside. Their families were branded "enemies of the people." For thousands of China's brightest intellectuals, people such as Wang Meng, it would be at least twenty years, until the end of the Cultural Revolution, before they could resume their careers and return to some semblance of a normal life.

Chinese scholars have long debated the reasons behind the calling of the "Hundred Flowers Movement" and the quick smashing of those who responded to the call. Some argue that the party was over-confident, and believed the intellectuals would meekly follow the party line. When intellectuals reacted with a torrent of criticism and pent-up dissatisfaction, the party struck back using its tried-and-true methods of force and repression.

Others, however, argue that Mao had laid a clever trap for the intellectuals, giving them just enough rope to hang themselves. Mao himself gave credence to this argument in a speech at the third plenary session of the Eighth Party Congress that September in which he said the purpose of the campaign was "to let demons and devils, ghosts and monsters, air views freely and let poisonous weeds sprout and grow in profusion so that the people, now shocked to find these ugly things still exist in the world, would take action to wipe them out."

The answer probably lies somewhere in the middle. The party does appear to have been shocked by the scale of the "Hundred Flowers" outcry. Mao then took advantage of this dismay to teach dissenting intellectuals a decisive lesson and reassert his basic premise that "class struggle" must still be the key principle guiding party actions. China's main battle, he told the congress, was between the proletariat and the bourgeoisie, between the socialist and capitalist roads.

A year earlier, in September 1956, the first session of the Eighth Party Congress had dealt that premise a defeat, issuing a statement that the main contradiction was no longer between the working class and the bourgeoisie, but between people's rapidly growing economic and cultural needs and the inability to meet them.

The idea, to be resurrected more than two dec-

ades later when Deng Xiaoping came to power, reflected the thinking of pragmatists who were rising in the party hierarchy. The 1956 congress named Deng to be general secretary of the party, replacing

Mao, and elected Chou, Liu Shaoqi, Chu Teh and Chen Yun, all known for their more measured approach to revolution, as vice chairmen. Mao remained as chairman, but Mao Tse-tung Thought

Chinese farmers tilling the soil near Hankow in 1957.

Chinese peasants of the Wei Hsing People's Commune working on a reservoir for irrigation in 1959.

At a Communist Youth meeting in 1957 (l. to r.): Chou En-lai, Chu Teh, Mao Tse-tung, and Liu Shaoqi, who had just been named president. Mao became Chairman of the Communist Party.

was dropped as a guiding principle in the party and Mao retreated to the "second line" in party affairs, letting Liu and Deng handle day-to-day business. The congress called for development of people's democracy and opposition to personality cults, an obvious reference to Mao.

Mao's seeming political defeat in 1956 was directly related to the difficulties in the economy. The "High Tide" movement of rapid collectivization was abandoned by the summer of 1956 because of persistent resistance and problems. The agricultural producers cooperatives were failing to meet expectations. There were serious management problems, resulting in improper distribution of income, inefficient planting and harvesting and poor care of livestock. Some cooperatives were underreporting their yields to save on taxes and allow farmers to sell more on the free markets. Despite figures showing good harvests, rationing increased in the cities. There were reports of food shortages. The stress on developing

heavy industry had also left agriculture short of investment funds, a problem shared by consumer and construction industries.

As in 1955 when Mao launched the High Tide movement, he believed the problem lay not in the nature of the reforms but in the failure of the government to carry them out with speed and decisiveness. In the summer of 1957, at the same time he was cracking down on "rightist" intellectuals, Mao gave orders for a major rural rectification campaign to straighten out lassitude and wrong-thinking among rural leaders. That August the State Council ordered the closure of all rural free markets, cutting off a major incentive for the spurning of the cooperative movement. At the third plenum of the Eighth Party Congress the next month, a regenerated Mao pushed through plans for a comprehensive mobilization in the countryside. In the following months millions of cadres were sent into rural areas to propagate and enforce government policies.

Mao traveled to Moscow in November 1957 for a conclave marking the fortieth anniversity of the So-

Chinese girls using an old-fashioned irrigation waterwheel at a farm near Hangkow in 1956.

viet revolution. While there, his disputes with Khrushchev over peaceful coexistence with the West and the gradual transition to socialism became increasingly strident. The trip reinforced Mao's belief that the Soviets had become incorrigibly revisionist, and that Beijing, rather than Moscow, must

be the lodestar of world communism.

Mao was also convinced that the Soviet models of heavy industry and central planning were not appropriate for China. After the "Hundred Flowers" movement he was also disillusioned with intellectuals and their promise of providing expertise to the nation. Instead, Mao believed, China must fall back on its one unquestionable resource, its unlimited manpower. Like the Chinese emperors of the past who mobilized the nation's vast population to built the Great Wall and the Grand Canal, Mao believed that the grand structures of a modern nation could be built on the backs of millions of peasants. The result was the disastrous 1958-59 Great Leap Forward.

Great Leap Forward

The Great Leap Forward was launched on the premise that rapid modernization could be accomplished better through mobilization of the unskilled masses than introduction of technology, better through ideology and politics than economic planning. It was a two-pronged attack, with people told they must learn to "walk on two legs" by gaining self-sufficiency in both agriculture and industry. Material incentives were shunned under the belief that the revivalist spirit engendered by the campaign and patriotic appeals to work for the nation and the common good would sustain the movement.

The goal was to increase industrial output by 33 percent in 1958 and to surpass Britain as an industrial power in 15 years. At the end of 1958 the government claimed that output had actually grown a remarkable 65 percent, a highly suspect figure since Mao had abolished the Central Statistical Bureau and officials in the field were grossly exaggerating production figures in order to meet unrealistically high targets.

The first commune, the Weixing People's Commune in Henan province, was established on April 20, 1958, and in the following months cooperatives were organized into communes at a frantic rate. By November almost all peasants were relegated to some twentuy-six thousand communes across the country, with each composed of about thirty cooperatives and twenty-five thousand people. People

Women of the Shihchiching People's Commune harvest the corn crop in one of the farm communes established throughout China in 1958.

Workers planning their day's chores on a collective farm in 1958. Combines in background were brought from the Soviet Union. In efforts to boost sagging food production, the government confiscated nearly 120 million acres of land between 1950 and 1953 and parceled it out, with machinery and animals, to the peasants.

lived in their own homes, but the commune confiscated almost all private property and took over administration of nurseries, schools, health care, banking, supplies and most other basic needs. People ate in communal kitchens and were paid in accordance with the number of work points they earned.

A secret party meeting that May adopted Mao's line of "going all out, aiming high and achieving greater, faster, better and more economic results to build socialism." Liu, falling in line with Mao, delivered the main speech, while Chen Yun, the economist who opposed radical economic changes, was safely away on a trip to Moscow. Marshal Lin Biao, whose support of Mao's leftist policies was tied to his political ambitions, was named to the Politburo Standing Committee.

"Going all out" meant bold experiments in every aspect of Chinese society. Besides starting up the communes, millions of peasants were organized to build dams and water conservancy projects. Education was revamped to downplay academics and give greater importance to work-study programs and providing schooling to the children of workers and peasants. Small-scale urban and rural industries mushroomed, and millions of women entered the work force for the first time because of the demand for labor. Egalitarianism reached new heights, with millions of cadres forced to join in physical labor and peasants with little education given major managerial roles. Millions of students and soldiers were sent to the countryside to haul dirt along with their peasant comrades.

Spectacular results were recorded in industrial production, public works projects and agricultural output. Under the Three Banners of the General Line, the Great Leap Forward and the People's Communes, agricultural and industrial output was said to have more than doubled. But the costs were extremely heavy, as exemplified by the backyard steel furnaces that became the symbol of the movement. By the end of 1958 it was reported that farmers and workers had built 600,000 backyard iron and steel plants, helping to double the nation's steel output in one year. But despite the heroic efforts of the people, who scoured for pots and pans and metal scraps to feed their furnaces, much of the steel was of such low quality that it was unusable. Moreover, peasants ordered to keep their furnace fires burning did irreparable damage to the environment, with entire forests being denuded for fuel.

Another example of waste and mismanagement was the "four pests" campaign in which millions were sent out to destroy flies, mosquitoes, rats and sparrows. The campaign upset the ecological balance, because sparrows eat bugs and other pests, and in the end the pest problem only became worse. Centralization was at times carried to extremes as when farmers around the country were given orders to carry out deep plowing and close planting. This recipe for high yields proved totally unsuitable for some places, and caused serious erosion in others.

Mechanized rice planter is used in efforts to grow more food during the Great Leap Forward in agriculture.

The most critical mistake was to take millions of peasants away from the land for months at a time to work in city factories and on public works projects. Cities had to cut rations because of the increased population and there was marked deterioration of farmland because the best workers were gone. The environmental damage caused by the Great Leap, and inadequate attention to the land, were major factors in the flooding and pest infestation during the next three years when China suffered through a major agricultural crisis.

Chinese laborers, working by hand, lay the groundwork for expansion at the Wuhan steel complex. The expansion, in 1958, was part of a campaign to double steel production in one year.

Workers at a steel producing center being built in 1958 at Wuhan.

Chinese peasants laboring with a primitive forge to turn out steel in 1958. At this village blast furnace, the two men at right turn a wheel by hand to run the belt that operates the blower.

Nikita Khrushchev greeted by Mao on a September 30, 1959 visit to mark ten years of Communist rule in China.

The nation's emotional high was given another boost by armed conflicts between China and the Nationalist forces on Taiwan centering around Nationalist-held islands off the coast. Khrushchev, fearing the fighting could escalate into a larger conflict with U.S. involvement, made a secret visit to Beijing in July 1958 to urge caution. He was ignored by the Chinese side, who called on the nation to double steel production to prepare for all-out war.

By the end of the year, with the chaos created by the Great Leap becoming obvious, Mao was again on the defensive. Neither Mao nor the party was in a position to repudiate the Great Leap because of their major commitment to radical modernization. However, at a conference in November Mao ad-

mitted to serious mistakes and said others in the party had been too eager for the communes to assume all public ownership rights and to make a quick transition to communism. Mao also refuted party ideologist Chen Boda's attempt to abandon all commodity production.

A Central Committee plenum in December 1958 took measures to decentralize the commune system and accepted Mao's request to step down as state chairman, or head of state, ostensibly so he could devote less time to ceremony and more to policy.

But as Mao later wrote, he was treated "like a dead man at his own funeral."

As the new year began, the party wavered, unsure of where it was heading. At the grassroots level, momentum for the Great Leap was still strong, with thousands of local leaders gearing up for another year of superhuman achievements. At the same time, many communes were beginning to revert back to a more decentralized structure, with production brigades, the former cooperatives, regaining control over planning and decision-making. Divisions were equally intense at the top, with some leaders urging that the Great Leap be carried forward with adjustments while others, at least privately, wanting it scrubbed. Mao, still trying to cover his losses, said at a February Central Committee meeting that the trend toward excessive egalitarianism and centralism should be corrected. But he continued to insist that the Great Leap with its mass mobilization represented the best way to override bureaucratic and naysaying tendencies on the road to quick political and economic victories.

The debate came to a head at an enlarged meeting of the Politburo in Lushan in July and August 1959. Defense Minister Peng Dehuai, regarded as China's second greatest military hero after Chu Teh, wrote a letter to Mao, presenting his views of the "leftist" errors committed during the Great Leap. Peng was backed up by other party leaders, including Chen Yun, who called for the cooperatives to be restored and for greater emphasis on expertise rather than "redness." Peng, in addition to taking the highly risky step of directly confronting Mao, was in a precarious position because he had recently returned from a tour of East Europe, which included a meeting with Khrushchev in Tirana, Albania. Peng had informed Khrushchev of the serious economic problems China was encountering and the Soviet leader had advised him to oppose Mao.

Mao, accusing Peng of conspiring against the party with Soviet backing, turned the party against the veteran revolutionary. His letter was branded as a "right opportunist anti-party program," and on August 2 the party purged Peng and three of his supporters from all their party and government posts.

On August 16, Mao stated: "The struggle at Lushan is a classic struggle, a continuation of the life-and-death struggle between the two major antagonistic classes, the bourgeoisie and the proletariat, a struggle which has been going on in the socialist revolution for the last 10 years."

Peng, who played an important role in the 1934-35 Long March and led Chinese forces in the Korean War, was replaced as defense minister by Lin Biao. He was arrested at the beginning of the Cultural Revolution in 1966 and died in 1974 while still in disgrace.

V

The Great Cultural Revolution

It was one of the sad ironies of Mao's radical approach to socialism that the masses—in particular the peasants—whom he saw as his rock and salvation, were the people he hurt the most.

Throughout his political career Mao had sought to politically energize the masses in his losing battle against bureaucratism, statism and official distortions of his revolutionary goals. Yet Mao, a child of the countryside and the first to give communism a strong rural dimension, failed to grasp the basic needs and rhythms of life of the peasantry, and in his drive to push them into the political vanguard was guilty of causing them great suffering.

Much of the good will engendered from the land reforms of the 1950s, when centuries of inequality were rectified, was dissipated by the forced collectivization of the following years. Farmers resented the confiscation of their mules, hoes and their few other private possessions. People who had always worked at their own pace for their own personal gain balked at being given assigned tasks to complete in a designated period. Moreover, any advantages that communal farming might have offered were often wiped out as a result of the excessive speed in which the communes were established. The hastily organized communes were plagued by poor planning, poor management and poor use of manpower.

The problems were exacerbated by the launching of the Great Leap Forward at the same time the

In an unchanging China, a farmer tills the soil in the ancient way, with a wooden plow and a water buffalo.

communes were getting off the ground. Millions of peasants and workers were marched off in 1958 and 1959 for months of participation in public works projects. Land conditions deteriorated and communes floundered from lack of leadership, disorganization and the demands for industrial as well as agricultural production.

By 1959 it was evident that the countryside was in serious trouble, and by 1960 large areas of the nation were beset by famine. Bad weather—three hundred and twenty million were affected by drought in 1959 and millions more were hit by flooding and pest infestation the next year—was in part responsible for the disaster. But even here, man-made destruction of the environment, one big side-effect of the Great Leap Forward, and the slighting of agricultural investment with the promotion of heavy industry, heightened the tragedy.

Estimates of the number of deaths from the effects of malnutrition during the "three hard years" of 1959 to 1961 run as high as twenty million to thirty million. Millions of people were out of work, and there were reports of rising crime and social unrest.

Production figures at the time were often inflated, and it is difficult to obtain a definite sense of the extent of the disaster. Official figures show that grain production fell from 195 million tons in 1957 to 160 million tons in 1962. Fruit production dropped from 3.2 to 2.7 million tons in that period and the output of pork, beef and mutton plunged from 4 million tons to less than 2 million.

The leaders in Beijing, when they spoke of the crisis at all, blamed it on natural disasters, but they were fully aware of the realities and the causes of

A state goal of Chinese industrialization in the late 1950's was to surpass Great Britain in steel production.

Relatively modern blast furnaces started to replace the small, crude furnaces of the start of the crash industrialization program of 1959.

Liu Shaoqi in 1950.

the problems. Chou En-lai and his wife Deng Ying-chao stopped eating meat and eggs for the three-year period to show their sympathy to the hungry masses. Liu Shaoqi, by nature a cold, stone-faced man, was said to have been deeply moved by the extent of the disaster during a six-week trip to the southern province of Hunan in the spring of 1961. In visits to numerous villages, including his birth-place, Liu found extensive malnutrition, a wide-spread breakdown of irrigation and water conser-vancy systems, and a general sense of bitterness among peasants who felt they had worked like slaves during the Great Leap Forward and now were being repaid with food shortages. "The prob-lems were not caused by natural calamities," Liu reportedly said. "They were man-made." The men he was referring to were quite plainly Mao and his radical supporters.

Role Model

Saints, martyrs and spirits have been brought to life as China's modern leaders try to teach their people to be good Communists in times of sinking fortunes for communism around the world.

The role model—selfless, hard-working, plain-living and loyal unto death—is a time-honored educational tool in Communist China. As China's hardline leaders seek absolute allegiance to their system, the party has again called on its paragons to lead the way.

They are a counterweight both to the anti-party, pro-West sentiments of the crushed pro-democracy movement of Tiananmen Square in 1989 and the political changes that swept Eastern Europe.

The perfect soldier, Lei Feng, perennially returns at times of ideological strife.

Nearly two decades after his death, Chinese today offer blood, sweep streets and give free haircuts in the name of peasant soldier Lei Feng.

Lei, who according to a children's song "walks a thousand miles and does a thousand good deeds," was killed in 1962 at age twenty-two when he backed his truck into a utility pole. But a year later, Chairman Mao Tse-tung proclaimed him a Communist saint in the first of many campaigns titled "Learn from Lei Feng."

According to legend, the fervent patriot secretly washed the clothes of his comrades, donated his savings to help peasants hit by floods and once gave his coat to a woman and her child during a freezing rainstorm.

For his latest reincarnation, the People's Liberation Army has distributed three hundred thousands copies of his diary "with a view to launching a new upsurge in the army on learning from Lei Feng."

The *PLA Daily*, newspaper of the People's Liberation Army, said some supporters of "degenerate Western bourgeois concepts" have tried to denigrate Lei by saying he's outdated. But it added: "If all soldiers can be like Lei Feng, have unparalleled loyalty to the party and the people, and give matchless love to socialism . . . then our army will become an indestructible steel Great Wall."

Adding to China's difficulties as the new decade began was the final collapse of relations with the Soviet Union. Relations had gone steadily downhill since Khrushchev's 1956 defrocking of Stalin. Mao's assertions that the Soviet Union had become mired in revisionism and that China was now the center of world communism irritated the Kremlin, as did China's increasing truculence in international affairs. Khrushchev said Mao's people's communes were "nonsense," an idea that had failed in the Soviet Union a generation earlier.

In 1959, Moscow angered the Chinese by taking a neutral stand toward rising Sino-Indian tensions resulting from Chinese military action in Tibet. In March that year the PLA crushed an abortive uprising by anti-Chinese Tibetans that sent the Dalai Lama and thousands of his followers into exile in India.

That same year the Kremlin reneged on an agreement to provide China with a sample atomic bomb and assist in China's nuclear weapons program. The final blow came in the summer of 1960, when the Kremlin withdrew its entire contingent of about fourteen hundred Soviet experts, leading to the suspension of some two hundred industrial and military projects being built with Soviet aid. The party acknowledged that the Soviet withdrawal had "disrupted China's original national economic plan and inflicted enormous losses upon China's socialist construction."

The Central Committee met at the summer resort of Beidaihe in July 1960 to assess the damage wrought by natural disasters, the "leftist" mistakes of the previous years and the withdrawal of Soviet technical and financial assistance. Once again, when times were at their worst, realists such as Liu, Deng and Chen Yun tried to moderate the excesses of the radicals and set the Chinese economy on a more stable and even keel.

The committee resolved that agriculture had been

Children and old housing in Shanghai in 1961.

overlooked in the push to develop heavy industry, and that industrial growth must be tempered to match that in the countryside. Capital construction projects were cut and urban workers were mobilized to help out in agricultural projects. Chen and Deng also pressed for further decentralization of the communes to give authority to the production team, made up of twenty to forty households, rather than the production brigade, a grouping of about ten teams, or the communes, comprised of ten to fifteen brigades.

The "modern" women of 1961 China working in a steel factory in a people's commune in Shanghai.

In November 1960 the Central Committee issued an "emergency letter" on commune policies, stating that the production team would be the basic unit for the ownership of commune property and that commune members would be allowed to cultivate a small plot for their private use. Families were also permitted to operate small sideline businesses. In January the committee formally adopted a policy of "readjustment, consolidation, filling out and improvement" to overcome the difficulties of the "three hard years."

Serious divisions remained over the proper approaches to revolution and modernization, but the economy did begin to recover in the early 1960s as the pragmatists generally held sway and new political campaigns were kept to a minimum. The mood was reflected in a September 1961 speech by Foreign Minister Chen Yi to Beijing University graduate students, in which he said there was nothing wrong with intellectuals "taking part in political activities

less frequently" because they must work to develop expertise applicable to building the nation. "Who wants to fly with a pilot who is ideologically pure but cannot manage the controls?" he asked.

In the following months some intellectuals who had been purged during the "anti-rightist" campaign were rehabilitated, and there was a short respite from the ideological onslaught of recent years. Vice Premier Lu Dingyi reduced the amoung of time students spent in political studies and manual labor, and brought back lessons in calligraphy and the classics in elementary schools.

The Central Committee convened a work conference of seven thousand senior cadres in January 1962 for a session during which Mao's policies were criticized for bringing China "to the brink of collapse." The moderates dominated the meeting, with decisions reached to guarantee peasants some 5 percent of arable land for their private use and to give further powers to the smaller production team. In foreign policy, the meeting adopted a policy of "three reconciliations and one reduction," moderating conflicts with imperialists, reactionaries and re-

A performance of a traditional Chinese dramatic sword dance in a Beijing theater.

visionists and reducing aid to foreign liberation movements.

Liu, who succeeded Mao as head of state in 1959 and was Mao's heir-apparent, and Deng were clearing steering the country in the first years of the 1960s, but Mao remained the "Great Helmsman." Despite his defeats, Mao's political clout remained on a different level from that of his rivals for power, and the all-important PLA, under Lin Biao, was firmly in Mao's camp.

At the Tenth Central Committee Plenum of the Eighth National Congress in September 1962, Mao was still straddling the "two lines" that had emerged in the debate over domestic policy. He acknowledged the importance of modernization and economic development, but hammered home that the revolutionary ideals forged in Yenan would not be allowed to fade away. He asserted that the main contradiction was still between the proletariat and the bourgeoisie, that there was a danger of capitalist restoration and that revisionism had crept into the heart of the party. The party must never forget class struggle, he said.

The struggle began again within months with the start that winter of the protracted "Socialist Education Movement." The movement, inspired by Mao,

was aimed at keeping the class struggle concept alive, eliminating unhealthy cultural trends and preventing the emergence of revisionism. Programs of "xiafang" or "sending down" to the countryside were arranged so cadres could learn from the masses while propagating the party line.

Under the "first ten points," an outline of the movement drawn up in February 1963, poor and lower-middle peasants were to organize teams to help expose and correct cadre problems. Cadres in turn were to spend more time working in the fields. However, when neither peasants nor cadres demonstrated much enthusiasm for the campaign, Mao called on Beijing Mayor and Politburo member Peng Zhen to come up with a "second ten points" to enforce its objectives. Peng's plan called for work teams to be sent into communes to link up with peasants to investigate how local officials were conducting their affairs.

However, the tendency of the work teams to gloss over problems at the local level became evident in early 1964 when Wang Guangmei, wife of Liu Shaoqi, concealed her identity and spent weeks with a work team sent to Peach Blossom Commune near Beijing. She came back with a shocking report of rampant cadre corruption and resurgent capitalism among the peasants. Her report confirmed to Mao that the bureaucracy was ignoring his will and that party leaders, in this case namely Peng Zhen, were not carrying out his orders.

In September 1964, Liu took over the movement, revising Peng's "second ten points" and calling for "human sea" work teams to move in and take over local units. Up to one million party officials lost their positions in the ensuing purge and crackdown on abuse of power.

Mao still was not satisfied. In late 1964 he oversaw the drafting of the "23 Points," a more populist program that called for the pullout of the rectification teams and more mass participation in weeding out undesirable cadres. However, the popular uprising against the new warlords that Mao had hoped for never got off the ground, leaving him further embittered and divided with Liu and others who he believed were thwarting him with their bureaucratic approach to problems.

The Central Committee in January 1965, in a reassessment of the Socialist Education Movement, decided it should henceforth be called the "four cleanups" concerned with eradicating problems in politics, economics, organization and ideology. The party also suggested that the movement had gone too far in attacking officials, and reiterated that its purpose was to expose "people in power within the party who have taken the capitalist road."

Another original goal of the movement was to clean up unhealthy cultural tendencies, an ominous throwback to the 1957 anti-rightist movement. There were as yet no major campaigns against writers and intellectuals, although in June 1964 Mao warned that literature and art associations had failed to carry out party policies and had slid to the brink of revisionism. Mao's leftist wife Jiang Qing also moved into the forefront, complaining about the dominance of classical themes in Beijing opera and demanding the introduction of new operas with revolutionary storylines. In December 1965, at her urging, the Shanghai Propaganda Department organized a drama competition for new plays with revolutionary themes.

Mao also continued to battle what he considered were the elitist trends of educators trying to improve educational standards and reduce time spent on ideology and manual labor. He sought to expand the school system to include more children of workers and peasants in higher education, and told students it was right to rebel against school authorities.

Diplomatically, Mao resisted pressure from within the army and the party for some sort of reconciliation with the Soviet Union. In July 1964, Mao made his point clear in a speech entitled "on Khrushchev's phony communism and its historical lessons for the world." China, Mao said, must not only be in the forefront of world communism but must become a leader of the Third World battling both U.S. and Soviet oppression. China began to champion Third World causes, as witnessed by an extended tour of eleven African nations by Chou En-lai and Chen Yi in 1965.

Mao's argument that China could survive without Soviet assistance was bolstered when the nation exploded its first atomic bomb on October 16, 1964, just five years after the Soviet Union had terminated its help for China's nuclear program. Three years later, at the height of the Cultural Revolution, China staged its first successful test of a hydrogen bomb.

The People's Liberation Army, behind Defense Minister Lin Biao, had also come down solidly behind Mao's assertion that self-reliance and the building of a politically enlightened "people's army" were the keys to military success. Lin, his reputation boosted by China's successes in its 1962 border war with India, was unfailingly loyal to Mao and his trust in guerrilla warfare. By relying on the strength of the masses and not depending on outside aid, Lin said in 1965, the people's army will inevitably be victorious. Lin showed his determination to put these theories into practice when he abolished all military ranks in 1965.

Some military officers, who witnessed the heavy losses in personnel China sustained in the Korean War and saw China lagging behind many nations of the world in the technology of modern warfare, quietly opposed Lin's policies and hoped for improved relations with the Soviet Union, formerly China's chief source of weapons technology. Peng Dehuai was purged in 1959 partly for courting relations with the Soviets, and in 1965 Chief of Staff Luo Ruiqing ran into trouble for advocating a better equipped, more modern and less politicized army. Luo was fired from his job in December 1965 and forced to make a self-criticism. He later retracted his confession and tried to commit suicide, making him one of the first victims of the Cultural Revolution.

Others were soon to follow. The first big salvo of the impending explosion came on November 10, 1965, when Shanghai's *Wenhui Daily* published an article criticizing Beijing Vice Mayor Wu Han of making veiled criticisms of Mao in his play "Hai Rui

Mao wears armband of the Red Guards as he waves to crowd.

A 1966 photo purports to show Mao Tse-tung swimming in the Yangtze River near Wuhan, dispelling rumors of his illness at the time.

Slogans calling for the long life of Mao Tse-tung and the Communist Party adorn the walls of a Beijing building in 1966.

Dismissed From Office." The play, which was first published in 1961, tells the story of an honest 16th century Ming Dynasty official, Hai Rui, who loses his job after telling the emperor "you think you alone are right, you refuse to accept criticism and your mistakes are many."

According to the daily, Hai Rui represented Peng Dehuai, who was dismissed from office after speaking his mind to the emperor, Mao. The article was written by Yao Wenyuan, a leftist polemicist from Shanghai, reportedly at the bidding of Mao's wife Jiang Qing and Shanghai Party Propaganda Department chief Zhang Chunqiao. Yao, Jiang and Zhang were three members of the group that one day would be known as the reviled "gang of four."

Other reports followed, naming Wu and others in Beijing under Mayor Peng Zhen of being a "black gang" out to falsify historical figures in order to blacken the reputation of Mao. The articles said Wu was preaching the virtues of the feudal system and ignoring the issue of class struggle.

Wu publicly repented in December, saying he had failed to use Mao's theory of class struggle in the play. But the campaign against him had greater goals than merely extracting a confession. Wu was a former university professor, with close ties to the intellectual community. He was also a friend and bridge partner of Deng Xiaoping, whom the leftists increasingly saw as one of their prime adversaries in the power struggle. Perhaps most important, he

was the protege of Peng Zhen, whose power base in Beijing was a major obstacle to the Shanghai radicals in their quest for greater influence over policy.

Mao, using one of his favorite tactics for exposing his enemies, gave the job of investigating the Wu Han case to Peng Zhen. Peng was serving in his capacity as head of a five-member "Leading Group of Cultural Revolution" set up by Mao in 1964 to oversee cultural activities. Instead of attacking Wu, however, Peng tried to have disciplinary action taken against the Shanghai group for failing to receive authorization before publishing the Wu Han criticism. But Peng had not bargained on Mao's strong support for the Shanghai view. In February Peng won Politburo approval for a document calling for open debate and equality before the truth on academic matters, but he was quickly countermanded by another document drawn up by Jiang Qiang at a conference on literature and art for the armed forces and edited by Mao. Jiang's document contradicted Peng, stressed the continuation of the class struggle and renewed criticism of Wu Han and his associates. It called for the start of a "Great Socialist Cultural Revolution."

On March 26, 1966, the day Peng's ally Liu Shaoqi left on a prescheduled trip to Pakistan and Afghanistan, the Beijing mayor disappeared. Several months later he was formally removed from all his posts and at the end of the year arrested on criminal charges.

VI

The Great Proletarian Cultural Revolution

The Great Proletarian Cultural Revolution was Mao Tse-tung's final, cataclysmic attempt to kindle the fading fires of revolution and roust out the bureaucrats who had settled into power across the country.

In its patterns, it resembled the numerous other movements, from the "three antis" to the "Socialist Education Movement" that had periodically disrupted the nation since 1949. Once again the masses were being urged to rise up, to drive out the fat, the complacent and the corrupt, and restore the militant revolutionary ideals upon which the nation was founded. This time, however, things went very badly out of control. Having unleashed the forces to tear down the party structure, Mao suddenly found himself faced with chaos that threatened to tear the entire nation asunder. In the process, nearly every Chinese citizen suffered, from the "lost generation" of young people deprived of a decade of education to the scholar tormented for owning Western books to the peasant unable to raise a pig out of fear of being labeled a capitalist. Among the most prominent victims was Mao himself, who as his health declined saw the Cultural Revolution deteriorate into a sometimes violent power struggle that could only be resolved with his death.

The political infighting and push for a confrontation reached the critical point in May 1966, when an enlarged meeting of the Politburo was convened to issue what came to be called the "May 16th Circular." The document condemned Peng's February

Carrying little red books of "Quotations from Chairman Mao," Chinese youths celebrate National Day in 1966.

document and disbanded his five-member Cultural Revolution group. Peng, Chief of Staff Luo Ruiqing, Culture Minister Lu Dingyi and Yang Shangkun, head of the Central Committee General Office, were all formally removed from their posts. It also called upon party committees to seize leadership over cultural matters and attack "representatives of bourgeoisie" who had infiltrated party, government, army and cultural circles.

A new Central Cultural Revolution Group was set up, headed by Mao's secretary Chen Boda. Security chief Kang Sheng, another radical, was adviser and Jiang Qing and Zhang Chunqiao were deputy leaders. Yao Wenyuan, another from the Shanghai group, was also a member.

The first object of attack was the universities, with Mao's persistent strain of anti-intellectualism being given full play. Mao encouraged students to carry forth the Cultural Revolution by criticizing teachers and administrators and they responded with surprising force. The best known young radical was Nie Yuanzi, a philosophy instructor at Beijing University who on May 25 with six students put up a poster lambasting the university president for suppressing student activities. Mao ordered the press and radio to carry full accounts of Nie's activities on June 1. Also on June 1 the *People's Daily*, now under the control of Chen Boda, published an inflammatory editorial "Sweep Away All Monsters."

Universities, and a growing number of factories and offices, quickly descended into mayhem, with walls and sidewalks covered with accusatory posters, classes cancelled and many teachers and officials subjected to namecalling and persecution.

and spiritual regeneration is more important than economic progress.

Mao on August 1 wrote to Red Guards at a middle school attached to Qinghua University supporting their rebellion against "reactionaries." Red Guard groups had been forming at schools since the beginning of the year, their numbers consisting of ideologically upright young people loyal to Mao and with the proper parentage—workers, peasants, army or party. With Mao's endorsement, Red Guard groups quickly formed around the country, with millions converging on Beijing to receive the blessings of their great leader. Between August and November on eight occasions Mao, often accompanied by Lin Biao, reviewed wildly cheering Red Guard rallies on Tiananmen Square. More than thirteen million people attended those rallies.

Millions more took advantage of free train rides to travel around the country to join in campaigns in the provinces and "exchange revolutionary experiences." Apart from the bitter feelings universally shared toward the Cultural Revolution, many middle-aged Chinese today look back on those anything-goes days of the summer and fall of 1966 as the most free and exciting time of their lives.

Mao's personality cult reached new heights, with statues appearing on central squares and portraits appearing on the walls of every home desiring to show its revolutionary fervor. Millions made pilgrimages to Mao's birthplace in Shaoshan, Hunan province, or to Yenan and other scenes of his great exploits. In 1967, three hundred and fifty million copies of Mao's Little Red Book, "Quotations from Chairman Mao," were published, their contents memorized by his loyal followers. Preface inscriptions were written by Lin Biao, who urged Chinese to act according to Mao's instructions and "be his good fighters." In a 1967 inscription, Lin wrote, "sailing the seas depends on the helmsman, making revolution depends on Mao Tse-tung Thought."

On August 1, Mao convened the first Central Committee plenum in four years, with the express aim of attacking two men he now considered his principal adversaries, Liu Shaoqi and Deng Xiaoping. Mao wrote a big-character poster saying "bomb the headquarters," urging frontal attacks on party leaders at the highest level. The session agreed that the purpose of the Cultural Revolution was to struggle against and overthrow "those persons in power

Member of the Red Guards places armband on Chairman Mao.

Liu Shaoqi, in a move reminiscent of past campaigns, tried to control the ferment and turn it to the party's advantage by dispatching work teams into institutions to supervise the rectification work. Radical students, however, accused the work teams of trying to usurp their new powers of action. At Beijing's prestigious Qinghua University, Mao personally intervened on the side of the students and a work team led by Liu's wife Wang Guangmei was forced to withdraw.

In July, newspapers reported with banner headlines that Mao, who had kept a low profile and had made few public appearances during the past months of political strife, had successfully swum across the Yangtze River. Mao, displaying his restored political and physical vigor, urged young people to join with him in "advancing in the teeth of great storms and waves." It is right to rebel, he said,

Students at Beijing University read student newspapers in front of wall posters in 1967. The university was closed during the Cultural Revolution.

Passerby stops to read posters on Beijing walls during the Cultural Revolution. The large Chinese characters are the sayings of Mao Tse-tung.

Red Guards lined up at the side of Mao portrait.

Red Guards, wearing armbands and carrying portraits of Mao Tse-tung and little red books of his sayings, parade through Beijing in 1966.

who are taking the capitalist road" and to criticize "reactionary bourgeois academic authorities. It also issued a directive called the "16 Points" that encouraged creation of mass organizations to criticize the establishment. Lin moved up to the number two position on the Politburo Standing Committee, behind Mao, and Liu was demoted from second place to eighth.

The Red Guards that fall went on a nationwide rampage of destruction, abuse and persecution. Millions were humiliated, tortured and often driven to suicide. Anyone who had Western friends, books or clothing was subject to persecution, their homes ransacked. Books were burned, antiques and ancient art destroyed, historical sites vandalized and places of worship torn down. Minorities such as the Tibetans were punished for speaking their native languages and following their religious beliefs. Millions of scholars and officials were tormented as the Red Guards carried out their attacks on the "four olds"—thought, culture, customs and habits.

Violence against individuals quickly turned into armed conflicts as students and workers organized

CHINA

CHEN YI   CHOU EN-LAI   LIN PIAO

PENG CHEN   TAO CHU   PO I-PO

KAO KANG   PENG TEH-HUAI   JAO SHU-SHIH

LIU SHAO-CHI   TENG HSIAO-PING   CHU TEH

Liu Shaoqi was reported "dead physically as well as politically" in a Communist newspaper in Hong Kong in 1974.

competing groups and began vying for power and influence. Each claimed that it represented Mao Tse-tung Thought and the true spirit of the revolution. Cadres put together their own slogan-shouting groups in an attempt to defend their turf from rivals trying to drive them from power.

Their efforts failed in Shanghai, where radical workers, leading a rally of one million people, forced the Shanghai party leadership to resign in the "January (1967) Storm." The leftist victory was applauded by Beijing.

Liu and Deng were coming under increasing attack in wall posters and in the radical-controlled media, and in October were forced to make self-criticisms. Foreign Minister Chen Yi was also dragged before ten thousand people for a struggle session after radicals seized the Foreign Ministry on January 18.

Chinese leaders involved in power struggle in late 1960s.

Deng's self-criticism read, in part: "Liu Shaoqi and I represent the capitalist, reactionary line in the Cultural Revolution. My thoughts and deeds are not directed by the thoughts of Mao Tse-tung. My alienation from the masses denies me the right to carry out the tasks assigned to me by the Central Committee."

Deng was criticized throughout the Cultural Revolution as the "No. 2 Capitalist Roader" beside Liu. Among the numerous charges brought against him were that he had propagated the ideologically repugnant slogan, in reference to agricultural policy that "as long as the cat catches mice it doesn't matter if it is a white cat or a black cat." Deng was last seen in public on December 14, 1966.

Senior leaders, while publicly mouthing approval of the aims of the Cultural Revolution, were deeply concerned as more ministries were seized by young leftists and the nation slid toward total anarchy. Chou En-lai convened a meeting of top party leaders in February 1967 to criticize the Cultural Revolution Group for throwing the party, government, industry, agriculture and army into disarray. But Mao was firmly behind the radicals. Chou, who was widely respected and regarded as a crucial aide to Mao, received only mild rebuke but other moderates, such as Marshal Chu Teh and Chen Yun, were strongly criticized. The Politburo was in effect inactivated and replaced by the Cultural Revolution Group.

The violence and bloodshed in some cities, however, had become so serious that by early 1967 Mao was forced to send in the army to restore order. Never before had the PLA been given such wide powers to determine political destinies in the country, and this new authority added to the rising influence of Lin Biao. It also threatened to overturn the basic principle that the party must always retain control over the army and Mao's dictum that "the party commands the gun and the gun will never be allowed to command the party."

In some places the army merely joined in the factional fighting, providing arms and support to help one group eliminate another. But for the most part the PLA ultimately succeeded in averting full civil war in Chinese cities. In January, Heilongjiang province set up the first Provincial Revolutionary Committee, a loosely organized coalition of young revolutionaries, leftist cadres and PLA officers. This tripartite grouping became the accepted formula for new governments throughout the country, with all provinces establishing revolutionary committees by September 1968.

The attacks against Liu Shaoqi escalated in 1967,

with the earlier charges of revisionism being upgraded to include alleged acts of treason. The *People's Daily* in April attacked Liu as the top party member taking the capitalist road and issued a call to "liquidate the bourgeois reactionary line of seventeen years represented by Liu Shaoqi." Hundreds of mass rallies were staged throughout the country denouncing Liu, and he and his wife were subject to Red Guard struggle sessions and public humiliations.

The *People's Daily* in May published an editorial signed by Chou calling for an immediate end to violence, but fighting intensified in many parts of the country over the summer. Some of the worst

fighting erupted in the central city of Wuhan and in Canton, where weapons bound for the Vietnam War were stolen by rival combatants. Even Chou was locked up in his State Council office for two days, besieged by Red Guards.

Mao as well was stunned by the violence and turmoil he had wrought. On October 1, 1967, he issued a "great strategic plan" calling for factionalism to end and for general self-criticism. People were to channel their energies into Mao Tse-Tung

Young Red Guard during a demonstration in a Beijing street in 1966. Red Guards behind him show Mao books.

study classes organized around the country. Bloody fighting continued through the summer of 1968, with Canton and the southern province of Guangxi among the hardest hit, but gradually the PLA was restoring peace in most Chinese cities.

With the Red Guard fury and factional fighting beginning to wind down, the Cultural Revolution in mid-1968 took on new forms. Mao in May called on all cadres to "engage in agricultural labor and learn from the poor and lower middle peasants." In subsequent years millions of these "May 7 Cadre School" officials would be sent down to the countryside, many for periods that stretched into years.

The campaign against the politically suspect continued unabated, with the radicals demanding exposure of all those with landlord background, rich peasants, counter-revolutionaries, bad elements, rightists, spies, capitalist roaders, bourgeois reactionary academic authorities and the "stinking ninth category"—intellectuals with ideological problems.

Red Guards carry giant portrait of Karl Marx in demonstrations against "revisionism."

Mao effectively demobilized the Red Guards in July, after a talk with five Red Guard student leaders in which he chastised them for "ultra-leftism, sectarianism and mad fraticidal fighting." The next month Mao, who two years before had blasted Liu for sending work teams into the universities, dispatched worker propaganda teams to take control over all universities and other educational units.

The Central Committee in October formally passed a resolution to expel Liu from the party forever after approving a "report on the crimes of the traitor, enemy agent and scab Liu Shaoqi." Liu was arrested and eventually sent to Kaifeng, in Henan province, where he died on November 12, 1969, of pneumonia resulting from his persecution and mistreatment. The Central Committee endorsed Lin Biao as Mao's "close comrade" and eventual successor.

The *People's Daily* on December 22, 1968, published a directive by Mao stating that "educated young people should go to the countryside to be re-educated by poor and lower-middle class peasants." Mao's aim was to deal a final blow to the Red Guards and their capacity for disruption by dispers-

Quotes from Mao

Some quotes from Chairman Mao:

"A well-disciplined party armed with the theory of Marxism-Leninism, using the method of self-criticism and linked with the masses of the people; an army under the leadership of such a party; a united front of all revolutionary classes and all revolutionary groups under the leadership of such a party—these are the three main weapons with which we have defeated the enemy."

"We should support whatever the enemy opposes and oppose whatever the enemy supports."

"War is the highest form of struggle for resolving contradictions, when they have developed to a certain stage, between classes, nations, states, or political groups, and it has existed ever since the emergence of private property and classes."

"War is the continuation of politics. In this sense war is politics and war itself is a political action; since ancient times there has never been a war that did not have a political character. . . . But war has its own particular characteristics and in this sense it cannot be equated with politics in general. War is the continuation of politics by other . . . means."

"Every Communist must grasp the truth, 'Political power grows out of the barrel of a gun.'"

"We are advocates of the abolition of war; we do not want war, but war can only be aolished through war, and in order to get rid of the gun it is necessary to take up the gun."

"Letting a hundred flowers blossom and a hunded schools of thought contend is the policy for promoting the progress of the artss and the sciences and a flourishing socialist culture in our land. Different forms and styles in art should develop freely and different schools in science should contend freely. We think that it is harmful to the growth of art and science if administratie measures are used to impose one particular style of art or school of thought and to ban another. Questions of right and wrong in the arts and sciences should be settled through free discussion in artistic and scientific circles and through practical work in these fields. They should not be settled in summary fashion."

"I have said that all the reputedly powerful reactionaries are merely paper tigers. The reason is that they are divorced from the people. Look! Was not Hitler a paper tiger? Was Hitler not overthrown? I also said that the czar of Russia, the emperor of China and Japanese imperialism were all paper tigers. As we know, they were all overthrown. U.S. imperialism has not yet been overthrown and it has the atom bomb. I believe it also will be overthrown. It, too, is a paper tiger."

"The people, and the people alone, are the motive force in the making of world history."

Red Guards hold up Mao booklets in demonstration in front of the Soviet Embassy in Beijing in 1966.

Crowds get the news on posters pasted to the wall
by Red Guards.

Portraits of Mao and books of his sayings were
featured in most Red Guard demonstrations.

ing youth to remote mountain and rural areas where they would be required to release their political passions in a more constructive way.

Even more than the "xiafang" of the May 7 Cadre Schools, this decision was to have a profound influence on the lives of millions of people and affect the national psyche. Millions of young people were confined for years to lives of unimaginable poverty, backwardness and isolation. For many it was years after the Cultural Revolution ended before they finally obtained permission to return to their families and homes in the cities. They returned home too old to receive the educations they had missed, lacking in usable skills and deeply resentful of the government that was responsible for their years of suffering.

Red Guards walk through Canton, carrying excerpts from Mao books on their knapsacks.

Meanwhile, long-smoldering tensions with the Soviet Union were threatening to escalate into all-out war. The Soviet invasion of Czechoslovakia in August 1968 and the announcement of the Brezhnev Doctrine shortly thereafter that asserted the Soviet right to invade rebellious Communist states reaffirmed Chinese fears of a Soviet attack. Prompted by Mao's inherent suspicions of the Kremlin, foreign policymakers in the late 1960s made a major shift in world outlook. Despite the presence of U.S. troops battling the North Vietnamese on China's southern border, the Soviet Union was judged the main military threat to China, and Soviet hegemonism became a greater evil to the world than American imperialism.

As the Vietnam War intensified in the mid-1960s, Mao was under pressure to send in troops in aid of China's socialist brother, just as it had done in Korea fifteen years before. Chief of Staff Luo Ruiqing, supported by Liu Shaoqi, had also pushed for reconcili-

ation with the Soviet Union to present a united front against American aggression. But Mao, far more concerned with the Cultural Revolution and domestic matters, adamantly rejected both ideas. Mao even denied the Soviets the use of Chinese airfields and airspace to fly supplies to North Vietnam. His reason, Mao told the Soviets, was "frankly speaking, we do not trust you. We and other fraternal countries have learned bitter lessons in the past from Khrushchev's evil practice of control under the cover of aid."

The two sides came to blows on March 2, 1969, on Chenbao (Damansky) Island, a small piece of disputed land in the Ussuri River on Chinese Manchuria's northeast border with the Soviet Union. The two sides clashed again on March 14-15, with the use of tanks and large numbers of troops on both sides. Sporadic battles continued along the border in the coming months, and Mao, amid a feverish anti-Soviet propaganda campaign, ordered the na-

tion to prepare for war. Extensive networks of air raid tunnels were built under major cities and key military and industrial equipment plants were moved into the hinterlands, safe from invading armies. The imminent threat of war eased somewhat when Soviet Premier Alexei Kosygin made an unscheduled stop in Beijing on September 11, 1969, while on his way back from Ho Chi Minh's funeral in Hanoi, for a three-hour meeting at the airport with Chou. The two agreed that efforts should be made to disengage troops on the border, maintain the status quo of the frontiers and open talks on territorial disputes. Border talks resumed the next month, but made no progress, and by the early 1970s both sides had at least one million troops and heavy armaments facing off against each other along the border.

Child Red Guard takes notes from wall newspaper in Canton.

Chinese and Soviet frontier guards in border discussion in 1969.

Chinese frontier guards on the Soviet-Manchurian border in 1969. River is the Ussuri, with the disputed Chenpao Island at center.

Soviet guards on alert at the Chinese-Soviet border.

By contrast, even during the most virulent years of the anti-capitalist Cultural Revolution, Mao was edging toward a rapprochement with the United States. Mao saw the Vietnam War as winding down, and regarded the "American card" as crucial as Sino-Soviet relations deteriorated.

In November, 1968, China suggested to the United States that ambassadorial level talks be resumed in Warsaw, and in July the next year President Nixon relaxed travel and trade restrictions for China. The next October, *Red Star Over China* writer Edgar Snow was given a prominent seat on a reviewing stand between Mao and Chou, and told by Mao that China would welcome a visit by Nixon. The next diplomatic foray was the sudden invitation to an American ping-pong team in Japan for a tournament to visit China, where they were given a warm welcome by Chou. On June 9-11 National Security Adviser Henry Kissinger made a secret visit to Beijing for talks with Chou that culminated a week later in the announcement that Nixon would visit China. That October, the United States offered little resistance when the United Nations decided to give the People's Republic the seat in the General Assembly and the U.N. Security Council held by the Nationalist government on Taiwan.

Nixon arrived on February 27, 1972, for a historical visit ending with the signing of the Shanghai Communique in which the United States recognized that there was only one China and Taiwan is a part of China. The U.S. side said the question of Taiwan should be settled peacefully by the Chinese themselves and pledged to progressively reduce U.S. military installations on Taiwan. Economic and cultural contacts between China and the United States were resumed. The following spring a U.S. liaison office opened in Beijing, although formal relations were not established until January 1, 1979.

The world that watched with fascination the TV coverage of Nixon in China and read of a great nation re-opening its arms to the world was unaware that China had just undergone the most dangerous political crisis during the first quarter-century of Communist rule, with Lin Biao attempting to overthrow and murder Mao.

Chou En-lai and Richard Nixon review honor guard of the People's Liberation Army at Beijing airport on the U.S. president's arrival.

President Nixon is greeted by Premier Chou En-lai at Beijing airport in February 1972.

Nixon meets Mao during the U.S. president's historic trip to China.

Chou En-lai and Richard Nixon share a toast on the plane that carried them from Beijing to Hangchow.

President Nixon meets with Chairman Mao as Premier Chou En-lai looks on. Woman is interpreter Tang Wen Shen.

End of an Era

Deng Xiaoping in 1951.

Chou En-lai was the great survivor of the Cultural Revolution. He never spoke out against it, yet did more than any other man to modify its excesses. He is credited, perhaps with some exaggeration, with personally saving thousands of people from persecution and arrest, and with preserving countless historical treasures from the marauding bands of Red Guards. What is unassailable was that he possessed tremendous personal charm and prestige, was incorruptible and a tireless worker, and held Mao's lifelong trust. He never attempted to supersede or succeed Mao, thus escaping the fates of Liu Shaoqi and Lin Biao, and skillfully stayed aloof from factional struggles, thus managing to keep his posts when all around him were being purged.

Following the downfall of Lin in 1971, Chou was clearly in the ascendancy. His diplomatic skills had played a major role in bringing about Nixon's visit in 1972 and the restoration of Sino-American ties. Later that year he also hosted Japanese Premier Kakuei Tanaka, accomplishing the normalization of diplomatic relations with Japan.

Domestically, his influence was being felt in a shift away from the extremist policies of the late 1960s. Greater stress was being put on economic efficiency and central planning, getting away from the radical decentralization and moral incentives of the past. Mao's clarion call to "learn from Dazhai," the poor commune in Shanxi province that reputedly made extraordinary progress through political enlightenment and self-reliance, was heard less often. Under Chou's cautious guidance, more emphasis was being given to technology and science, and grain production per capita was finally returning to pre-Great Leap Forward levels.

But in 1972, Chou was diagnosed as having stomach cancer. He continued to function, but was hospitalized for long periods of time and was gradually losing his vaunted capacity for work. It is difficult to say whether Deng Xiaoping's remarkable comeback was in any way related to Chou's illness, but Deng quickly stepped in after his rehabilitation in April 1973 to become Chou's right-hand man and the chief representative of the moderate policies supported by Chou.

Lin Biao, Mao's sycophantic supporter, reached the epitome of his power at the Ninth Communist Party Congress which convened in April 1969. The new party constitution named Lin as Mao's close comrade and successor, and Lin gave a key speech

The downfalls of Lin and Chen were major blows to the radicals. Jiang Qing aspired to be the new voice of the ailing Mao, but was regarded with suspicion by her husband. Still, the Cultural Revolution rolled on with formidable force. The Central Committee had ordered institutes of higher learning to resume classes, but with the caveat that they abolish exam systems and enroll students from worker, peasant and soldier classes who were recommended by the masses. A national conference on education in the summer of 1971 said people educated prior to the Cultural Revolution are "basically bourgeois in their world outlook."

But the momentum was slowly shifting to the moderates. In April, 1972, the *People's Daily* printed an editorial edited by Chou saying that cadres and party members should be correctly treated and veteran cadres are the wealth of the party. The rehabilitation of purged leaders began, with Chen Yun and others restored to their posts. A year later Deng Xiaoping was to make a dramatic comeback.

Mao is flanked by his deputy, Lin Biao (r.), and Premier Chou En-lai in 1967 photo.

praising the accomplishments of the Cultural Revolution. Lin's PLA was rewarded for dousing the nationwide fires of strife and rebellion by being given enormous power within the party. Of the all the members of the new Central Committee, 44 percent were military. The twenty-one-member Politburo included four marshals, one of course being Lin, six generals and Lin's wife Ye Qun. Jiang Qing also joined the Politburo.

With the Congress, the Cultural Revolution was declared at an end, but in effect it had merely entered a new and more complicated phase. For the next seven years, as Mao progressively weakened physically and mentally, a fierce power struggle raged between the leftists who saw the continuance of radical policies as the key to their hold on power and the moderates who sought to restore the gradualist policies of the early 1960s.

Lin made the first and most dramatic play for power. Following the congress, Lin began pressing Mao to resurrect the position of chairman of the

PRC, or head of state, that had been vacated since the purge of Liu Shaoqi. Lin and Chen Boda were also pushing a theory that Mao was a "genius" of a level that appears on the human scene only once every several centuries. Mao resisted both ideas, seeing the first as Lin's desire to be named head of state to further his ultimate grab for power. Lin sought to deify Mao, it was thought, so Lin as second-in-command could become his oracle, the man responsible for interpreting the words from above.

Mao openly opposed Lin and Chen over the head of state issue at a plenum of the Central Committee meeting in Lushan in August and September 1970. He was not yet ready to directly attack Lin, but had fewer compunctions about Chen. Soon after the plenum ended, Chen was branded an "ultra-leftist" and "political swindler" and disappeared from public view. He was expelled from the party in 1973.

It was obvious to Lin that he was fast losing Mao's favor, particularly after January 1971 when key supporters in the Beijing Military Region were removed from office or transferred. In March Lin met with his son, Air Force Major General Lin Liguo, and other sympathetic military officers to plan a military coup under the code name of "Operation 571," the numbers being a homonym for "armed uprising."

According to Chinese official accounts, Lin and his co-conspirators tried to blow up Mao's Hangzhou-to-Shanghai train on September 8, 1971. The attack was called off at the last minute, and on September 12, with their plot about to be exposed, Lin, his wife, his son and others tried to flee to the Soviet Union. They were killed when their plane ran out of fuel and crashed in Mongolia. Mass criticism of Lin began in November, but it was almost a year before details of his attempted coup and his demise began to be made public.

Deng, like Chou, developed his leftist sympathies while on a work-study program in France in the 1920s. He joined Chou and Mao on the Long March in 1934-35 and earned a reputation as a skilled political commissar and military strategist. After 1949 he

Mao and Lin Biao (r.) review demonstration by Red Guards in January 1967.

returned to his native province of Sichuan as a party leader, but was quickly recalled to Beijing, where he was appointed vice premier, minister of finance, and, in 1954, took the important post of general secretary for the party. Although his support for Mao back in the 1930s had been instrumental to his rapid political advance, in the 1950s and 1960s Mao came to distrust Deng's pragmatic, non-ideological approach to problems. Deng's frankness and blunt manner, such as when he belittled Jiang Qing's revolutionary operas, were also to make him an obvious target for the radicals.

The showdown between the radicals and the moderates was clearly revealed when the 10th Party Congress was held August 24-28, 1973. The crimes of Lin Biao's "counter-revolutionary clique" were criticized, but the Cultural Revolution line of "continuing revolution under the dictatorship of the proletariat" was reaffirmed. Deng, his post of vice premier already restored, rejoined the Central Committee, as did other senior leaders who had disap-

peared during the height of the Cultural Revolution. But the radicals, now led by Jiang Qing and Zhang Chunqiao, remained a formidable force.

Because of the purge of military leaders associated with Lin, only ten of twenty-one Politburo posts were filled when the congress opened. In the five-member Politburo Standing Committee, only Mao, Chou and the ailing security chief Kang Sheng held on to their seats. The military was a big loser in the new appointments, and the moderates made gains, but generally the moderates and the radicals were about even in strength, creating an uneasy balance of power.

The continued strength of the radicals was demonstrated by the precipitous rise of Wang Hongwen, a Jiang Qing protege and later to be branded as a member of her "Gang of Four." Wang was a security guard at a Shanghai cotton mill when the Cultural Revolution began. He gained prominence by organizing the Shanghai Workers Rebellion Headquarters in its successful drive to overthrow the mayor of the city. He became known as the "helicopter" because of his rapid political rise, climaxed when he was named by the congress to be vice chairman of the party, second to Mao, and appointed to the new six-member Politburo Standing Committee. He was thirty-seven years old.

Wang was joined on the Standing Committee by fellow radicals Kang Sheng and Zhang Chunqiao. On the moderate side were Chou and newly rehabilitated Chu Teh, with Mao the final arbiter of policy.

Another new name on the Politburo was Hua Guofeng, an obscure party official from Mao's native province of Hunan who apparently was promoted partly because of his work in investigating the Lin Biao case.

Deng's position as the nation's top administrator was confirmed in December when he was named to the Politburo and appointed chief of the PLA General Staff. Deng thus held senior positions in the government, the military and the party, giving him the leverage needed to repair damages to the bureaucratic structure sustained during the previous years.

The radicals, however, launched a fresh attack with the initiation in October 1973 of the "Criticize Lin Biao, Criticize Confucius" campaign. The professed purpose was to expose the reactionary roots of Lin by associating him with the scholar's two thousand-year-old ideas on human relations and dynastic rule. But as in all such campaigns in China, there were deeper meanings and veiled allusions. The radicals who led the campaign obviously hoped to disavow any relationship with the disgraced Lin,

Mao and his wife, Jiang Qing.

who for years had shared their ideological views of perpetual revolution and been an ally in their campaigns against entrenched bureaucrats and pragmatists.

The campaign had ominous overtones of the first days of the Cultural Revolution, with walls plastered with sloganeering posters and the official media filled with strident condemnations of Lin and Confucius. As in the earlier period, the campaign attacked those who would obscure the class struggle and descend into support for feudalism, capitalism and revisionism. Evidence was produced to show that Lin worshipped Confucian tenets such as filial piety and loyalty to one's rulers, with the conclusion that he was seeking to subvert the proletarian dictatorship, restore a class society and introduce capitalism in China.

The movement's leaders said Confucius was introduced into the campaign to highlight the perfidy of Lin, but in actuality it appears to have been a means to attack the radicals' most powerful adver-

Mao and his wife in Yenan, about 1945.

sary, Chou En-lai. At a mobilization meeting in January 1974, Jiang, Wang Hongwen and others criticized "Duke Chou of the Western Chou Dynasty" and "the great contemporary Confucianist," a scarcely concealed reference to Chou En-lai. One pro-Chinese Hong Kong paper in February said the real target of the campaign "is very careful and prudent but inside his bones are full of tricks. On all occasions he appears to be humble and loyal to the king, but that is solely for the purpose of preserving his official position."

The Lin-Confucius campaign was accompanied by new attacks on Western culture and society. The *People's Daily* in February attacked the music of Beethoven and Schubert, signalling an effective ban on the playing of classical pieces. The leftist-controlled daily also denounced as "vicious weeds" backers of a new opera entitled "Three Trips to Dao Feng." The opera was sponsored by a cultural section of the State Council headed by Chou En-lai.

In attempting to undermine Chou, however, the radicals were overreaching themselves. They also may have overestimated the capacity of the politically exhausted nation to sustain yet another political campaign. By the summer, the Lin-Confucius movement was running out of steam, and in July Mao is said to have warned Jiang, Zhang, Wang and Yao against forming a four-member clique.

Even Mao, looking noticeably weaker in his public appearances and said to be suffering from Parkinson's disease, appeared to be fed up with the constant political upheavals. The Central Committee in October released Mao's instructions that "the proletarian cultural revolution has continued for eight years. Now is the crucial moment to emphasize stability and unity. The whole party and army must be united." Later that month, Wang Hongwen traveled to Changsha for a meeting with Mao, during which he criticized Chou and tried to elicit Mao's support for blocking Deng's appointment as first vice premier. Mao, however, would not listen, and the following January Deng was named first vice premier and promoted to the Standing Committee of the Politburo.

Although some China watchers were speculating that Mao was sinking into senility, his mental faculties were sharp enough to realize that Jiang was using her position as his wife to further her own political ambitions. "You are not to form a cabinet"—be the behind-the-scenes manipulator—he wrote on a letter from her in November. He later stated: "Jiang Qing is ambitious. She actually wants Wang Hongwen to be chairman of the Standing Committee of the National People's Congress and herself to be chairman of the Party."

The Fourth National People's Congress convened in January 1975, the first meeting of China's rubber stamp parliament in ten years. Chou rose from his sickbed to deliver a speech on the need to modernize agriculture, industry, national defense and science and technology by the end of the century, goals that came to be known as the "Four Modernizations." Deng was elected first vice premier and Chou remained premier, but the radicals maintained their presence with the appointment of Zhang Chunqiao as second vice premier and chief political commissar of the army.

In May, according to official histories, Mao convened a meeting of the Politburo and criticized Jiang and her colleagues, identifying them as the "Gang of Four." Mao and Chou agreed that Deng should be responsible for a meeting criticizing the "gang" and take over daily affairs of the Central Committee. Deng also called an enlarged meeting of the Central Military Commission, the powerful party body overseeing military matters, and appealed for professionalism and modernization in the armed forces. He rehabilitated Luo Ruiqing, the former chief of staff who was purged after differing with Lin Biao in the early 1960s over whether China should have a professional or people's army.

Deng's next decline was to be as rapid as his rise. Mao, whether lacking the mental powers to resist the manipulation of Jiang and her group or miffed by Deng's energetic efforts to blot out the aims and results of the Cultural Revolution, suddenly began to tolerate new criticism of Deng.

In August, the former actress Jiang came up with a new literary vehicle, the classic novel "Outlaws of the Marsh," through which to snipe at Deng. The nationwide campaign to criticize Song Jiang, the leading character in the novel, was easily identifiable as an attack on Deng and his supposed capitulation to the emperor, Chou.

In November, Mao himself issued a statement urging people to "criticize Deng and the counter-right deviationist trend to reverse correct verdicts." On November 26 the Central Committee started yet another movement to criticize Deng.

The New Year's Day edition of the *People's Daily* carried another statement by Mao saying that "stability and unity do not mean writing off class struggle. Class struggle is the key link and everything else hinges on it."

Yet this precept to which Mao had dedicated his life was once again to be proved wrong in coming weeks as the nation showed that far more hinged on personal loyalties and non-dialectical affection for one man, Chou En-lai.

VII

The Year of the Dragon

Eight days into 1976, a nation exhausted by endless revolutionary campaigns and an economy bordering on collapse received some of the worst news yet: debonair Chou En-lai, premier since the founding of the People's Republic and one of the few beloved Chinese leaders, was dead of cancer at age seventy-seven.

It was no secret that Chou had been wasting away slowly in a Beijing hospital. But even from his deathbed he had been working, receiving guests and dictating letters.

His death marked an ominous prelude to the Year of the Dragon, sending shock waves around the world and causing an enormous outpouring of grief at home.

Nearly a million ordinary Chinese shivering in winter overcoats wept as Chou's flower-draped funeral convoy crawled through the windswept, dusty capital. No other modern Chinese leader had every received such popular adulation.

For Chairman Mao's wife, Jiang Qing, and fellow radical leftists struggling for primacy in the government at that time, Chou's death signaled an important opportunity.

They despised Chou because he had been a powerful voice of moderation that had persistently and shrewdly blocked their political agenda. He was one of the few leaders outside of their influence who had always enjoyed easy access to the chairman.

Even while aligning himself with the now-feeble Mao, Chou had deftly managed to minimize the impact of Mao's disastrous decrees, from the anti-rightist purges and catastrophic Great Leap Forward of the late 1950s to the excesses of the Cultural Revolution incited by his wife and her political allies.

With Chou now gone, it was a moment for the radicals to prevent what they feared most: an extended outpouring of grief for Chou and the appointment of his protege, first vice premier Deng Xiaoping, as the new premier.

"Hitherto I was locked in a cage," Jiang Qing reportedly exclaimed when Chou died. "Now I can come out and speak!"

Jiang Qing and her associates made sure only a perfunctory mourning period was allowed. Unlike other revolutionary heroes, Chou wasn't buried in the Babaoshan (Eight Precious Mountain) cemetery on the outskirts of Beijing, but his body cremated and its ashes strewn from a plane.

In fact, many Chinese believed the cremation was not Chou's wish but a plot by Jiang Qing, and at one point during the funeral procession crowds blocked his hearse from moving forward.

It was only after Chou's widow, Deng Yingchao, personally assured the crowds that Chou had willed his ashes to be scattered over "the rivers and soil of the motherland" did the mourners let the hearse proceed.

In Shanghai, historical powerbase of the radicals, it was clear from the press reaction to Chou's death that no mass memorial would take place.

The teeming city's main newspaper the *Liberation Daily* gave the obituary front-page but terse treatment, forcing Chou to share space with propaganda about industrial production and the familiar feats of revolutionary zeal elsewhere in the country.

Shanghai's ruling revolutionary committee, as the municipal governments throughout China were then called, refused to sanction the use of special paper and cloth for making mourning wreaths and black armbands. But millions of defiant and grief-stricken ordinary citizens made their own anyway.

Deng Xiaoping, making his most important public appearance since he was rescued by Chou from

Youths crowd against Martyrs' Monument to honor Premier Chou En-lai, who died in 1976.

Dazhai Commune

No other place in China symbolized the vision of selfless toil and egalitarianism more than Dazhai, a people's commune in the rugged hills of remote Shanxi province that became a Maoist mecca and a model for others to emulate through most of the 1960s and '70s, until it was labeled as a fraud and sham by Deng Xiaoping.

Dazhai, also known as Tachai, means "Big Fortress" or "Big Stockade." It became a routine stopover for thousands of Chinese officials, study groups and foreign visitors after Mao decreed the two hundred and fifty-acre commune a model in 1964.

The community of more than four hundred peasants, who had once lived in dank caves hidden among the eroded slopes and rock-filled gullies, created a new prosperity by what was officially described as heroic efforts against nature.

They had to rebuild from scratch three times because of violent floods, government propaganda claimed. They toiled for years to clear boulders and earth by hand. They vacated the caves and moved into solid, spacious huts built of heavy stones.

They dug irrigation canals, terraced mountains and transformed what had been a lifeless semi-desert into green fields of corn, wheat, millet, soybeans and nut trees.

Dazhai's party secretary, a leathery, chain-smoking peasant named Chen Yonggui, also became a model of idealism. For years his portrait

hung beside Mao's on walls throughout the country.

He quickly rose to membership in the Central Committee and later a vice premier. In 1973 he was elected to the Politburo, the highest organ of political power.

When Chen greeted visitors or was shown on national television at formal state dinners or important work conferences, he always wore his trademark, a simple checkered peasant's sweat towel wrapped around his bearded, sunburned head.

Dazhai became a pillar of China's political culture and educational curriculum. Elementary Chinese language textbooks contained lessons on Dazhai's glorious achievements.

By the early 1970s, more than 4.5 million people had toured Dazhai. It was receiving four thousand visitors a day.

The Committee of Concerned Asian Scholars, a group of Western educators who toured China in 1971, was so impressed with Dazhai and Chen Yonggui that it devoted most of a chapter to them in a book on the trip, marveling at how the commune treated guests to luscious banquets of noodles, pork, chicken and fresh vegetables.

"How has this village gone from being poor and food-deficient to having a secure if simple life and a spirit of persistent hard work filled with confidence and hope?," the committee wrote.

"First of all, the people of Tachai say, they have

Cultural Revolution exile a year earlier, delivered Chou's eulogy.

This was watched with close interest by foreigners trying to decipher the nuances of China's clandestine politics. It possibly meant that Deng, earlier branded a "capitalist roader" by Mao himself, might take Chou's place.

But there also was evidence that behind the guarded walls of Beijing's Zhongnanhai compound, the former imperial residence where the communist leaders now lived and worked, Jiang Qing and her cohorts were engaged in an intense power struggle

Chinese leaders, holding copies of Mao's sayings (from left): Chou En-lai, Jiang Qing, Kang Sheng, Chang Chun-chiao, Wang Li.

with Deng.

The most obvious signal was that nearly a month went by before the outside world got its first significant hint of who would inherit Chou's position. To some of even the most seasoned China experts, the choice was a surprise.

It was Hua Guofeng, a virtual unknown, the burly chief of public security from Mao's home province of Hunan. At age fifty-six, he was considered an inexperienced rookie politician among the core leadership of aging revolutionaries.

The state-run press said Hua had been elevated to the post of acting premier, indicating a compromise had been reached between the pro-Deng and radical factions, at least for the time being.

What wasn't clear, however, was how long such a

studied and tried to put into practice the teachings of Mao Tse-tung. They have learned to put the needs of the collective first, to work together (as they have in transforming the land and building their homes), and not to fear hardship or death."

The slogan, "In agriculture, learn from Dazhai," was plastered on buildings, bridges and propaganda posters throughout the country. The campaign to study Dazhai's spirit of self-reliance, like other Maoist movements, reached a feverish level.

Because the poor Dazhai peasants shared equally and abandoned private plots, other communes blindly copied this practice, merging richer and poorer households into single production units, much to the resentment of the richer.

They also followed Dazhai's farming strategy, often recklessly clearing away valuable trees and grassland to make room for grain.

By the time Mao died in 1976, Dazhai was such an imbedded part of China's political propaganda that a few years passed before it was reevaluated and ultimately discredited.

For awhile, Mao's handpicked successor Hua Guofeng was intent on preserving the sanctity of Dazhai, part of the reason why Hua did not last long. One of his first acts as new chairman was to choose Dazhai as the site of a national conference on agriculture.

Even Deng Xiaoping, who later made it known

that he despised the Dazhai campaign, had to make a few obligatory visits there himself.

By late 1978, however, when Deng had taken effective control of the government, the word was put out that only the "spirit" of Dazhai, not its actual working methods, should be copied.

A year later, the state-run press reported shocking news. Dazhai really hadn't relied on its own efforts after all.

The commune which had immortalized the famous "Three Refusals"—no money, food or material from the outside—had in truth accepted millions of dollars worth of state subsidies and help from battalions of army ditch-diggers to make the land livable.

Moreover, the *People's Daily* newspaper admitted, Chen Yonggui had deliberately falsified Dazhai's production output, persecuted more than one hundred people to death during the Cultural Revolution and protected his "moral degenerate" son from arrest after he raped and robbed a number of Dazhai peasants.

In 1980 Chen, one of Hua Guofeng's few remaining Politburo allies, was dismissed from all posts and ordered to undergo "re-education."

The "learn from Dazhai" posters also are gone, and the place once exalted as a national symbol of pride is rarely mentioned.

bland and undistinguished functionary could last in such a powerful position unchallenged. Hua was about to be put to the test.

First Blood on the Square

In the weeks following Chou's death, intense political maneuvering became increasingly evident via hints dropped in the *People's Daily* and other party mouthpieces.

Perhaps the most telling message was the vitriolic denunciations of "capitalist roaders," a code-word for the group of Communist Party leaders led by Deng who opposed political campaigns like the Cultural Revolution, wanted to modernize China and integrate it into a rapidly advancing world.

At the same time, Jiang Qing began to cultivate herself as the emerging supreme leader of China. In direct and obscure hints, Mao's fourth wife was preparing to assume the position of "the great helmsman" when he died.

Besides receiving visiting dignitaries in her position as a Politburo standing committee member and cultural commissar, Jiang Qing ensured that the role of powerful women in Chinese history became an important topic in newspapers.

For example, articles appeared extolling the Han Dynasty Empress Lu, who ruled from 241-180 B.C., and Tang Dynasty Empress Wu, 624-705. Both women succeeded their husbands as China's rulers.

For many Chinese, the combination of Chou's death and the political scheming by Mao's arrogant wife signaled alarming trouble for the country.

It was against this background that China celebrated the festival known in Chinese as "Qingming," which means "clear and bright." It usually falls in early April, when families visit the graves of their ancestors, sweep them clean, lay food and flowers in homage and bow three times in a firmly entrenched Confucian ritual.

Unlike many of China's cultural traditions pilloried and banned during the Cultural Revolution, the Qingming festival had survived relatively unscathed, although it had been renamed "Martyrs Day."

Workers and peasants took time off, stores closed, relatives visited. Over the tortuous ten years of political convulsions, Qingming was almost a blissful respite from grim reality.

So it wasn't surprising that in early April 1976, many Chinese viewed Qingming as an opportunity to bestow a measure of dignity on their beloved Chou En-lai, a dignity that they believed had been cruelly denied by Chou's radical enemies after his painful death.

In Beijing's vast Tiananmen Square, where Chou had stood beside Mao to proclaim the establishment of the People's Republic in 1949, a couple of hundred ordinary Beijing residents held an impromptu memorial service at the Monument to People's Heroes, a granite column honoring revolutionary martyrs.

But by late Friday April 2, word had spread fast about this display of political defiance of the radicals and thousands more people massed in the square. They laid paper-flower wreaths at the monument exalting Chou Ye-Ye—"Grandpa Chou."

By Sunday, the crowd in the square had swelled to a hundred thousand, by far the biggest gathering since the orchestrated rallies at the height of the Cultural Revolution.

To Beijing's revolutionary committee first secretary Wu De, who was the equivalent of the mayor, the situation was out of control. As a Jiang Qing associate who got the powerful post largely through her influence, this mass outpouring had to be contained and defused.

"Don't be deceived by bad people," Wu decreed in a warning broadcast via the loudspeakers stationed throughout the square. "This is a subversive

Workers carry a portrait of Chou En-lai in a 1977 tribute on the first anniversary of his death.

activity against chairman Mao Tse-tung and the party central committee."

The throngs ignored him. By Sunday night, the square was overflowing with people and wreaths for Chou. More importantly, a few posters and banners appeared criticizing Jiang Qing and other radical leftists.

Like most other news in China, none of this extaordinary activity was reported by the government press, but it traveled fast by word of mouth.

Tens of thousands of young people in Beijing, many of them students whose studies had been curtailed by the Cultural Revolution, traveled to the square to honor Chou.

Trains arriving in Beijing's railway station about a mile east of the square were crammed with people who had heard about the mass display of emotion and anti-radical protest. Some had even hung banners outside the train windows, a few criticizing Mao himself.

This was unprecedented, and to Jiang Qing it was outrageous, intolerable and almost certainly the devious work of her old enemy, that irrepressible little man from Sichuan, Deng Xiaoping.

What exactly happened next in the square has never been fully documented. Most accounts have come from anonymous Chinese witnesses, passed along second and third hand. But most agree that it was a violent, ugly and then deadly confrontation.

On Monday April 5, the People's Militia, controlled by Jiang Qing loyalists, began to surround the square. They forced their way to the People's Monument and removed the wreaths honoring Chou.

Outraged, thousands of demonstrators lobbed rocks at the militiamen, set several of their vehicles ablaze and torched a nearby government building.

The militiamen responded with clubs, pickax handles and gunfire, scattering the demonstrators and shooting many down as they fled.

By some estimates, thousands were killed or wounded, left for dead on the square's littered grounds, though others contend there were far fewer casualties.

Some witnesses claimed that demonstrators found with pro-Chou leaflets or poems were seized, hauled to the Public Security Bureau and shot.

Armed police and troops cordoned off the square for two days, the few foreigners in the capital were told to stay indoors, and cleanup crews worked around the clock, hosing blood off the square's stone-slab surface and hauling away corpses.

The Communist Party organ *People's Daily* did not give details of the bloodletting but referred vaguely to the demonstration, branding it a counter–revolutionary act. The newspaper warned against what it called "rabid resistance and troublemaking from class enemies at home and abroad."

It also directly criticized Deng by name, accusing Chou's seventy-two-year-old disciple of scheming to subvert the goals of the Communist Party with his avowed emphasis on economic modernization.

Foreigners in Beijing and abroad speculated it was highly unlikely that Deng himself had organized what appeared to be a spontaneous outburst against the radicals.

But the crushing of the Tiananmen demonstration and the intensified propaganda campaign against Deng bode ill for the diminutive, scrappy leader who already had been purged twice.

A few days after the April 5 confrontation on the Square, Mao himself ordered the Politburo to strip Deng of all posts and appoint Hua as premier and first deputy chairman of the party, in effect making Hua the next paramount leader of the country.

There was no indication of what had befallen Deng, and rumors swept the capital and the nation over his whereabouts. By some accounts he had been imprisoned or even assassinated.

There were rumors he was hiding out in his native Sichuan, or had sought refuge with former army colleagues in the southern city of Canton. An old military associate and Long March comrade-in-arms, senior Politburo member Ye Jianying, was protective of Deng and resented the way he'd been treated for years.

Although there was no official account of the Tiananmen incident, the promulgation of Deng's dismissal was swiftly carried out via the newspapers, Beijing Radio and state television.

Tens of thousands of Chinese citizens, from major cities to the remote Western provinces, were mobilized to show support for Mao's decree in yet another tired display of revolutionary zeal that had become part of their daily routines. Broadcasts referred to the April 5 riot as a grave crime incited by Deng himself.

"Having discussed the counter–revolutionary incident which took place at Tiananmen Square and Deng Xiaoping's latest behaviors, the political bureau of the Central Committee of the Communist Party of China holds that the nature of the Deng Xiaoping problem has turned into one of antagonistic contradiction," the party's ruling body proclaimed a few days afterward.

"Antagonistic contradiction" was the key phrase in that proclamation. To veteran China watchers, it meant Deng no longer was considered a wayward comrade but an enemy of the party.

A few weeks later, Jiang Qing and her allies made their first public appearance, clearly intended to show they were behind the suppression of Deng.

Jiang Qing, party vice chairman Wang Hongwen, party theorist Yao Wenyuan and Shanghai mayor and propaganda strategist Zhang Chunqiao, appeared with Premier Hua at a reception for more than a hundred people who had "gloriously performed meritorious exploits for the party and the people in the struggle to smash the counter–revolutionary political incident at Tiananmen Square."

Meanwhile, more horrifying details of the killings in the square spread surreptitiously, by letters, poems and word of mouth. Some ex-militiamen, for example, told foreign correspondents in Beijing that they personally wiped brains and blood off the square and that hundreds of demonstrators were shot in cold blood.

Not a word of this was ever reported in the official press and none could be verified.

The nation seemed to be lapsing into a sullen stagnation while rival party leaders warred behind the one-time imperial confines in the capital, maneuvering for position to await that inevitable day when Mao himself, sickly and isolated, would die.

Beijing's spring, birdless from Maoist campaigns to rid the land of sparrows and crows, gave way to a dusty, sultry summer in 1976. It was about to be-

Thousands of Chinese gathered outside Martyrs Monument in January 1979 to mark the third anniversary of the death of Chou En-lai.

come a summer of sorrow and nature's fury.

First Marshal Chu Teh, Mao's close comrade in arms and the strategist behind the Eighth Route Army's triumph in the Chinese civil war, died after a prolonged illness at the age of ninety. Shortly there-

Shortly thereafter, on the hot sticky night of July 28, all over the North China plain, millions of houses began to heave uncontrollably in what the Chinese call a "di zhen"—an "earth terror" or earthquake.

The quake measured 8.3 on the Richter scale of ground motion, rivaling the great San Francisco earthquake of 1906 but many times more deadly.

The brunt of the temblor flattened the industrial city of Tangshan northeast of Beijing, killing at least two hundred and forty thousand people, most of them crushed to death in their flimsy brick-and-mud homes.

But many thousands more were killed in a wide swathe of cities and villages that extended through much of Hebei province, including suburbs of Beijing. Many buildings were severely damaged in the major port of Tianjin about seventy miles east on the Bohai Gulf.

It was a disaster of such profound and stupefying magnitude that the government seemed paralyzed, almost helpless. First reports of the quake's intensity came from abroad and Chinese officials refused to even confirm anything had happened, considering it an internal affair and no business of foreigners.

For millions of ordinary citizens, raised with deeply ingrained folk religion and superstitions about nature's relationship to man, the horror of the earthquake only reinforced an underlying fear about what lie ahead.

To many it was a signal that Mao, the modern-day ruler of China, had lost the mandate of heaven upon which emperors always had relied for their legitimacy.

For a government preoccupied with factional bickering, a much more serious problem was at hand: helping quake victims bury the dead and resurrect their shattered lives.

But officials seemed more fearful that the scope of the disaster would reach the outside world, as if it were an embarrassment that must be kept secret. One of the first official moves was to impose a news blackout, deny a crisis existed and close affected areas to foreigners.

It wasn't until years later that more substantial information about the effects of the earthquake were disclosed. One government document estimated the death toll at more than six hundred and fifty-five thousand killed and seven hundred and seventy-nine injured.

Foreign visitors eventually were given chaperoned tours of Tangshan, much of it under reconstruction. To some people seeing Tangshan for the first time in the post-quake years, it was difficult to tell what had befallen the city, except for a vast mangle of wrecked railroad cars serving as a disaster memorial.

In Tianjin, a grimy city of 7.7 million that once was a pre-revolutionary colonial enclave, foreigners were banned until 1978 because of the widespread destruction and masses of people literally bivouacked in the streets.

By 1981 there were still at least a hundred and fifty

thousand people living in raggedy makeshift hovels, waiting for new housing. The housing problem was compounded by tens of thousands of so-called "rusticated youths" who streamed back to the city after they had been exiled to the countryside during the Cultural Revolution.

The severity of the destruction and the regime's inability to deal with it efficiently became a new source of frustration among the Chinese and reinforced a growing bitterness that had been accumulating for years about the tortuous path of Maoist China.

There was a widespread feeling that the quake was not an isolated event. It was just too coincidental to the other problems besetting the country, ranging from severe food rationing to hordes of unemployed troublemaking ex-Red Guards.

To many Chinese, the quake signaled an unknown political change. They already had lost two respected leaders during the year.

The rumors of Chairman Mao's imminent death began to circulate within weeks of the quake. He had not been seen in public for months. Prominent

Soldiers of the People's Liberation Army pay respects to Mao Tse-tung, who died in 1976.

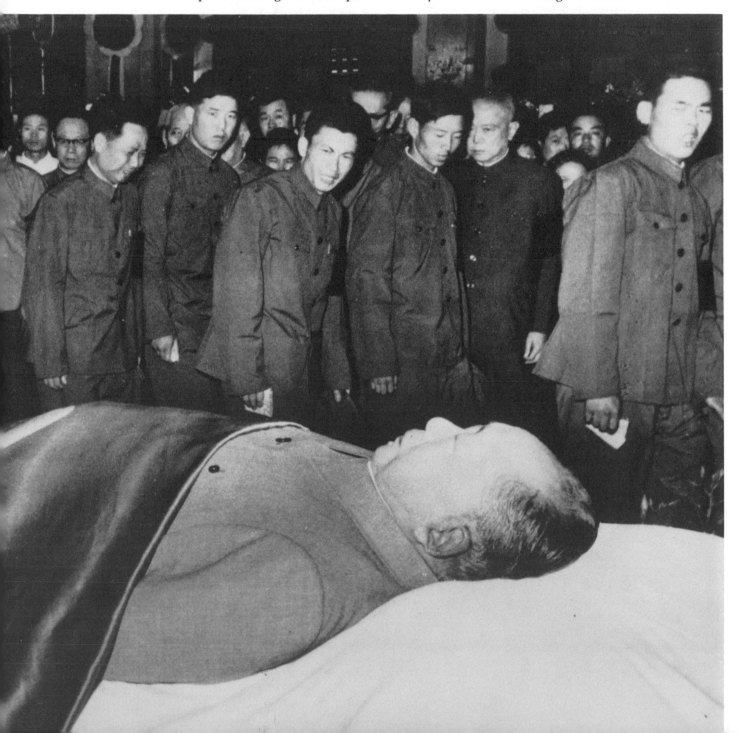

visitors who'd had audiences with "the Great Helmsman" earlier in the year reported him to be feeble, flaccid, drooling at the mouth and unable to stand without the help of his young women aides.

On Monday September 9, workers and peasants were told to go home and listen to their radios or neighborhood loudspeakers for an important announcement.

It came as little surprise when the official news agency Xinhua proclaimed solemnly and with "extreme grief" that Chairman Mao Tse-tung, the shining star of new China, brilliant revolutionary and impassioned political tactician, had died at age eighty-two. No cause of death was given.

Even to Mao's enemies, rivals and critics, this was an electrifying and historical moment, like the death of an emperor.

Despite his massive failures, vindictive political purges and ill-concieved economic ideas, Mao was revered as the founder of modern China, the man who resurrected respect for a nation and people humiliated for generations by foreign invaders.

Tributes began pouring in from around the world, even a condolence from the Soviet Union, the only foreign country Mao had ever visited, China's erstwhile ally and now its menacing, revisionist neighbor to the north.

In the United States, President Gerald Ford, one of the last foreign leaders to have seen Mao in person, called his death a tragedy and described Mao as a "remarkable and very great man."

Former President Richard Nixon, who had pioneered the resurrection of U.S.-China relations with his history-making trip four years earlier, hailed what he called Mao's far-sighted vision in wishing to normalize ties with America.

So brought an end to the reign of a man whose thoughts and actions became the guide for everything that nearly one fourth of the world's population said and did.

His quotes, embodied in a little red book printed by the hundreds of millions and flailed fanatically by screaming Red Guards, were famous around the world.

"A revolution is not the same as inviting people to dinner or writing an essay or painting a picture or doing fancy needlework," Mao wrote in one oft-quoted passage. "It cannot be anything so refined, so calm and gentle, so mild, kind, courteous, restrained and magnanimous. A revolution is an uprising, an act of violence whereby one class overthrows another."

"Gang of Four" arrested on charges of plotting a coup.

Perhaps Mao's most famous quote was this: "Political power grows out of the barrel of a gun."

To foreigners in Beijing, Mao's death cast an eerie, uneasy pall over the capital, where the nights were already growing chilly with impending fall and the streets were beginning to reek with the rotting smell of harvested cabbage.

It was an awkward time for foreigners to be in China, almost as if they were witnessing a death in a stranger's family. Indeed, the government did not allow non-Chinese to attend the funeral and did not invite foreign heads of state.

One reason for that exclusion, China specialists believed, was the intensified power struggle set off by the chairman's death. The problem of rival factions at the highest levels was hinted at by the party's Central Committee, which took the unusual step of appealing for unity almost immediately after Mao died.

A week later, after a period of national mourning, a mass funeral was held in Tiananmen, attended by half a million carefully selected workers, peasants and soldiers. There was to be no repeat of another spontaneous "counter–revolutionary incident" this time.

Hua Guofeng, as first vice chairman of the party, delivered the televised eulogy. He was flanked by youthful vice chairman Wang Hongwen, dressed in military fatigues, and Jiang Qing, wearing stark black widow's clothes. Deng Xiaoping was nowhere to be seen. It was later learned that he was barred from the proceedings.

"We want Marxism, not revisionism," Hua intoned, quoting from a speech Mao had made during the Cultural Revolution. "We want unity, not dissension. We want to be open and aboveboard, not scheming and intriguing."

Even as Hua spoke those words, however, the scheming and intriguing was about to reach a dramatic turning point that would signal a stunning setback for Mao's radical disciples and a new era for the world's most populous nation.

The "Gang of Four"

With his nondescript country-bumpkin background, bulldog jowls and burly torso, Hua Guofeng did not exactly strike the Chinese people as a rightful inheritor of Chairman Mao's position.

Hua had written no flowery poetry, no catchy slogans. He had espoused no creative political philosophy. He played a relatively obscure role in the Chinese revolution.

About the only obvious connections between the late Chairman Mao and his apparent successor were their thick Hunanese drawls and Hua's work to create irrigation projects in their home province, where he became a leading party functionary in the 1960s.

After the discovery of the alleged plot by the late Defense Minister Lin Biao to assassinate Mao in 1971, the chairman recruited Hua to lead a special investigation.

As a result, Hua later became a vice premier and security minister, an important post that effectively put him in charge of the nation's vast network of uniformed and plainclothes police.

Hua was said to be among those advisers closest to Mao, partly because of an unquestioned loyalty and an adherence to what would later become known as the "two whatevers" or "whateverist" philosophy: "Whatever Chairman Mao said and did was right."

It was understandable that Mao, confronting his own death and what he feared would be the death of China's revolution, saw Hua as a logical choice to succeed him.

In what are Mao's now-famous deathbed words, whether he actually spoke them or not, he told Hua: "With you in charge, my heart is at ease."

But even as Mao's corpse and was prepared for preservation in a crystal sarcophagus tomb to be erected in Tiananmen Square, Hua was facing the battle of his political life.

He had always been the compromise choice to take Mao's place. Months earlier, when the party Politburo was debating who should succeed the late Chou as premier, Hua was selected because of a deadlock between moderates who wanted Deng and radicals who favored Zhang Chunqiao, one of the Cultural Revolution's main figures.

Hua was in the no-man's land, between a powerful group of leftist radicals led by Jiang Qing, and a rival group of party elders who remained loyal to Deng, wanted to rehabilitate him, close the books on the Cultural Revolution and get on with the "Four Modernization" goals first advanced by Chou in 1975.

The big question was with which faction would Hua align himself now that Mao was gone.

The answer came with stunning dispatch October 6, less than a month after Mao's death, at a special meeting of the Politburo's standing committee.

As Zhang Chunqiao and his allies Wang Hongwen and Yao Wenyuan arrived, they were seized by

Hua's security men.

It was a carefully organized arrest aided by senior Politburo member Marshal Ye Jianying, the crusty old revolutionary colleague of Chou En-lai's who was believed to have personally sheltered Deng Xiaoping after he was blamed for the Tiananmen incident and sacked.ÉThe fourth and most powerful member of the radical clique, Jiang Qing herself, reportedly had been tipped about the plot to arrest her and didn't attend the meeting.

Security agents led by Mao's personal bodyguard Wang Dongxing, who had been believed loyal to the radicals but abruptly switched sides, seized Mao's widow at home.

So marked the arrest of the "Four Scoundrels," later dubbed the "Shanghai Four" and "Gang of Four," accused of plotting to seize power and anoint Jiang Qing as Mao's rightful successor.

Ultimately the "gang" would be blamed for one of the darkest and deadliest periods in Communist China's short turbulent history, the Great Proletarian Cultural Revolution launched by Mao himself.

The immediate impact of the arrests was a common outpouring of spontaneous joy and emotion nationwide, as if a hated dictatorship had been overthrown. In many cities, workers were given more than a week off just to celebrate.

In the southern city of Canton, where Deng himself reportedly hid after he was dismissed, hundreds of thousands of residents swarmed through the streets, beating drums, clashing cymbals and blowing trumpets to show support for the arrests. Even in Shanghai, the home-base of the radicals, where one-time movie starlet Jiang Qing had begun her ambitious political career, there was an overwhelming feeling of relief and joy that the "gang" had been deposed.

It took nearly two weeks for the state media to officially announce what had happened, partly because the press and radio had been under the control of the radicals for more than a year and it took some time to remove them.

On October 18, the *People's Daily* proclaimed in a front-page editorial that "a firm campaign must be waged to thoroughly expose and criticize those who attempted to snatch power from the party." It was the first reference to the Gang of Four's coup attempt.

A few days later state radio confirmed that Hua had officially been appointed to replace the late Chairman Mao and had crushed a "conspiratorial clique" led by Mao's widow.

Hua thus earned his place in history as a key collaborator in ending the period of radical leftism that had isolated China, crippled its economy and left its people desperate for change.

In the days and months that followed the arrest of the Gang of Four, most of the nation's problems were attributed to them. To many Chinese, the blame was justified.

The gang was accused, for example, of relentlessly persecuting prominent intellectuals, artists and scientists as the "stinking No. 9" category, vilified like the other "stinking" categories of landlords, rich peasants, counter-revolutionaries, bad elements, rightists, renegades, enemy agents and "capitalist roaders."

They sought audiences with communist officials, people's prosecutors and judges for word on when their property would be returned, their reputations restored, the killers of their relatives brought to justice.

In the meantime, China's economy continued to stagnate and delays in ambitious plans to modernize antiquated factories were prolonged. There were increasing reports of local military commanders in China's far-flung provinces carving out their own fiefdoms like feudal warlords, ignoring directives from Beijing.

Moreover, there remained pockets of deep-seated support for the deposed radicals. Many local party functionaries had gained power during the years Jiang Qing and her associates were in command and were not about to relinquish their status. Some even resorted to arming themselves in preparation for civil war.

In Shanghai, for example, pro-radical militia units considered commandeering the railroad line to Beijing but were quickly disarmed, Chinese witnesses reported later.

In Baoding, about a hundred miles from Beijing, Gang of Four loyalists raided ammunition factories, grain stores and shops in preparation for a battle with pro-government party factions.

The government had to send troops to quell that insurrection, one of a series of disturbances reported in at least twelve of China's twenty-nine provinces in the months following the gang's arrest.

Hua Guofeng, meanwhile, behaved increasingly as though he were trying to become the reincarnation of Chairman Mao himself and prolong the type of cultism created by China's No. 1 revolutionary, who in his waning years became divorced from reality and had little knowledge of what was happening in his own country.

Effigies of the "Gang of Four" hanging from a tree, with name tags.

Posters of "the wise leader Chairman Hua Guofeng," smiling and reading scriptures by Chairman Mao, began appearing in major cities. Hua even commissioned an oil painting showing a dying Mao telling his protege that China's future was in his hands.

Hua's portrait hung beside Mao's at important party meetings and his utterances were printed atop the *People's Daily*. Hua cut his hair like Mao and wrote inscriptions at Communist shrines.

It also was believed to be at Hua's personal behest that Mao's body was pickled for eternal preservation, mirroring what the Soviets did with their revolutionary idol Vladimir Lenin and the Vietnamese with theirs, Ho Chi Minh.

One of Hua's first acts as top leader was to take charge of a huge construction project to display Mao's corpse in an imposing marble mausoleum built on the southern rim of Tiananmen Square.

Many Chinese, including some prominent leaders, were known to be deeply offended at this arbitrary decision, partly because it destroyed the square's picturesque symmetry and exalted a figure whose final place in Chinese history had yet to be fully judged.

Eventually, Hua's inability to control the aftermath of the Cultural Revolution, his clinging insistence on worshipping everything Chairman Mao said and did, and his questionable decision to construct a Mao tomb forced him to compromise with Deng supporters in the Politburo.

By the middle of 1977, leading veteran Politburo members wanted to bring back Deng to run the day-to-day affairs of the party, the country and the army. They wanted to reverse Mao's decree that the Tiananmen riot more than a year earlier had been a counterrevolutionary act.

Although it was not clear at the time, Deng already had made somewhat of a comeback, even if he wasn't seen publicly.

Talks and speeches of Deng's published years later suggested he was regularly sought for advice on running government and party affairs. He also seemed to be maneuvering for a power struggle with Hua over the critical question of Mao's legacy.

The gang was accused of devastating China's cultural treasures and setting back by a generation or more the national effort to become a powerful socialist state by the year 2000.

The squalid life in the countryside where 800 million peasants subsisted, the low factory pay in the cities, the stifling bureaucracy, housing and food shortages, unfair privileges for party members, all were ascribed to the Gang of Four.

Some of the blame bordered on the absurd and reflected a deliberate party attempt to make the radicals responsible for all of China's problems. Beijing's recurrent dust storms, for example, a phenomenon caused by generations of tree-cutting, soil erosion and over-farming that predated the communists, were blamed on the gang. The failure of the nation's scientists to accurately predict the Tangshan quake likewise was blamed on the gang.

This systematic scapegoating would last for years and touch every facet of what was wrong with the country, no matter how petty, inconsequential or irrelevant.

When the Chinese national basketball team toured the United States in 1978, for example, the coach blamed its spotty performance directly on "the pernicious influence of the Gang of Four." Ever since the gang's demise, he said, Chinese basketball players had been growing taller and stronger.

The most venomous and personal criticism was directed at Jiang Qing herself. A second-rate film actress, she was despised for her arrogant self-appointment as China's cultural arbiter, determining what the people should see, hear, wear and think.

Tales of Jiang Qing's own vanity, extravagance, hypocrisy and vulgarity abounded in the press after her arrest and was one the most popular topics of conversation in China.

It was claimed, for example, that she had not lived with Mao for years, ignored his warnings against political scheming, tampered with his writing and monopolized access to him.

While Jiang Qing required the women of China to wear shapeless baggy pants and cut their hair in peasant's pigtails, her personal retinue of women servants wore white lace dresses and watched private screenings of Greta Garbo films—Madame Mao's favorite. She was accused of forcing peasants to chop down their trees so she could take better landscape photographs. She made soldiers lock their arms in a protective ring around her when she swam at Beidaihe, the party's seaside resort on the Bohai Gulf.

About a month after the gang was arrested, the Chinese press announced that Jiang and her three alleged co-conspirators, along with Mao's former secretary Chen Boda and five senior generals, would face trial. Marshal Ye was to head a special investigation to gather evidence against the defendants, who would remain in prison or under house arrest.

Deng Xiaoping's role in the gang's arrest never has been fully revealed. But it was clear that the five-foot-tall leader, who once said, "when the sky falls, the giants get hit first," possessed enormous influence behind the scenes during this period. It was only a matter of time before he was officially rehabilitated.

By the beginning of 1977, it was clear that Hua Guofeng was in political difficulty.

Although his arrest of the gang lifted an enormous weight off China, it was also like popping a cork on a champagne bottle over which he had no control.

For millions of Cultural Revolution victims, this was a time to demand redress, compensation and vengeance for the terror and waste of the previous ten years.

Many besieged government and party offices, wrote letters to Beijing and camped outside the guarded Zhongnanhai compound for leaders in the capital. From elderly couples to unrequited lovers, they carried tales of murder, exile, persecution, shattered relationships and broken dreams.

"We cannot mechanically apply what Comrade Mao Tse-tung said about a particular question to another question, what he said in a particular place to another place, what he said at a particular time to another time, or what he said under particular circumstances to other circumstances," Deng said. "Comrade Mao Tse-tung himself said repeatedly that some of his own statements were wrong."

At an important Central Committee meeting in July 1977, Hua was formally named to the country's top positions as party chairman and premier. But this was seen largely as a symbolic showing of unity.

The more significant event of that session was the formal restoration of Deng to his jobs as party vice chairman, vice chairman of the Central Military Commission and vice premier.

On its face this made Deng the No. 2 man, but in reality Deng had triumphantly returned to power for the third time in Communist China's history.

His rising position was further reinforced by a party congress a month later that decreed a "collective leadership" comprised of Hua, Deng, Marshal Ye and other senior Politburo members was running the country, a further slap at Hua.

Deng's comeback meant it was only a matter of time before "the wise leader comrade Hua Guofeng" would become a footnote.

In a September 1980 session of the National People's Congress, China's largely ceremonial legislature, Hua resigned as premier, replaced by a top Deng lieutenant, Zhao Ziyang. In a June 1981 Central Committee session he resigned as head of the Communist Party, replaced by another key Deng

man, Hu Yaobang.

Perhaps as a face-saving gesture, in recognition of his role in toppling the Gang of Four radicals, Hua was given the title of a party vice chairman. But even that was taken away from him at the Communist Party Congress of September 1982.

He has rarely been seen since. Government spokesmen, occasionally asked by foreign journalists about the status or whereabouts of the man Mao once anointed as his successor, have said Hua is "recovering from an illness," a euphemism for leaders relieved of their power.

The Emergence of Deng Xiaoping

The People's Republic of China that Deng took control of in the last half of 1977 was even more fragile and weakened than when he was abruptly sacked more than a year earlier.

Domestically, the situation was basically out of control. The peasants and factory laborers, tired and cynical from the "big pot" system that gave them equal compensation regardless of how hard they worked, weren't working that hard. The country was dipping into foreign exchange reserves to import necessities like grain.

A wave of lawlessness inspired partly by the freewheeling Cultural Revolution had created a generation of young people with little respect for authority or the value of their own lives. Violent crimes ranging from murder to rape to robbery, previously unheard of or unreported in Mao's China, were on the increase.

The deposed radical regime's obsession with building showcase heavy industries like steel mills, fulfilling quotas, subsidizing prices, insisting on Mao's dictum of "self reliance" and shunning foreign investment had severely hurt the economy and largely isolated China from the commercial world.

The menacing Soviet Union, meanwhile, continued to mass troops along the vast Sino-Soviet frontier and turn Vietnam into a Pacific military base in the aftermath of the American retreat.

China's own relations with the United States had stumbled over the sticky problem of Taiwan.

Despite a U.S. commitment to normalize ties with Beijing made in the historic Shanghai Communique five years earlier, there had been little movement, partly because of the Chinese Communists' refusal

Trial of the Gang of Four

The dramatic and vindictive tone of China's most sensational trial was established at the outset, when armed guards hauled Mao Tse-tung's grim-faced handcuffed widow Jiang Qing, three radical cohorts and other former high-ranking defendants into a packed Beijing courtroom on a cold fall day in 1980.

So marked the start of the five-week trial of the "Gang of Four" and their subordinates, who included six co-conspirators in an assassination scheme by the late Defense Minister Lin Biao to dynamite Mao's train and seize power in 1971.

The defendants, some of them frail old men already imprisoned for years, finally faced formal charges that ranged from mass murder to plotting the violent overthrow of the government.

It soon became clear to the hundreds of millions of Chinese following the unprecedented proceeding that an entire decade was on trial, a decade of madness, turmoil and terror formerly known as the Cultural Revolution, now considered an unmitigated disaster.

For Mao's pragmatic successor Deng Xiaoping and his colleagues, purged and mistreated during the 1966-76 campaign, there was no question the defendants were guilty of high crimes. There was no possibility of acquittal and little room for leniency. Most members of the thirty-five-judge panel in the Supreme People's Court were Cultural Revolution victims themselves.

The trial, held in a converted auditorium at No. 1 Justice Road in Beijing, had all the makings of an officially orchestrated vendetta, from the chief judge's somber intonations to the stern guards who led the shackled defendants to and from their chairs.

The proceeding was meant partly as a demonstration of China's newly enacted legal codes aimed at showing the country was ruled by law, not personality cults or capricious politics. But it also was a message of warning to Gang of Four supporters who had risen to prominent positions during the Cultural Revolution that they no longer had protectors in high places.

To a great extent, the trial also was a repudiation of Mao himself, although his stature was so great it was impossible to directly impugn him. Still, many Chinese said privately, the defendants should have been called the "Gang of Five."

Glum and bitter, the accused mostly just stared aimlessly while prosecutors spent hours reading the charges in the twenty thousand-word indictment, assembled by a special investigation team that had spent years gathering evidence and deposing witnesses.

Television cameras panned the courtroom, crammed with more than eight hundred spectators including prominent widows and widowers of the Gang's alleged victims. Carefully edited excerpts of the testimony dominated the TV news every night.

Jiang Qing, then sixty-seven, was the alleged ringleader, the cultural commissar charged with personally overseeing frame-ups, extorted confessions and mass persecutions of innocent officials, intellectuals, teachers, writers and artists that resulted in at least thirty-five thousand deaths and more than half a million shattered careers. The former Shanghai movie starlet was further accused of deceiving and isolating Mao in his sickly final years and plotting to anoint herself his successor as he gasped his last breaths.

One count accused her of ransacking homes of former costars to seize any compromising photographs they may have kept of the ex-actress, who used to call herself by the stage name "Lan Ping" or "Blue Apple" during her film days in pre-revolutionary Shanghai.

Prosecutors likened Jiang Qing to the tyrannical Empress Dowager for her cunning and scheming. She also was the most defiant during the trial and provided most of the surprises in what otherwise seemed a carefully rehearsed show.

She broke into sobs as the indictment was read against her. She spurned state-appointed defense lawyers, spoke on her own behalf, screamed epithets at the judges, challenged the charges and denounced her captors as revisionists, spies and thugs.

Sometimes Jiang said she couldn't remember anything about the accusations. Sometimes Jiang claimed she was hard of hearing and asked for a re-reading.

At one point she interrupted a sobbing prosecution witness and was dragged from the court as the audience applauded. On other occasions she quibbled, tried to shift blame to others or claimed everything she said and did had her husband's explicit approval.

"I was Chairman Mao's dog," Jiang told the court in her high-pitched tinny voice. "Whomever he told me to bite, I bit."

The other principal members of the gang were Zhang Chunqiao, a leading radical theorist and former Shanghai mayor; Wang Hongwen, a young ex-textile mill worker in Shanghai who had struck Mao's fancy and risen to the No. 3 spot in the party hierarchy; and Yao Wenyuan, a propaganda specialist whose writings played an important role at the beginning of the Cultural Revolution.

Also on trial were Chen Boda, Mao's former private secretary who ghostwrote many of his speeches and commentaries, and five former military commanders, including former air force chief Wu Faxian and former chief of staff Huang Yongsheng, who were accused of participating in the Lin Biao conspiracy to assassinate Mao.

Defendant Zhang refused to cooperate during the trial by simply ignoring all questions put to him and staring ahead silently. The others either babbled out confessions or nodded in acquiescence to the charges when their turns came.

Chen, a crippled seventy-seven-year-old with rotting teeth, was so eager to please the judges he told them death by firing squad was too good and they should behead him instead.

He readily admitted helping carry out the purges of the late President Liu Shaoqi, as well as Deng Xiaoping and others since restored to power.

Chen also admitted authorizing an infamous editorial in the *People's Daily* in June 1966 that exhorted Chinese to "sweep away all monsters and demons." The editorial was subsequently blamed for inciting extremist upheavals that caused many deaths.

As the trial dragged on, the biggest question was not guilt or innocence but the severity of the sentences. All faced possible death penalties, but the Chinese Communists never had executed any former leaders.

In Jiang's case at least, it seemed highly unlikely that the court would order the death penalty, in grudging deference to her position as Mao's widow.

Moreover, execution created the possibility of martyrdom for Jiang should the political winds of China shift yet again. Deng Xiaoping himself had said Jiang and her codefendants would never be treated with the same harshness as their alleged victims.

Still, when the trial ended December 29 the prosecutors urged the death penalty for Jiang. In another vitriolic display, she dared the court to execute her and said she would gladly march to the killing ground after the masses had debated her fate.

"You are trying to put Mao on trial through me," she said. "You are trying to destroy me because you know you never will be able to destroy Mao."

A month later, the special court announced it had sentenced Jiang to death and suspended the punishment to give her a chance to "reform through labor."

to renounce the use of force to "liberate" the island from their old wartime enemies, the Chinese Nationalists.

The communists were getting impatient for a breakthrough not only because of the enormous economic opportunities an American relationship offered, but from its strategic value as a counterweight to the growing Soviet influence in Asia.

These were only Deng's immediate, urgent problems. He faced several subtle but potentially more alarming crises as a result of the Maoist era over which he'd had limited influence.

Perhaps the most insidious and pervasive problem, and in many ways the key to the other challenges, was China's rampant population explosion encouraged by Mao himself.

In 1949 a census showed there were 540 million people in China. By the late 1970s the population had nearly doubled to 1 billion in a country only slightly larger than the United States and with only a fraction of land suitable for farming.

Put another way, China's population comprises nearly one-quarter of mankind living on just 7 percent of the world's arable land.

Mao had insisted that more people mean more production, one of the tenets in his catastrophic "Great Leap Forward" campaign of 1958, aimed at overtaking the capitalist world and making China a workers paradise of plenty.

"With many people, there's lots of power," Mao had once said.

An estimated ten million people perished from starvation in that debacle, the worst famine of modern times, yet Mao never retracted his exhortations for more births.

It was not be until nearly three years after Mao's death that the communists would take draconian measures to reverse the country's birth time bomb and hold the population to 1.2 billion by the year 2000. These measures included a widely unpopular one-child limit on new families, which resulted in an alarming number of female infanticides by parents who wanted sons, the traditional preference in Chinese families.

Despite government denials, there also were persistent reports of officially sanctioned forced abortions and forced sterilization in the countryside to contain the burgeoning population.

Another crisis faced by Deng left by the Mao legacy was China's rapidly deteriorating environment, especially its serious air and water pollution.

Under Mao, China had no environmental protection measures. Industrial waste, contamination and erosion were deemed problems exclusive to capitalist countries.

Propaganda posters showed lush forests, fish-filled lakes, verdant valleys, man and nature in harmony. Foreign visitors were shown how the Chinese recycle waste, use natural fertilizer and terrace farmland to prevent erosion.

This Maoist achievement turned out to be a monumental fiction. Although Mao cannot be blamed for the enormous environmental damage China has suffered over centuries of deforestation and over-farming, his policies worsened the problems.

Perhaps the most disastrous was Mao's decree to "take grain as the key link" to prosperity and grow it everywhere. The result was massive destruction of what few forests China had left.

These were daunting, awesome problems facing Deng Xiaoping in a government that wasn't even thirty years old.

But for Deng, perhaps the most daunting and awesome of all was how to reverse nearly everything Mao stood for without repudiating "the Great Helmsman" himself, and thereby remove the Communist Party's own claim to political legitimacy.

Deng decided it would have to be done patiently, gradually, subtly and without violence if possible. It also would mean rewriting history with the help of the dead Chairman Mao's own words and making serious overtures for much closer relations with two foreign powers Mao once despised, the United States and Japan.

America and Japan: "Old Friends"

By late 1977 there was no question that the Chinese people were enthusiastic to expand and embellish their disrupted ties with America, known in Chinese as "Meiguo" or "Beautiful Country."

Many Chinese had relatives in the United States; tidbits of American culture banned during the Cultural Revolution, from Charlie Chaplin films to jazz to classic stories like Huckleberry Finn, had been re-released and were enormously popular.

Chairman Deng Xiaoping (l.) and Party General Secretary Hu Yaobang at a meeting of the Central Military Commission in June 1985.

Limited numbers of American tourists were traveling in China as a result of President Nixon's groundbreaking 1972 trip, and drew large friendly crowds.

The government no longer made routine references to "Mei Di"—shorthand for "American imperialism," and was increasingly testy toward Vietnam, America's erstwhile enemy.

China's desire for closer relations with Japan, however, was riddled with ambivalence. This stemmed largely from the vivid memories older Chinese harbored of marauding Japanese imperial troops who raped and plundered their way through the Chinese countryside in the 1930s and 1940s. Many Chinese have said privately they are grateful the United States dropped atomic bombs on Japan to force it into surrender at the end of World War II.

But senior Chinese leaders such as Deng, who had fought the Japanese invaders, concluded that China simply could not achieve its stated modernization goals without the enormous industrial and technological might Japan had to offer.

Moreover, ever since Prime Minister Kakuei Tanaka had visited in 1972 and laid the groundwork to normalize relations, the Japanese had made apologies for their past behavior and seemed ready to cultivate a longlasting friendship on equal terms. The Chinese and Japanese people were, after all, close cousins, with a common written language and many of the same traditions.

Japan also had rapidly become China's largest trading partner over the past few years. By the time the Chinese were ready to open their doors to Western countries in late 1978, U.S.-Japan trade already had reached $5 billion annually.

So with great fanfare on August 12, 1978, China and Japan signed a treaty of peace and friendship formally normalizing relations for the first time in more than half a century.

One of the keys to the China-Japan reconciliation was the Japanese willingness to sever a diplomatic relationship with the Nationalists on Taiwan, although Tokyo continued to maintain an unofficial presence there.

This was acceptable to Beijing and eventually would become part of the model for a blueprint to normalize relations with the United States.

But the U.S.-Taiwan connection was far more complex and delicate. For one thing, Taiwan had become one of the biggest U.S. trading partners and a big weapons customer. For another, the United States had a mutual defense treaty with the Nationalist government on Taiwan and had deployed military personnel there. This was a vestige of American

support for Chiang Kai-shek's government that fled the mainland when the communists triumphed in 1949. To Beijing, diplomatic recognition by the United States would require the Americans to terminate the military link with Taiwan.

Another problem facing normalization was the vocal opposition by a number of leading conservative U.S. politicians, notably Senator Barry Goldwater, a longtime friend of Taiwan's Nationalists, and former California Goveror Ronald Reagan, at

The world may know it as Coca-Cola, but to the Chinese it's "Tastes Good, Tastes Happy." This photo shows the first shipment of the soft drink to China being loaded in Hong Kong in January 1979.

Chinese Law

When Deng Xiaoping and other leaders who were imprisoned and disgraced during the Cultural Revolution re-emerged in the late 1970s and began to bury the radical policies of the past, one of their most important priorities was establishing a system of laws.

To the astonishment of many foreigners, China had no criminal or civil code of laws during the nearly three decades that Mao and his subordinates ruled the country.

The chairman's utterances, like those of the imperial emperors, were considered the law of the land, no matter how vague or illogical they may have seemed.

At the height of the Cultural Revolution in the late 1960s when China teetered on anarchy, the army basically ran the country in what amounted to martial law.

Mao himself considered laws a contemptuous tool of the rich and greedy to suppress the workers and peasants.

Likewise, he thought lawyers to be subversive, sly masters of twisting fiction into fact, confusing the masses and aiding counterrevolutionaries and common criminals. Lawyers were banned from practicing in China until 1978, two years after Mao's death.

When Deng became China's paramount leader, he presided over the construction of a new legal framework, new constitution, criminal code, civil and criminal procedure law, and more than three hundred economic laws, many designed to attract foreign investors.

Deng encouraged universities to establish law schools, invited foreign law experts to come teach and called for the training of thousands of lawyers, judges, prosecutors and investigators. He exhorted the mass media to promote the value of legal rights, once dismissed by Mao as the doubletalk of bourgeois "class enemies."

He assigned Peng Zhen, a close associate, Politburo member and former Beijing mayor whose dismissal in 1966 helped touch off the Cultural Revolution, to personally oversee the establishment of China's new body of laws, which were formally promulgated in 1980.

"It is necessary to switch from doing things according to policies to doing things both according to policies and in line with the law," Peng proclaimed.

Among the most significant elements of China's criminal code in the post-Mao period were the guarantees of an accused's right to a defense, including the right to hear the charges against him, question accusers and call witnesses.

The code promised public trials, a ban on forced confessions and strict limits on the pretrial detention of suspects.

Nonetheless, legal rights in China remain vastly different from their Western counterparts. China's system has been fraught with contradictions and growing pains, caused by the tradition of authoritarian rule and the Communists' own seesaw policies.

The most striking difference is the presumed guilt of the accused in criminal cases. The Justice Ministry has said that more than 95 percent of all people charged with crimes are convicted.

The best example of this was the trial of the notorious Gang of Four, the leftist followers of Mao blamed for the Cultural Revolution. Months before the televised proceeding began, the chief judge said the defendants were guilty.

In civil matters such as divorces, contract disputes or property damage, Chinese litigants are encouraged to settle differences through their local neighborhood committee or Communist Party secretary. The government also charges hefty fees for filing civil complaints, another reason to settle out of court.

In contrast to the Western legal system in which prior court rulings are used to interpret old laws and create new laws, Chinese judges do not necessarily cite previous cases in their decisions.

The Chinese also have expressed wariness over creating too many laws, which they see as a Western affliction. The Communist Party journal Red Flag once warned that China could face the same problem as the United States, where there are "more laws than the hairs on a cow."

Although lawyers once again are allowed to practice, they are still considered government employees, sworn to protect the interest of the state.

They usually get the same menial pay as factory laborers and are highly reluctant to aggressively defend their clients, partly out of fear this will only provoke judges into ordering heavier punishment. Most lawyers restrict themselves to pleading for mercy and leniency from the courts if their clients have confessed.

Despite the guarantee of public trials, most courts are in guarded, fenced compounds. Many trials are announced only after courts announce the verdicts in public posters pasted outside.

The police still retain extraordinary power to imprison people for petty crimes, such as burglary, public drunkenness or vandalism. They can summarily sentence suspects to up to three years of "lao jiao," or "reform through labor."

Human rights groups have continued to assert that Chinese prisoners are often mistreated and arbitrarily executed, depending on the nature of their alleged crimes.

After the government began an intense campaign against violent lawbreakers in 1983, Amnesty International said thousands of suspects were shot without trial. China denied this.

Foreigners who have run into legal trouble in China since the new code of laws were created often have found themselves at the mercy of a system riddled with double standards, confusion and arbitrary procedures.

Perhaps the best example of this came in 1985, when an American businessman named Richard Ondrik was detained without trial in the northeast city of Harbin after a fire in his hotel killed ten people, including his business partner, four Chinese employees and five visiting North Korean officials. Local police suspected Ondrik had started the fire by smoking in bed.

It was only after foreign news organizations reported his detention that the Chinese announced he would be tried on unspecified charges of criminal negligence. At first the local people's court refused to allow foreigners to attend but later reversed the restriction, evidently on orders from Beijing.

At the trial, hotel officials admitted they had purchased smoke detectors and sprinklers but failed to install them, the telephone didn't work so the fire department arrived late, and the employee assigned to security had been drinking in the hotel bar.

Nonetheless, prosecutors insisted that Ondrik had started the blaze, although the defendant couldn't remember whether he'd been smoking. On the advice of his Chinese lawyer, Ondrik elected not to challenge the prosecution's case and instead pleaded for leniency. He received an eighteen-month prison term and a $52,000 fine.

the time a Republican presidential contender. Both said such a move would be like stabbing old friends in the back after thirty years.

But by late 1978, Deng Xiaoping, flush with success in strengthening ties to Japan and clearly the leader in charge of integrating China into the world, was impatient for a breakthrough with the Americans.

It had been nearly seven years since both countries had established liaison offices in each other's capitals as part of the reconciliation process.

Two-way trade had grown from zero to several hundred million dollars a year. A few prominent American companies were even negotiating trade and investment deals over products ranging from Chinese silk and "Qingdao" beer to U.S. locomotives and Coca-Cola. Nonetheless, talks over Taiwan had foundered. For Deng, there could be no further development of China-U.S. ties without normalization.

In May, President Carter had sent National Security Adviser Zbigniew Brzezinski on a mission to Beijing, followed by visits from a few ranking Cabinet members. The Americans again stressed their wish for the Taiwan question to be resolved peacefully.

Exactly when the deadlock broke is unclear but it evidently happened in October, when Deng made a triumphant and eye-opening tour of Japan to celebrate the treaty of peace and friendship their countries had recently concluded.

It was on that trip that Deng saw with his own eyes the gleaming skyscrapers, superhighways, automated assembly lines and high-speed bullet trains for which Japan was famous. China's wartime nemesis, humbled and devastated at the end of World War II, had made a stunning comeback that vaulted it to the most advanced and richest nation in Asia.

For Deng, this remarkable change made it even more imperative that his own backward and impoverished homeland bury the turbulent past and get on with the task of catching up. He needed help more than ever not only from Japan but the United States too.

In subtle Chinese fashion, Deng dropped a diplomatic bomb. He told Prime Minister Takeo Fukuda that despite the relentless mainland propaganda threats to retake Taiwan, there would be no military conquest of the island. He clearly meant for Fukuda to convey that message to the Americans.

This set in motion an exchange of diplomatic notes and meetings that reached a crescendo a little more than a month later in Beijing, when Deng abruptly summoned Leonard Woodcock, the former United Autoworkers Union president who was now chief of the U.S. mission. Such an audience could only mean something important.

On December 15, Carter asked the three major U.S. television networks for broadcast time and told the American people that a profound and history-making change in relations was about to take place with the People's Republic of China.

The White House issued a joint communique proclaiming the United States and China "have agreed to recognize each other and establish diplomatic relations as of January 1, 1979." In the process, the White House said, it would terminate diplomatic relations with Taiwan and withdraw the seven hundred and fifty military personnel deployed on the island.

The news was announced at the same time in China via state-radio hookups to loudspeakers throughout the country and an unprecedented news conference given by Premier Hua Guofeng, who called the reconciliation "a historic event.'

But Deng was the driving force behind the normalization, one of the unrealized goals of his old mentor, Chou En-lai.

In recognition of Deng's role, he was chosen to accept an invitation to confer with Carter in January, making him the highest-ranking Chinese Communist to visit the United States.

For Carter, the change illustrated what he called "the simple reality" that the United States could no longer act as though one-fourth of mankind didn't matter.

But his action incurred the wrath of conservative political opponents who already perceived him as weak and yielding in the face of foreign pressure.

Their anger intensified when the State Department disclosed it had received no explicit assurances from the Chinese Communists about Taiwan's security.

Nor was their anger mollified by a Pentagon disclosure that the United States was still committed to supply Taiwan with more than half a billion dollars in weapons over the next five years, including forty-four advanced F-5 fighters, missiles, tanks, torpedos, amd laser-guided bombs.

Senator Goldwater immediately vowed to take Carter to court and challenge his authority to grant diplomatic relations without congressional approv-

Man shows off English language textbook he bought to use with language lessons offered by the government. The study of English increased in popularity in the late 1970s.

al. "This is a dangerous thing because it puts fear in our allies, especially our small allies, as to how the U.S. will keep its word," Goldwater said. But there was little the senator could do to block diplomatic recognition of Beijing, except stall the confirmation of an ambassador.

Reagan, seizing the normalization as a campaign issue, decried Carter's action as an "outright betrayal of our close friend and ally, the Republic of China on Taiwan."

In an ironic twist of history, the anti-communist Republicans found themselves on the same side of the China issue as the Soviet Union.

The Soviets were especially critical of U.S.-Chinese normalization because of its obvious strategic implications, and they warned Beijing and Washington that a military alliance between the two would be "a big mistake."

On Taiwan, the mood was violent and ugly. Protesters rallied outside the U.S. Embassy and tried to crash the front gate but Marines repelled them with teargas. The demonstrators burned American flags, smashed diplomat car windows and screamed "Down with the Communist and American bandits!"

Taiwan military police were forced to guard the residence of U.S. Ambassador Leonard Unger, and American citizens in the capital Taipei were warned to stay off the streets until tempers settled.

On January 1, 1979, U.S. Marines lowered the American flag for the last time at the embassy in Taiwan and removed signs from the gates under heavy guard.

One of Deng's main hopes was that the U.S. diplomatic and military abandonment of Taiwan would isolate the Nationalists and force them to negotiate on reunification with Beijing, ending the "Two China" stigma of postwar history. But Deng was premature.

"Our anti-communist struggle will never cease until the Chinese Communist regime has been destroyed," Taiwan President Chiang Ching-kuo, son of the man who'd lost China to the communists thirty years earlier, said in rejecting Deng's overtures for talks.

"We do not deny that our country is again distressed and assaulted by adversity," Chiang said in a reference to the American departure. "But our ancient sages have told us that a country thrives on distress."

Behind the rhetoric, however, the Americans worked intensively to assure Chiang that he had little to worry about. Besides the continuation of weapons sales, the State Department developed

what officials called a "crash program" to leave intact all existing commercial, cultural and education agreements with Taiwan.

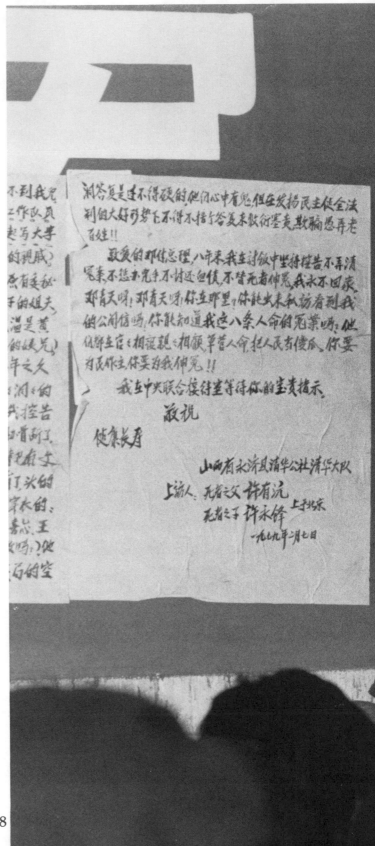

Protest poster goes up on Democracy Wall in Beijing in 1979. This one was headlined in blood, *from one of the young protesters who cut his finger to supply it.*

The key mechanism was the establishment of a private corporation chartered by Congress to conduct business on Taiwan, functioning much like an embassy. This was similar to what the Japanese did in their diplomatic reconciliation with Beijing.

Despite the conservative clamor that the United States had doublecrossed Taiwan, the U.S.-China normalization created a honeymoon atmosphere that excited enormous American interest in the land of one billion and the five-foot-tall man in charge.

One sign of respect for Deng was Time magazine's decision to name him 1978 "Man of the Year" for his roles in normalizing relations with the United States and ending China's isolation.

The choice of Deng, announced shortly before his visit to the United States, was notable because Time publisher Henry Luce had been closely associated with the Nationalists on Taiwan.

"As a party member for more than fifty years and a veteran of Mao's original Long March, he also possesses a moral authority that no other Chinese leader can command, an authority based partly on his refusal to bow to the political winds of the past two decades," Time proclaimed. Ironically, Deng was the first Asian picked for the Time honor since it had chosen Chiang Kai-shek in 1938.

For his part, Deng hoped to make the most of a visit he saw as an opportunity to send shivers into the Kremlin, despite the shrill Soviet warnings about strengthening U.S.-China ties.

Of course, Deng realized that not everyone in America would welcome him. He knew Carter had faced blistering criticism from anti-communist Republicans and Taiwan loyalists over the normalization issue. But what Deng may not have anticipated were the demonstrations against him by American Maoists who thought he had betrayed the Chinese revolution.

When Deng's entourage arrived in Washington January 29 for a red carpet tour, the vice premier got his first personal dose of how democracy works in America, which must have been both amusing and disconcerting. Hundreds of leftists demonstrated against him outside the White House, chanting "Long Live Mao Tse-tung!" and waving the English translation of Mao's little red book.

They tried to rush a police line and hurled rocks, bottles, firebombs and bags filled with fishhooks into the White House grounds. At least forty people were arrested.

Meanwhile, two members of the "Committee for a Fitting Welcome," a radical group that opposed Deng's policies, were arrested for disrupting the White House reception for Deng posing as journalists. They screamed "Deng Xiaoping, you are a murderer," before Secret Service agents hauled them away.

Deng was as diplomatic about the disruption as he was in his remarks about the budding U.S.-China friendship, referring to the three previous decades of hostility, including the Korean War and Vietnam War, simply as "a period of unpleasantness."

The Democracy Wall Movement

As China increasingly courted the United States, Japan, and other industrialized democracies under the budding era of Deng Xiaoping pragmatism, the communists inched open a domestic political floodgate that included demands for democracy at home.

The roots were based on government criticism of the Gang of Four and Cultural Revolution. As this intensified, tales of persecution, death and destruction from that era surfaced daily.

Millions of people, intimidated and silent for years but now allowed to speak out, poured forth their bitterness in letters to the party and so-called "Da Zi Bao" or "Big Character Posters," a traditional form of public expression, often written anonymously and tacked up in gathering places.

With the government tolerating and even encouraging this emotional release, it was perhaps inevitable that bolder criticisms would arise questioning the legitimacy of party authority and the nature of the entire system.

Thus was born China's fledgling democracy movement, a loosely organized network of political dissidents that consisted of at least thirty groups and publications in a half dozen cities.

Their focal point became what's known as "Democracy Wall," a yellow and gray brick facade running two hundred yards along western Beijing's Changan Jie or Avenue of Eternal Peace, not far from the headquarters of state power, where young men and women would gather in the cold winter of 1978-79 to read big character posters addressing a range of political questions once unmentionable.

At first, Deng Xiaoping regarded this movement with perhaps bemused interest. But many foreign historians of Chinese affairs now believe he even actively encouraged the dissidents for his own political agenda.

Deng thought the dissidents were voicing popular criticism of the era spawned by the Gang of Four and its radical followers, some of whom were stubbornly clinging to power in the party Politburo.

Chief among these were Wang Dongxing, Mao's former bodyguard, who harbored deep-seated loyalty to the late chairman although he participated in the plot to arrest the Gang of Four.

Another key Deng foe was former Beijing mayor Wu De, the first to call the April 1976 Tiananmen riot a counter-revolutionary act. The third important Deng opponent was Mao's anointed successor Hua Guofeng, who thought China was straying from strict adherence to Mao's philosophy of constant revolution and "class struggle."

So the dissident call for greater democracy and freedom suited Deng fine because it helped to discredit Hua, Wang and Wu, known as the "fan-shipai" or "whateverist" faction for arguing that whatever Chairman Mao said and did was incontrovertible.

The dissidents discussed matters of political freedom and human rights in ways not seen in China since the short-lived "Hundred Flowers" movement more than two decades earlier. They called for freedom of speech, religion, travel and assembly.

They challenged the Communist Party's monopoly on power and asked why other political parties could not participate in running the government.

They freely quoted passages from the Western pillars of democratic freedoms in their posters, ranging from the Magna Carta to the American Declaration of Independence.

Moreover, the young men and women who plastered their messages and frustrations on Democracy Wall were bold enough to engage not only other Chinese in discussions but foreigners as well.

Some took the unheard-of step of inviting foreigners to their homes and showing them the crude inking contraptions and antiquated Chinese typewriters on which they printed their unofficial journals. Others were bolder and visited foreigners in the guarded diplomatic housing compounds reserved for envoys and journalists.

The most outspoken and articulate of these audacious young dissenters was Wei Jingsheng, a twenty-eight-year-old electrician at the Beijing Zoo, the disillusioned son of a Communist Party functionary who as a child had been forced to memorize Chairman Mao passages.

Wei published a crudely printed journal known as "Tansuo" or "Explorations." He also authored a politically explosive wall poster that attracted excited crowds to Democracy Wall in December 1978. It was called "The Fifth Modernization."

In that essay, Wei argued that China's Four Modernization goals of transforming agriculture, industry, science and the military by the end of the century would fail without a fifth modernization, democracy.

When people demand democracy, Wei wrote, "they are only asking for something they rightfully own. Anyone refusing to give them democracy is a shamelss bandit no better than a capitalist who robs workers of their money earned with their sweat and blood."

The appearance of the Fifth Modernization poster perhaps marked the height of a euphoria about a new level of tolerance for political dissent that was making Deng Xiaoping enormously popular.

Just a month earlier, Deng had told visiting Japanese dignitaries that the appearance of wall posters reflected the normal expression of a variety of views and marked a new era of political stability in China.

Besides, Deng said, such activity was guaranteed by the Constitution.

"We have no right to deny this or criticize the masses for making use of democracy and putting up big character posters," Deng said. "If the masses feel some anger we must let them express it."

Deng's popularity over the democracy issue was perhaps widely misunderstood or misinterpreted in the West, as well as by many of the dissenters themselves, who thought he was acknowledging the failure of communism as a political system.

Many later concluded he tolerated the dissident movement largely because it helped him confront and isolate his "whateverist faction" adversaries at an important party Central Committee meeting in December 1978.

"When it comes to emancipating our minds, using our heads, seeking truth from facts and uniting as one in looking to the future, the primary task is to emancipate our minds," Deng said at that meeting.

"The emancipation of minds has not been completely achieved among our cadres, particularly our leading cadres," Deng said. "Indeed, many comrades have not yet set their brains going."

Deng triumphed at that party meeting, marking Hua Guofeng, Wang Dongxing their associates for demotion.

With that out of the way, Deng abandoned his tolerance for the democracy movement and turned against it, calling the dissenters anarchists and subversives.

On March 29, 1979, agents of the Beijing Public Security Bureau quietly arrested Wei Jingsheng on charges of disclosing state military secrets to a foreigner and engaging in counter-revolutionary agita-

Unauthorized magazine is sold at the Democracy Wall. Such literature was usually announced by a poster pasted to the wall the day before the sale.

tion "for the overthrow of the dicatorship of the proletariat."

His arrest and the charges against him and another prominent dissenter named Fu Yuehua signaled the demise of the democracy movement, at least for awhile.

The day after Wei's arrest, at a special expanded Politburo meeting, Deng officially signaled he was tightening the reins on liberalization by announcing that China would modernize within what he called the "Four Cardinal Principles." These were upholding socialism, upholding the dictatorship of the proletariat, upholding the leadership of the Communist Party and upholding Marxism-Leninism and Mao Tse-tung thought. They also came to be known as the "Four Upholds."

In December 1979, nearly a year after Deng gave public assurances about freedom of expression in China, Democracy Wall was closed down, its political posters removed and replaced by dull Chinese factory advertisements for industrial machinery.

Wei was among at least forty political critics silenced or arrested during that period, but his case became a cause celebre in the West and was scrutinized by prominent human rights groups such as Amnesty International, much to the government's annoyance.

The prosecution of Wei Jingsheng attracted enormous attention for another reason. The Deng regime had promised a sweeping reform of the judicial system that included new laws, new curbs on arbitrary police power and guarantees for the rights of the accused, including the right to defend themselves. Wei Jingsheng became a test of that commitment.

Still, as far as Deng was concerned, the Wei Jingsheng affair was an internal matter and no business of foreigners, to be settled in a Chinese way.

To the dissidents, that meant Wei's conviction was a foregone conclusion. They knew this was now a classic case of warning by example regardless of whether Wei was guilty, according to the old axiom of feudal Chinese law and order: "Punish one, teach one hundred."

The Justice Ministry never disclosed the precise charges against Wei or his place of confinement, though he was believed to be incarcerated in Ancient Virtue Forest No. 1 Prison on the outskirts of Beijing, a place reserved for political prisoners.

Public security agents banned foreigners and most of Wei's friends from his six-hour trial on October 17, 1979, which ended conveniently at the daily quitting time for government bureaucrats.

Hundreds of Chinese packed the room in the two-

Workers tear off all wall posters—except an official notice banning posters at the famous Democracy Wall.

story concrete Beijing Intermediate People's Court to watch. Many were evidently planted there by the government as "members of the public."

But some of the bolder spectators related the proceedings to foreign journalists outside and smuggled out a copy of the indictment.

The first charge accused Wei of supplying a foreigner with the names of military commanders, troop strength and casualties in China's border war with Vietnam in February of that year, violating a law on disclosing state secrets.

But prosecutors never identified the foreigner, never explained how Wei could have known such information and never explained how he could have known it was classified.

The second and more serious charge accused Wei of seditious writing that was widely circulated in Beijing and another center of dissident agitation, Tianjin. It said his articles "slandered Marxism and Mao Tse-tung thought as a prescription only slightly better than the medicine peddled by charlatans."

Acting as his own defense counsel, Wei methodically denied the charges, which may have partly accounted for the stiff sentence he received.

Wei said he shared general hear-say information about the China-Vietnam war, but how was he to know any of it was secret? Besides, Wei argued, under the Constitution it was his right to talk with anyone he pleased, including foreigners.

As for the sedition and agitation charge, Wei again invoked the Constitution, saying it "gives the people the right to criticize leaders, because they are human beings and not deities."

In words reminiscent of what Deng himself had proclaimed at the height of the democracy movement, Wei said "Criticism cannot possibly be nice and appealing to the ear, or all correct. To require criticism to be entirely correct, and to inflict punishment if it is not, is the same as prohibiting criticism."

At 5:30 p.m., without taking a recess to decide Wei's fate, the court reached its verdict: fifteen years in prison.

The sentence was read on Beijing radio and in factory and farm loudspeakers around the country, even though most Chinese still didn't know who Wei Jingsheng was.

Soon after the verdict, the official news agency Xinhua published a detailed account of the trial, a strong indication that the entire proceeding had been a rehearsed show. Wei's defense arguments weren't reported.

Foreign reaction was swift and critical. The State Department protested the sentence, calling it harsh and disappointing. Amnesty International request-

ed that China publish a trial transcript. The government rejected the criticisms as interference in its affairs.

Wei appealed the sentence but the Beijing People's High Court upheld it a few weeks later. He had no right of further appeal.

The spawning of the dissident movement in China deeply disturbed Deng. He saw elements of Cultural Revolution-style anarchy in allowing young people to challenge authority.

He may also have seen the potential for an enormous political problem later, similar to what Poland's Communist Party was facing at the time with the popular trade union Solidarity, an alliance of dissident intellectuals and workers fed up with the system.

So Deng's crackdown on the democracy movement did not stop with the imprisonment of Wei Jingsheng and a few others. Irritated by the argument that the Constitution guaranteed their freedom to criticize, he had the Constitution revised.

In January 1980, Deng announced that the constitutional right to write big character posters and hold public debates would be expunged from Article 45, which guaranteed the "big freedoms" of expression to Chinese citizens. The next year, the government began referring to dissident groups and publications as illegal.

Between 1979 and 1981, police conducted what amounted to a mop-up campaign to crush the dissidents for good, and most went into hiding.

Among those seized were two prominent Beijing members of the "April 5 Forum," the editor of a critical journal in the coastal city of Qingdao known as "Sea Waves,' and the editor of the Canton dissident journal "People's Road."

The democracy movement and Deng's response to it raised many questions about the direction China was taking in the aftermath of the Cultural Revolution.

Was it possible for the government to tolerate any form of organized opposition? After thousands of years of authoritarian rule and three decades of upheaval, did Chinese society have the ability or even the energy for more unsettling political change?

Soon after Wei Jingsheng had been hauled off to prison and had become known around the world as China's most famous dissident, one of the last posters of the movement appeared on Democracy Wall, placed there by the "April Fifth Forum," named after the date of the Tiananmen Square uprising.

Titled, "In Memory of Democracy," the poster admitted that China probably was not ready for the kind of freewheeling criticism and debate raised by people like Wei Jingsheng. At least not yet.

VIII

Deng's Reforms

Deng's intolerance for political dissent may have been partly due to what he saw as a much more pressing and critical problem inherited from Mao: China's stagnant, isolated economy, a hodgepodge of rigid Soviet style planning, waste and mismanagement that had done little to raise the standard of living for thirty years.

In Deng's view, the No. 1 priority by late 1978 was to abandon Mao's exhortations of class struggle, self-reliance and "big pot" egalitarianism. Deng wanted to scrap the communes and restore family farming, allow a dose of private enterprise, and get Western and Japanese help to modernize the country's four hundred thousand dilapidated factories.

Before he could even begin such a heretical departure from Mao's vision of China, however, Deng had to carefully demystify the chairman and acknowledge Mao's errors. At the same time, Deng realized that without Chairman Mao there would have been no new China and no basis for the Communist Party's claim to power.

Therefore, Deng had to establish that he and his proteges were the true followers of Mao Tse-tung thought. It was a delicate and dangerous task that would take years, but Deng began it soon after he was rehabilitated himself.

The reassessment of Chairman Mao evidently was one of the biggest and most sensitive agenda items at the Third Plenum of the 11th Central Committee in December 1978.

These full sessions of the party's ruling body were closely watched in China and abroad. In the country's closed, secretive politics, the party plenums often were the forum for disclosing or hinting at important policy and leadership changes.

One of the most important results of the Third Plenum was the endorsement of Deng's guiding philosophy, "seek truth from facts" — adopt policies that work and abandon those that fail. This was considered an oblique rejection of Mao's dictum to always "put politics in command."

In other indirect but unmistakable stabs at Mao, the Third Plenum criticized the "whateverist" faction in the party, decreed the Tiananmen riot of April 1976 a revolutionary act instead of a crime, and rehabilitated nearly half a million victims of Mao's "anti-rightist campaign" purges nearly two decades earlier.

In addition, the Plenum rehabilitated two other prominent Mao victims, former Defense Minister Peng Dehuai, who was purged in 1959 because of his opposition to Mao's radical policies, and former Beijing Mayor Peng Zhen, whose dismissal in 1966 was one of the sparks that ignited the Cultural Revolution.

But perhaps the most significant downgrading of Mao at the Third Plenum was made not by Deng, but by Mao's hand-picked successor Hua Guofeng.

In a self-criticism that signaled Hua's own weakening position in the party and his ultimate downfall, Hua repudiated the personality cult that he had tried to emulate after Mao died.

Hua also decreed that no longer would his opinions be called "instructions," as Mao's were, and he would no longer go by the title "Chairman Hua Guofeng," but rather "Comrade Hua Guofeng."

The Third Plenum laid the basis for more criticism of Chairman Mao to come.

In a speech by Marshal Ye Jianying at the Fourth Plenum marking the thirtieth anniversary of the People's Republic of China in October 1979, Mao's transgressions were described as "faults" instead of

Top Chinese Communist Party leaders attending the fourth session of the Fifth National People's Congress. In front row (from 1. to r.) are Chairman Hu Yaobang, then Vice Chairman Deng Xiaoping (with earphones), and Li Xiennian.

"shortcomings." For the first time, Mao was directly and publicly blamed for launching the Cultural Revolution.

At the Fifth Plenum in February 1980, Mao's faults became "serious mistakes." They also were seriously broadened to include his persecution of the late President Liu Shaoqi, once reviled as China's chief "capitalist roader," who died in prison after he was stripped of all posts and expelled from the party in 1967.

Liu's posthumous rehabilitation into a revolutionary martyr presented an especially tricky problem for the Communist Party that went to the heart of its tortuous effort to rewrite history.

It was no secret that Liu and Mao had feuded bitterly and personally hated each other. During the height of the Cultural Revolution, Mao had referred to Liu as a "renegade, hidden traitor and scab."

Yet now, in an Orwellian transformation that turned black into white, the party felt obliged to present Liu as "the first to advance the concept of Mao Tse-tung thought." To avoid this contradiction, the "thought" was redefined for the first time as the collective wisdom of all top party leaders, not just Mao's.

Nonetheless, the leftover bitterness of the struggle between Mao and Liu was not erased for Liu's widow, Wang Guangmei, a sophisticated, Western-educated woman who had been imprisoned separately from her husband on fabricated charges of spying for foreigners. She was not even freed until two years after Mao died.

A memorial service held to honor Liu two months after his official rehabilitation reportedly was delayed because Wang Guangmei angrily opposed a line in the eulogy describing her husband as Mao's "close comrade in arms." The line was deleted.

Liu's posthumous funeral with honors showed dramatically how Deng Xiaoping, nail by nail, was sealing the coffin of the radical past, a political and personal vendetta that gave him and other victims of the Cultural Revolution an enormous satisfaction.

But the biggest display of repudiation was yet to come, a carefully orchestrated prosecution of Mao's widow Jiang Qing and her associates, the much vilified "Gang of Four," who were about to be marched into court, sullen and shackled, to face trial.

Senior Chinese officials had been hinting they would subject the Gang of Four to a public trial of spectacle proportions, like the Nuremberg war crimes prosecutions of Nazis in postwar Germany.

More than four years after their arrests, the trial finally was held in a special Beijing courtroom in

Defendants in the dock as the trials of the Gang of Four and Lin Biao Cliques began in Beijing in 1980 are (from left): Huang Yongsheng, once armed forces chief of staff; Wu Faxian, former air force commander; Chen Boda, former political secretary for Mao Tse-tung; and Li Zuopeng, former political commissar of the navy.

November 1980, replete with television cameras, hundreds of carefully selected spectators and predetermined verdicts of guilty.

By this time, Mao's previously infallible reputation had been sufficiently tainted in official print to set the stage for a fundamental re-evaluation of his role in history.

At the Sixth Plenum in June 1981, Mao was formally described as a great guerrilla tactician who helped expedite the Chinese revolution but made disastrous errors in his later years.

In what amounted to a blistering, devastating criticism that reportedly took more than a year to prepare, the Central Committee document on Mao's life described him as arbitrary, arrogant, capricious, smug, dictatorial and irrational late in life.

It credited Mao with rescuing the party and Red Army at two early points in the history of China's civil war: the 1927 campaign by Chiang Kai-shek's soldiers to surround and annihilate the guerrillas, and the 1935 Long March to Yenan.

But later, the document declared, Mao made one mistake after another, starting with the brutal anti-rightist campaign of the 1950s and ending with the Cultural Revolution, which was described as a "long, drawn out and grave blunder."

The repudiation of Mao and prosecution of his chief followers signaled the start of a much broader cleanup of leftist holdouts in the government and the party.

In 1982, Premier Zhao Ziyang began to streamline the bureaucracy, eliminating overlapping ministries and departments and easing many functionaries out. The number of ministers and vice ministers eventually was reduced by two-thirds.

In 1983, Party General Secretary Hu Yaobang announced that everyone in the forty million member

Chinese leaders of the 11th Central Committee of the Communist Party of China hold their First Plenary session in Beijing in 1977.

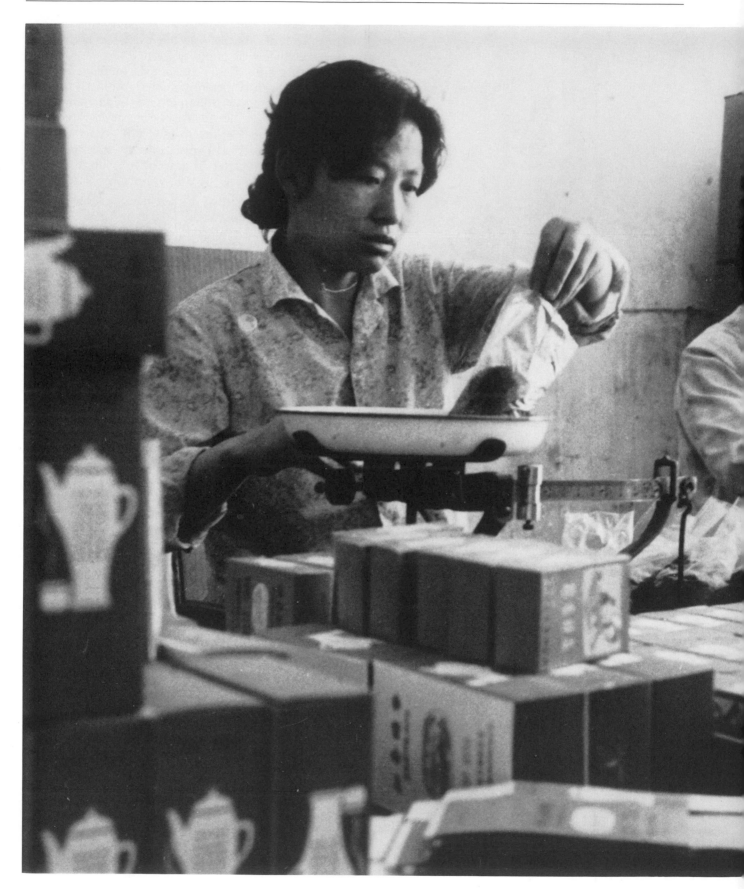

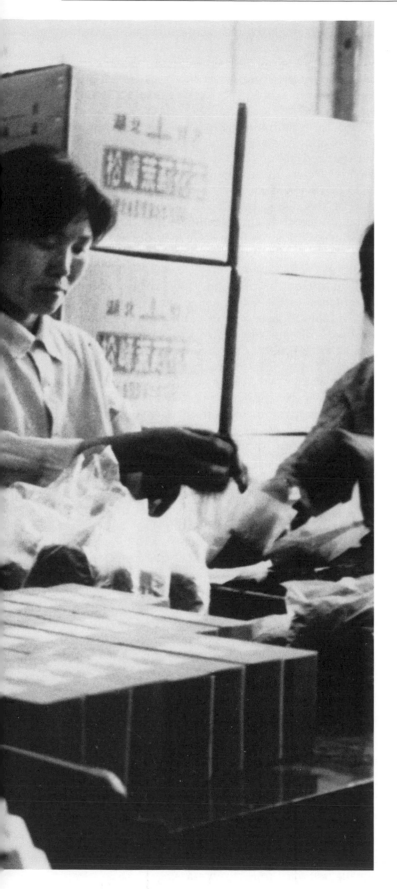

party would have to re-register, in what amounted to a quiet but systematic purge campaign to rid the party of leftover radicals from the Cultural Revolution. He estimted at least three million members would be expelled.

Even before Deng Xiaoping finished systematically unwrapping the cult of Chairman Mao, he began the daring dismantlement of his predecessor's most cherished accomplishment, the peasant communes in the vast Chinese countryside.

China's commune system, an entrenched vestige of the Great Leap Forward, was considered one of the most significant triumphs not only by Mao but many other Chinese and foreigners.

Even critics conceded that this radical redistribution of land and wealth, coupled with advances in irrigation and fertilizer use, evidently had enabled China to avoid the famines that had plagued the country for centuries under the old feudal landlord system.

Foreign visitors to China, even during the Cultural Revolution, marveled at the fat pigs, rosy peasant children and banquets of plenty on their chaperoned tours of model communes that the communists showcased to the world.

This perception, however, masked a sobering reality, particularly in the inland regions of the country that most foreigners never saw: the commune system wasn't working. Vast portions of the peasantry weren't getting enough to eat.

In the poorest areas, where per-capita income amounted to less than $10 a year, many families lived in mud hovels and foraged for food ranging from wild tuberous roots to field rats. Others were given permission by commune leaders to go begging in the cities.

Even the government's own statistics and simple arithmetic suggested the nation was barely able to feed itself after three decades of convulsions under the communists.

Although grain output had doubled since 1949, so had the number of mouths to feed. Per-capita annual income of one quarter of the rural population totaled less than $30.

One in six of China's two thousand counties had barely increased production since the early 1950s, the last years of individual farming. Per-capita grain supplies were less in 1976, when the Gang of Four was arrested, than they had been two decades earlier, just before Mao created the communes.

Packing tea at a tea factory in a town in Hubei province.

Other assessments of China's economic plight were even more sobering. For example, a study of China's food output by Nicholas Lardy, an economic professor at Yale University, suggested that by the end of the 1970s, per-capita farm production was no better than it had been during the Japanese occupation before World War II.

The system was hampered by another Maoist vestige, the fanatic emphasis on grain production. This was similar to the Soviet Union's obsession with steel production, aimed at showing the superiority of communism, but it masked horrendous problems.

Perhaps because of his training as a guerrilla fighter in the 1930s, Mao believed that grain was China's greatest storable asset — it could get the masses through drought, flood, invasion and war. He decreed that grain was the economy's "key link" and exhorted peasants to "store grain everywhere."

Like results of many other Maoist directives, grain growing reached a fanatic scale. Peasants chopped down fruit trees and filled in rivers to grow grain, even where the climate was inhospitable. Local communist leaders ordered peasants to terrace mountains and destroy valuable crops to make room for grain.

The results were disastrous. The mass conversion of grasslands into grain fields caused so much erosion that satellites could detect China's dust storms at plowing time. Beijing's own meteorological observatory, which recorded three dust storm days in the 1950s, reported twenty-six a year between 1974 and 1980.

In some areas, the grain just didn't grow, leaving the peasants with nothing to eat. In others, peasants were swamped with so much grain that much of it rotted and turned worthless.

Deng saw the commune system and the emphasis on grain production as illogical, wasteful and inconsistent with his dictum to "seek truth from facts."

But reforming the communes was a daunting task, just measured in numbers alone. By the end of the 1970s, nearly eight hundred million peasants were organized into fifty thousand people's communes stretched across the Chinese countryside.

The communes were sort of the rural equivalent of towns, with administrative responsibility for such things as schools, health care and mail service. In addition, the communes were responsible for paying grain taxes to the state. They also ran small sideline factories and mines to finance public works projects such as roads and canals.

Depending on its size, each commune was subdivided into a dozen or so production brigades. Each brigade was subdivided into a number of production teams, comprised of individual families.

Under a complicated system of "work points" awarded by the communes and brigades, each production team would receive wages and allotments of grain and other necessities.

But the system tended to discourage the peasants from working, since in the end the team members all received about the same amount of compensation regardless of how hard they toiled.

In 1979, peasant dissatisfaction was so widespread that Deng began a program to restore the type of incentives that he and Liu Shaoqi had tried to implement more than two decades earlier and again in the early 1960s, before they were sacked as traitors.

Under Deng's direction, the government split production teams into smaller units, in some cases individual families, as part of an effort to end what he called "da guo fan" - "the big pot."

The government also began to pay higher prices to the communes for their harvests and granted more leeway in what crops could be grown, raising the inducement for everyone to work harder.

Perhaps most important, it sanctioned the reestablishment of private plots and free markets banned by Mao, enabling families to grow food for themselves and sell the surplus in the cities.

This last step laid the basis for an even more radical departure from Maoism a year later, when Beijing began to abolish the collective system of work points and let many peasants farm larger plots of land individually under contract to the state, in what became known as the "contract responsibility system."

The result of these reforms was an enormous leap in farm production, peasant morale and income that startled Deng himself. It strengthened his popularity and further discredited the Maoists.

But the decollectivization of agriculture also spawned a number of other nettlesome side effects. It turned the communes into loosely organized townships with vague responsibilities, eroding the power of local communist officials. Many of them, especially those who rose in power during the Cultural Revolution era, resisted the change or simply ignored the orders from Beijing.

In addition, the communes were suddenly deprived of income from peasants now working for

Farm-scientist Ting Hsueh-li explains cross breeding of rice to members of a scientific experimental group as China sought to increase production with fine seed strains.

themselves, so they could no longer necessarily provide schools, medical care and social security, undermining the state's pledge to care for the sick and the needy.

For millions of peasant families, now able to grow their own food and sell what they couldn't eat, the reforms were an enormous opportunity to improve their standard of living.

Many began to keep their children out of school to work in the fields, threatening China with a new generation of illiterates.

Others began to ignore the new state population control directives, willing to pay the financial penalty for more children because bigger families still meant more hands and more income.

For the time being at least, these were considered manageable complications, part of the readjustment to a more market-oriented economy after years of stunted growth.

It was not until years later that far more serious problems with the reforms would emerge.

Deng did not single-handedly undertake the monumental task of burying the ghost of Mao, revamping the countryside economy and opening China to the outside world.

He had help from two increasingly prominent subordinates who, like Deng himself, had been purged and humiliated during the political spasms of the Mao years, accused of betraying the revolution and taking the "capitalist road."

Zhao Ziyang and Hu Yaobang were both about ten years younger than Deng. Both possessed the same bold way of thinking in practical terms and speaking their minds.

Both believed, like Deng did, that it made no sense to continue exhorting the peasants to produce more good without paying them more money.

Both believed it was politically acceptable, even desirable, to encourage the peasants to do a little business on their own and amass wealth, even if it meant some were richer than others.

They believed the most important measure of success was results, embracing Deng's now-famous words in the disastrous aftermath of the Great Leap Forward: "Private farming is all right as long as it raises production, just as it does not matter whether a cat is black or white, as long as it catches mice."

Zhao, born in 1919, was the son of a Henan provincial landowner and grain merchant. He renounced his wealthy lineage as a teen-ager and joined the Communist Party in 1938.

After the communists triumphed in 1949, Zhao supervised economic development in southern Guangdong province. He became known for his flexible ideas on mixing free enterprise with socialism as the provincial party secretary in the early 1960s. Like thousands of other bureaucrats victimized by the Maoist radicalism of the Cultural Revolution, Zhao was seized and manhandled by Red Guard fanatics. They labeled him a right-wing deviant and paraded him in the street wearing a dunce cap. He disappeared for a number of years but resurfaced in the waning stages of the Cultural Revolution, when the party desperately needed to reassert control over the stagnant economy and rehabilitated many formerly discredited party members.

In simple terms, this was the basis for Mao's successful peasant-led revolution that overthrew the landowners, educated wealthy and other "exploitative classes."

Those who weren't killed or imprisoned, Mao reasoned, must be constantly watched, their class background never forgotten, even if they swore loyalty to the communist cause. In his view, "class struggle" would last well beyond his lifetime.

For nearly three decades, the mistrust of former landlords, rich peasants, merchants and intellectuals was imbued into the system by Mao and his subordinates.

It was extended to include people with overseas connections, like relatives abroad, since they might be spies for the Nationalists on Taiwan, imperialists and other enemies of China.

People with suspicious or dangerous class backgrounds received fewer grain ration coupons, lower pay and the most menial jobs, from cleaning toilets to feeding pigs. They had trouble finding marriage partners and couldn't easily attend school.

During Mao's political campaigns, they were the first to be criticized in "struggle sessions." Untold numbers faced persecution, arrest and even death during the Cultural Revolution.

Their friends, children and grandchildren inherited the same taint, like the untouchables of a caste system, guilt by association and blood relations.

Even crimes like murder and rape were defined by class. A rich peasant accused of not shouting the praises of Chairman Mao loud enough conceivably might have been put to death during the Cultural Revolution, for example, while a party activist who killed an "enemy of the people" such as a former landlord would be pardoned.

In an effort to increase food production, Chinese scientific workers study fine seed strains adaptable for growing on the edge of the desert.

After Deng Xiaoping firmly established himself in power, he declared that class struggle in China was basically finished because its aims had been achieved. This was another stunning repudiation of the Mao era.

Yes, Deng said, there were still class enemies, but they were mostly common criminals and thugs who thrived from the breakdown in society order caused by the Cultural Revolution.

As for rich peasants, former landlords, intellectuals and others who had been labeled "rightists," Deng's decree seemed to spell the end of a nightmare that had lasted for thirty years.

The first to be liberated from this stigma were overseas Chinese, partly because Deng desperately needed them for their foreign business connections and access to hard currency to help fuel China's Four Modernizations drive.

No longer were overseas Chinese to be considered imperialist lackeys and traitors. Any property they might have owned in China before the communist takeover was returned. The government even opened special stores and hotels exclusively for them.

Next in line for redemption were the intellectuals, the artists, scientists and writers who had once dared to speak their minds during Mao's "Hundred Flowers" campaign but had largely remained silent, sullen and terrified since then.

In an important speech at a conference on science and technology in March 1978, Deng formally reclassified the intellectuals as members of the proletariat.

"They differ from the manual workers only insofar as they perform different roles in the social division of labor," Deng said. "Everyone who works, whether with his hands or with his brain, is part of the working people in a socialist society."

Later that year, the bad-class "rightist" category, in which Deng himself had once been classified, was formally abolished. Millions who had been labeled rightists were rehabilitated, their reputations, former job assignments and salaries restored.

In early 1979, the government announced that former landlords and rich peasants would have their rights as citizens restored as well. This meant they were entitled to reclaim at least some of the property seized from them after the revolution, although the state still retained title to their land.

Zhao was assigned to rescue Deng's home province of Sichuan province from disastrous radical policies that had left many people near starvation in China's most populated region.

He became Sichuan's party secretary and reversed the crisis by allowing peasants more freedom to grow what they wished, the prototype for reforms that later caught Deng's attention.

Deng was so impressed with Zhao that he maneuvered him into the party Politburo. Zhao, an urbane, affable man with a razor-sharp mind and a penchant for Western sports jackets and ties, replaced the hapless Hua Guofeng as China's premier in 1980.

Hu Yaobang, born in 1915 in Hunan province, also joined the Communist Party as a teen-ager and later held posts in its youth organization. He trudged alongside his elder comrades in the famed Long March in 1935. After 1949 Hu became a successful party administrator in Sichuan and was a member of several delegations dispatched to Eastern Europe in the 1950s, when China was friendly with the Soviet bloc.

Red Guards sacked Hu as a rightist in 1967 and he disappeared. But by 1972 he resurfaced and by 1977, he held important posts in the party's school and the Central Committee.

Hu was short like Deng, with a sassy, gregarious disposition and a mouth that sometimes got him into trouble. He ghost-wrote several important speeches and documents, including some key resolutions that discredited Mao and vilified the Gang of Four.

He became closely associated with Deng by 1978 and replaced Hua as head of the party three years later.

In recruiting these potential leaders, relatively young by Chinese standards, Deng seemed acutely aware of the looming succession problem that confronted the communists. Most of the senior revolutionaries still alive were in their late seventies and eighties.

Like Mao, many clung to their power and privilege, their villas and chauffeured limousines, until their last gasp of breath. Some, as Hu Yaobang once disclosed, showed symptoms of senility.

Deng was determined that his two proteges, whom he called the "twin pillars," would be the vanguard of a new generation of educated, competent leaders to take over in a smooth transition when he was too old.

Nonetheless, a peaceful transfer of political power in China had never been achieved during the Communist Party's relatively short tenure.

On the contrary, power struggles seemed endemic to the Communist Party because it lacked a formal system for succession. Deng himself would later be forced to swallow one of Mao's own slogans: "Political power grows out of the barrel of a gun."

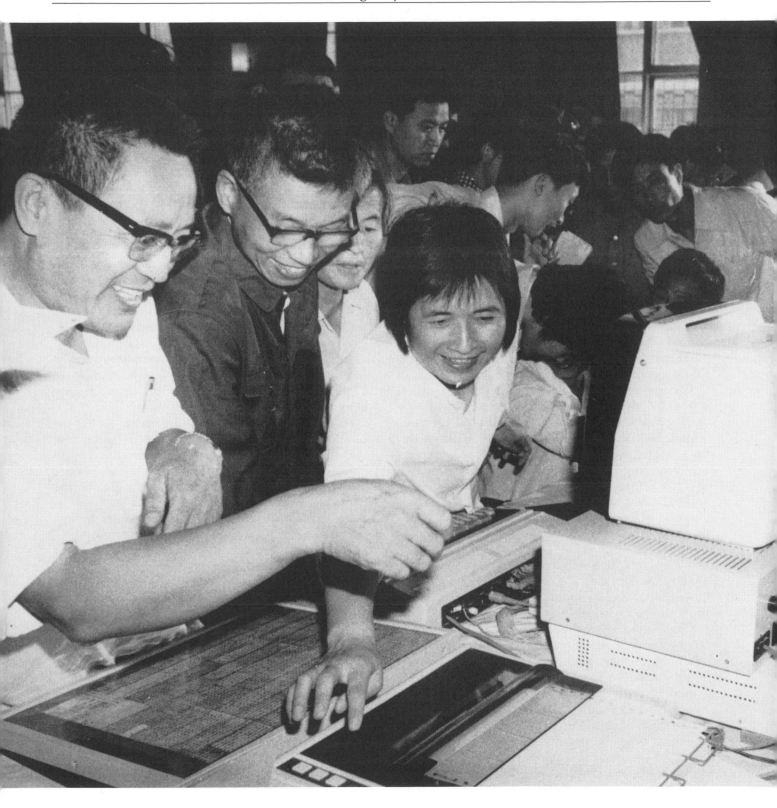

A new addition to China's industry in the early 1980s was a small-size Chinese language computer, suitable for wide use, here examined by technicians in Beijing.

The Official End of "Class Struggle"

For diehard Maoists, Deng's dismantling of the commune system was heretical enough, but it undercut an even more fundamental part of the late chairman's philosophy, the concept of class struggle, a concept that was one reason for the Chinese revolution itself.

Mao always had distrusted and despised the intellectual class, the learned officials of Mandarin China, whom he believed lived corrupted lives off the sweat of others. They traveled in shaded carriages and grew long fingernails to show they never had to work with their hands.

Though Mao came from a rich peasant background himself, he also hated the landowners, the barons who rented the fields to their poor illiterate neighbors and exacted exorbitant rents that kept the vast majority of rural Chinese virtually enslaved.

The government also announced that others whose belongings and money were seized by marauding Red Guards during the Cultural Revolution would get them back. State agencies were created for the purpose of identifying purloined property and returning it to the rightful owners, a process that took years.

Deng's decree closing the books on class struggle was part of a much broader relaxation of restrictions on some of the most basic and innocuous activities of daily life.

It was as if China were coming out of a long, deep tortuous nightmare, shaking herself awake, wondering what had happened for ten years, wondering if she had gone mad.

Chinese women, obliged to wear shapeless baggy fatigues and braid their hair in pigtails during the rule of Mao, began to put on touches of lipstick and eye shadow. Beauty parlors, once closed as a vain symbol of bourgeois decadence, were reopened.

Flowers and plants reappeared in apartment windows. Retired workers once again brought their caged birds to the parks in the mornings. Lovers snuggled on benches; children flew kites.

Musicians who had fearfully hidden their violins, flutes and other banned Western instruments—the only permissible one had been the piano—dusted them off and practiced openly.

State radio, which for years had played only politically correct songs like "When the Nightsoil Collectors Descend from the Mountain" and class-struggle arias from radical operas like "On the Docks" began to reintroduce Beethoven, Chopin and Mozart. Traditional Beijing operas reopened to enthusiastic crowds.

The tumultuous welcome in 1978 for violin virtuoso Isaac Stern, a tour that produced an emotional and award-winning documentary film called "From Mao to Mozart," dramatically illustrated the prolonged deprivation of the music-loving Chinese.

Nowhere was the emotional release stronger and more poignant than the relaxation on religion, once banned by Mao and his radical disciples as one of the "Four Olds"—out-of-date culture, ideas, customs and habits.

Under Deng there was a cautious relaxation on religious worship. Some churches, mosques and temples closed during the Cultural Revolution reopened on a limited basis. Many priests and monks who had been defrocked or imprisoned were allowed to resume practicing their beliefs.

What was extraordinary and even astonishing to the communists was the degree to which ordinary Chinese responded to this relaxation, embracing religion almost as a tool of quiet protest.

Millions of people, even children born during the tumultuous years of leftist upheavals, crammed places of worship, from the Catholic churches in Beijing, Shanghai and Canton, to the Islamic mosques of remote Xinjiang and Ningxia, to the Lama Buddhist shrines of Qinghai and Tibet.

It were as though decades of propaganda against religion and its foreign origins had done nothing.

This was especially remarkable in the case of Christianity, first brought to China by Jesuit priests in the 1500s. By the 19th century China was overrun with missionaries, who arrogated power and property, collaborated with the Japanese invaders and corrupt Nationalist government during the war and were widely despised by non-believers. Mao expelled nearly all the missionaries after 1949.

Yet Christianity not only survived three decades of communist convulsions, but some party members themselves quietly had become believers, in defiance of their own atheist vows.

Deng evidently sanctioned the religious revival for a couple of reasons. First, he saw it as a bold

Liu Wancong said he earned about $5,500 in 1984 by planting cotton under the government's touted "responsibility system," which aimed to increase production by stimulating private initiative.

demonstration to the outside world of his commitment to tolerance and flexibility, a way of luring foreign tourists and investors to help modernize China.

Second, the relaxation did not pose a significant threat to the communists' monopoly on political power. On the contrary, religion provided a stabilizing influence, allowing people a peaceful outlet to vent their troubles and frustrations.

Under Deng, the constitution was revised to allow more religious freedom, but with a couple of important qualifications.

It upheld the right of citizens to believe or not believe in religion. It also forbade what was described as "foreign domination" of Chinese religious affairs, a reference to China's resentment of Vatican influence that led to a break with Rome in the 1950s.

Moreover, all Catholics and Protestants had to belong to state-sponsored patriotic religious associations, and actively recruiting new parishioners was forbidden.

Estimates on the Catholic population ranged from three million by official count to more than six million by religious activists abroad. Protestants totaled between seven hundred thousand and one million. But those are tiny minorities in a land of one billion.

Of greater concern to Beijing were the Moslems, mostly in the central and western parts of the country, numbering at least ten million, as well as the three million Tibetans, virtually all of them devout Buddhists. These groups had a history of unruliness.

Deng saw the religious relaxation as a way of winning their support or at least defusing any dangerous hostility toward Beijing left over from the Cultural Revolution excesses.

The new policy also helped ingratiate China with other developing nations that had large Buddhist and Moslem populations. This was especially important for Deng, who wanted to chart an independent foreign policy and enhance China's image as a Third World leader.

The tolerance for religion under Deng had limits, however. The government did not go out of its way to carefully restore religious icons and shrines smashed during the Cultural Revolution. Some Catholic priests such as Shanghai's Monsignor Kong Pingmai, who had been imprisoned more than twenty years for refusing to renounce his allegiance to the pope, remained incarcerated. On several occasions, Beijing rejected Vatican overtures for reconciliation talks.

Despite an enormous demand for bibles, only one printing house in Shanghai was permitted to publish them after a ten-year lapse, and customs authorities restricted imports. Thousands were routinely smuggled in from Hong Kong.

Many places of worship, closed or used as granaries, machine shops or horse stables during the Mao era, were never restored to their former function. Others didn't reopen until two or three years after religious freedoms were expanded, a reflection of the underlying resistance to some of the changes Deng undertook.

The communists also railed against what appeared to be the post-Mao rebirth of China's own folk religions, which were convoluted mixtures of Buddhism, superstition, Taoism and Confucian ancestor worship that had evolved over centuries.

The state-run press began to frequently report arrests of self-proclaimed witches, warlocks and shaman priests in the countryside, who practiced banned rituals that ranged from fortune telling to animal sacrifices to communicating with the dead.

The *People's Daily* and other party propaganda outlets often warned against believing in the supernatural powers these people claimed to have, an indication of their prevalence, especially in the countryside. The press also regularly harped against revivals of common Chinese folk practices such as burning phony paper money at ancestor graves and other "feudal customs."

The momentous changes started by Deng Xiaoping had a profound impact on China's foreign relations. Its shift toward cordial ties with the United States and Japan, its desire for Western capital and technology, aggravated the strained relationship with the Soviet Union and led to the violent collapse of a friendship with southern neighbor and former ally, Vietnam.

Although China's reconciliation with the Americans angered the Vietnamese, the root of the China-Vietnam fallout began much earlier. It was based partly on the historical mistrust between the small countries of Southeast Asia and their giant neighbor.

A deep-seated Vietnamese resentment of the large population of Chinese in their country played an important role. These "hua qiao"—"Chinese sojourners"—owned many of the businesses and property in South Vietnam, which were seized by the North Vietnamese communists after they triumphed over the U.S.-backed south in 1975.

The regime of newly united Vietnam accused many ethnic Chinese of exploitation and collaboration with the departed American forces and soon began expelling them from the country.

There were other lingering resentments by the Vietnamese that directly stemmed from what they felt was China's hypocritical behavior during the war with the American enemy.

Though Mao had proclaimed Vietnam's struggle against U.S. forces a "storm center of world revolution," Beijing never sent troops to help, in contrast to its fraternal aid to North Korea during the 1950-53 Korean conflict. Vietnam also stewed over what it considered China's stingy support for postwar reconstruction. For its part, China had calculated long before the U.S. pullout from Vietnam that the Americans wanted to quit the war. The Chinese therefore chose to look the other way when American B-52s violated their airspace during bombing runs on North Vietnamese targets.

At the same time, the Chinese were growing worried about Hanoi's strengthening friendship with the Soviets, a concern that was elevated after Moscow quickly moved military forces into bases vacated by the departing Americans after 1975.

Three years later, at about the same time Deng Xiaoping was working feverishly to normalize China's relationship with the United States, Chinese-Vietnamese tensions worsened dramatically.

A key catalyst was Vietnam's arbitrary and sudden expulsion of two hundred and fifty thousand ethnic Chinese. Many fled across the "Friendship Bridge" from the north Vietnamese frontier into southwestern China, where they were resettled in makeshift border camps and state farms at considerable expense to China. Others joined throngs of so-called "boat people" fleeing Vietnam's harsh life for refuge in Hong Kong, Malaysia, Thailand and the Philippines.

China quickly reacted to the expulsions by moving troops and artillery into the four-hundred-and-fifty-mile-long remote Vietnamese border zone adjoining Yunnan province and the Guangxi Zhuang autonomous region. The Chinese also closed the Friendship Bridge and other border crossings that had once been unpatrolled, accusing the Vietnamese of sending spies and saboteurs masquerading as refugees into China to stir up trouble.

Still, it seemed unlikely at the time that China would take any military action, especially an invasion of its erstwhile ally. The Chinese had said many times before that they would not fight beyond their borders unless they were attacked first.

Then on Christmas Day 1988, Vietnam launched an ambitious invasion of neighboring Cambodia, with the avowed aim of toppling the Beijing-backed dictatorship of the radical Khmer Rouge.

Armed with modern Soviet weapons, a hundred thousand Vietnamese troops overran Khmer Rouge positions with surprising ease and speed, seizing

effective control of Cambodia within weeks. It was a stunning military victory and a significant loss of face for China.

Even more embarrassing to the Chinese was the Cambodian welcome for Vietnamese troops, hailed as liberators from a regime that had massacred Cambodians and buried them in mass graves in what emerged as one of the biggest atrocities of modern times.

While China denounced Vietnam's invasion and Soviet military support for it, there was little the Chinese military could do in Cambodia short of direct intervention.

The last thing Beijing wanted to do was get embroiled in a costly conflict, given its stated policy of never fighting on foreign soil unless it felt directly threatened. But defending Chinese soil was an entirely different matter.

So China laid the foundation for what it would call a "lesson" to Vietnam, a punitive strike into Vietnamese territory to stop what the Chinese called armed border provocations.

The People's Liberation Army, which hadn't fought a major battle since the Korean War, began massing an estimated two hundred thousand troops along the Vietnamese frontier, backed by hundreds of tactical warplanes. At the same time, Beijing Radio blasted shrill warnings to Vietnam to stay on its side of the border.

The Vietnamese at first thought the Chinese were bluffing. Even at this new low point in their relationship, Vietnam's veteran generals reasoned, it seemed highly unlikely that their neighbor and former ally would spill blood first.

After all, Deng Xiaoping himself had made it plain that economic development was China's top priority. Any prolonged military struggle could cripple his Four Modernizations plans.

Moreover, Vietnam had signed a mutual aid pact with the Soviet Union, making a Chinese strike even less logical.

The Soviets could easily distract China on their five thousand mile border, where they had deployed more than forty heavily armed divisions ever since a nasty border clash in 1969. Much of China's 3.3 million member armed forces presumably would be committed to defending the northern frontier first.

So Vietnam assigned no more than about fifty thousand troops to the one hundred-mile stretch between the Chinese frontier and Hanoi. Still, Vietnam's battle-seasoned strategists were taking few chances.

In case they had miscalculated China's intentions,

the Vietnamese redeployed most of their air force from Cambodia back home. They also stationed their first main line of troops well back from the border, in what military strategists call a "defense in depth," to avoid any shock assault that could overrun them. These precautionary steps turned out to be shrewd decisions.

The first word of a Chinese invasion was broadcast by Vietnam's state radio on February 17, 1979. Chinese troops supported by artillery, tanks and planes thrust deep into Vietnamese territory from more than a dozen points along the frontier. They outnumbered the defenders at least two-to-one.

China's official news agency called the invasion a "counterattack" and coupled it with an immediate proposal for border negotiations. "We do not want a single inch of Vietnamese territory, but neither will we tolerate wanton incursions into Chinese territory," the agency said. "All we want is a peaceful and stable border."

China had correctly guessed the superpowers would try to avoid involvement in this fight. The Kremlin made threatening statements but did little else except send Vietnam supplies. The United States, having just normalized relations with China

and still traumatized by the Vietnam War, issued lame calls for restraint.

The Chinese strategy seemed patterned on Beijing's armed foray into northeast India seventeen years earlier. Then, as now, a border spat was the pretext to thrash out other issues on the battlefield.

In 1962, the argument was over the MacMahon Line, the demarcation of India's northern frontier. But the real dispute was India's support for the Tibetan uprising against China.

The Chinese easily won the fight against their Indian counterparts in the thinly populated Himalayan area, partly because it was so remote that India had trouble sending in troops and supplies. Having made its point with a deep thrust, China withdrew.

But if the Chinese thought they would triumph with the same strategy against Vietnam, they were badly mistaken. They learned that the Vietnamese were gifted in the art of war, especially on their own turf.

Chinese news agency photo depicted mobile rocket unit fighting against the Vietnamese.

days of the Chinese army's penetration of [Viet]nese territory it got bogged down and suf[fered] enormous casualties. The veterans of the Viet[na]mese army and militia, skilled in guerrilla tactics and armed with superior Soviet weapons, outgunned the invaders and stopped them from ever getting close to Hanoi.

Less than three weeks later China withdrew, having pushed only a few miles into Vietnam. The cost was an estimated twenty-five thousand dead and wounded, plus an unknown quantity of military hardware that included tanks, artillery and planes.

The Chinese government tried to put the best face on the first major military confrontation outside its border in more than twenty-five years. Despite evidence the army had blundered its way in and out of Vietnam, the press extolled the bravery of the Chinese soldiers who "exploded the myth of invincibility of this Asian Cuba."

Nonetheless, the crisis smeared China's reputation as a self-proclaimed leader of developing nations, did nothing to stabilize the underlying political tensions in Southeast Asia, and fractured any lingering ideas about solidarity in the communist world.

It also led to a reassessment and streamlining of the People's Liberation Army, the world's largest fighting force, in what amounted to a tacit admission by the Chinese that the Vietnam border war exposed some glaring shortcomings in their military capability.

The end of China's short-lived Vietnam invasion seemed to mark the start of an intensified effort by Deng Xiaoping to focus almost exclusively on the country's pressing domestic problems, as well as resolve two burning emotional and historical issues within his lifetime, the future of Taiwan and Hong Kong.

Taiwan, seat of the rival Nationalist regime that had fled the mainland three decades earlier, seemed even more determined than before to reject calls for reunification, despite Deng's pledges to grant it a great deal of autonomy.

The island had grown from a poverty-stricken former colony of Japan into one of the most dynamic industrial centers in Asia, with a rapidly rising standard of living envied on the mainland.

But for Taiwan's nineteen million people, most of them weaned on the vitriolic anti-communism of the Nationalist regime, the prospect of re-incorporation with China seemed frightening and unthinkable. The problem was aggravated by what Deng considered a subversion of the Chinese-U.S. agreement that normalized relations in January 1979 and terminated Washington's diplomatic recognition of the Nationalists as China's legitimate government.

Shortly thereafter the U.S. Congress passed the Taiwan Relations Act, which among other things guaranteed continued sales of American defensive weapons sales to the island, including advanced jet fighters and anti-aircraft missiles.

In the Chinese view, this measure was outrageous, illegal and only hardened the intransigence of the Nationalists, who were still vowing one day to retake the mainland from the "communist bandits."

A few years later the Chinese successfully pressured the United States into promising that it would gradually end weapons sales to Taiwan. But the "Two-China" issue remained an emotional and thorny issue.

Chinese-Vietnamese fighting at the frontier was described by the Chinese news agency as "counterattack against the Vietnamese aggresssors" in February 1979.

Chinese and Vietnamese troops clash in Vietnam in 1979.

Vietnamese news agency photo showed fighting with Chinese troops in Lang Son province, about twelve miles from the border.

Vietnamese troops carrying part of an anti-tank gun in Vietnamese-Chinese clash of 1979.

184

Reforms Reshape Rural China

Deng Xiaoping and his radical Maoist predecessors battled over many points, but on one they agreed. The key to China's ultimate triumph over poverty and backwardness lay not in the cities, but in the countryside where 80 percent of the population lived.

Mao and his followers had wanted to instill the peasants with perpetual revolutionary zeal and self-lessness to modernize the country. Deng and his allies took another approach: Not only reward hard work with higher pay, but encourage peasants to "get rich," spend their money freely and spread the wealth around.

Deng's death knell for the egalitarian people's communes in 1978 came when the peasants were desperate for improvement in their living standards, but the change held enormous risks.

Not only did it amount to a break from the past, but smacked of a brazen return to capitalism, exactly what Mao had feared. Deng denied this, calling his reforms "socialism with Chinese characteristics."

Exhorting peasants to amass wealth raised another danger of the old society, a return to the classes of rich and poor, haves and have-nots, exploiters and exploited.

Peasants at a private market in Shantung province sell produce they grew privately on plots alloted to them by communes.

Egg Farmer Who Bought a Car

By the spring of 1984, the novelty of peasants purchasing televisions, washing machines and refrigerators with their wads of cash from private farming had largely worn off.

But when Beijing's Communist Party newspaper published a story of a peasant who made so much money she became the first in China to buy her own car, it turned into the sale heard around the world.

"Happy purchase of Toyota for Sun Guiyang, best chicken farmer in the country," said the *Beijing Daily* in a story widely reported by foreign news agencies. "Sun Guiyang will drive her silver Toyota around to make business contacts and promote egg sales."

Sun's egg farm in a Beijing suburb sold more than sixteen thousand pounds of eggs a year and her family's annual income totaled nearly $19,000, considered a fortune where many peasants still were earning less than $50 a year in the poorest regions of the country.

She spent about $4,700 cash for the car, the newspaper said. That would be an unusual feat even in some Western countries, where car buyers often must borrow from banks.

The story suggested that China's countryside, the biggest single market in the world with more than eight hundred million mouths to feed, had reached a point in its development where the once-unthinkable idea of private ownership of cars was now a reality.

It was a prospect that raised enormous business possibilities for foreign automakers, especially the Japanese, who already were selling thousands of vehicles to China's tourist agencies and industrial concerns.

The Chinese press already had reported instances of peasants who bought their own Chinese-made trucks. Earlier in the year it gave prominent coverage to a group of peasants who pooled their money to invest in a crop-dusting helicopter.

But the idea of private car ownership in China still was difficult to comprehend. Most Chinese never had ridden in a car, much less remotely considered buying one. Most rode bicycles.

Even party officials didn't have their own cars, though they traveled in curtained chauffered limousines that technically are owned by the state.

The story of Sun Guiyang's new car fit together just a little too neatly. Moreover it was published just a few weeks before the visit of President Reagan, a skeptic whom Chinese leaders wanted to impress with the pace and scope of their economic reforms.

Some members of the Beijing-based foreign press corps began to ask serious questions about Sun Guiyang.

How did she get the restricted-use foreign currency needed to buy a foreign car? How did she negotiate the $4,700 price, which sounded suspiciously cheap? Since there are no auto showrooms in Beijing, where did she buy it? Why didn't she buy a domestic car?

Foreign press requests to interview Sun Guiyang were rejected. But Chinese sources said privately the story was at best grossly exaggerated, at worst a fiction.

Some said Sun's egg farm was cooperatively owned by many peasant families, who had pooled some savings to purchase a used Toyota that once had belonged to a foreign embassy. Others said Sun claimed ownership of the car because her husband was a local Communist Party functionary.

Regardless of the real story, the *Beijing Daily's* version probably wasn't true. It's also a good example of how China's state-run press attempted to incite the people to work harder in those days, not for revolutionary glory, but material rewards.

Deng, who had proclaimed class struggle was basically over in late 1978, denied this would happen too. The state still owned the land, he emphasized. There would be no return to landlordism because individuals could not own the property they farmed.

Nonetheless, Deng's "get rich" strategy caused wrenching changes that would arouse jealousy among the millions of Chinese who saw others making more money than them.

For the first five years or so, the restoration of private farming and free enterprise in the countryside produced mostly good news that boosted Deng's image at home and abroad.

The leap in productivity and income was watched with fascination by other countries, including the Soviet Union, which also was desperate for ways to improve its stagnant economy.

By the end of 1983, average per-capita peasant income in China reached about $150, a 130 percent increase over 1978. The peasants' sale of food and other products increased 53.5 percent over 1978 when the reforms began.

Government banks loaned enormous amounts of money at low interest for peasant families to start "specialized households," the term for those that produce one commodity such as pigs or cotton. By 1983 more than twenty-four million had sprouted nationwide.

Some were doing quite well and became the new models for others to emulate, just as the now-discredited Dazhai commune had during the Mao years.

The press regularly reported on peasants known as the "tomato kings," "silk kings" and "egg kings" who reaped in the profits, built new houses for themselves and purchased the ultimate of status symbols, a Japanese color TV.

Provincial governments bestowed "millionaire" titles on peasants who contracted with the state and

Chinese leaders vote "yes" to the economic reports made by Premier Zhao Ziyang (bottom row, left) at the closing session of the fourth meeting of the Fifth National People's Congress in 1981. In the second row are (l. to r.) Hu Yaobang, Deng Xiaoping, Li Xiennian.

profitably managed fruit orchards, silk farms and fish hatcheries. Such people would have been thrown in jail as "capitalist roaders" a few years earlier.

Though they weren't technically millionaires, many were surprisingly rich by Chinese standards, earning the equivalent of $1,000, $2,000 and $5,000 a year. The government even disclosed a few cases of peasant families who were earning $10,000, $20,000 and even $50,000, although it said the number was "extremely small."

Deng sought a way to show Taiwan that China sincerely wanted peaceful reunification, preserving the island's prosperity and capitalist system. He found it, he thought, in his approach to the other big question from history that preoccupied him, Hong Kong.

The British Crown colony Hong Kong, a rocky island near the mouth of the Pearl River adjoining southern China's Guangdong Province, was seized in the 1840s as a prize in the first Opium War against the weak Ching Dynasty government, which had the temerity to challenge Britain's right to peddle opium to the Chinese and create a captive market of addicts.

As a result of agreements later forced on China at the turn of the century, Hong Kong was expanded to include a mainland peninsula known as Kowloon and larger stretch of land called the New Territories, with a ninety-nine-year lease that expires July 1, 1997. Together, they comprised 92 percent of the colony's total land mass.

To the Communists, Hong Kong symbolized the history of foreign bullying and exploitation that had humiliated the Chinese and helped perpetuate China's image as "the sick man of Asia."

After all, the Chinese surrendered Hong Kong in the notorious Treaty of Nanking, the first of the "Unequal Treaties" imposed on them by the British, French, American and German imperialist powers that created a necklace of semi-colonies along China's coast for trade in opium, tea and silk. Common hatred of these imperialist exploiters was one reason the communist revolution succeeded.

Nonetheless after their victory in 1949, the communists weren't eager to retake Hong Kong, despite taunts from other socialist governments, principally the Soviet Union, about China's reluctance to obliterate a bygone era's "colonial remnants."

On the contrary, China's new rulers quickly came to appreciate the value of leaving the colony alone, because of its role as an economically booming duty-free port, buyer of mainland goods and window of information on the freewheeling capitalist world.

Besides, the communists discovered, Hong Kong became a useful safety valve for their post-revolutionary political convulsions.

Its population went from about 1.5 million to more than 2.4 million in the early 1950s because of refugees from the mainland, mostly Chinese merchants and industrialists from Shanghai and other coastal cities fleeing the uncertainties of communist rule.

During the height of the Cultural Revolution, more than two hundred and fifty thousand Chinese a year were vacating the mainland, mostly into Hong Kong, sometimes at the rate of more than a thousand a day.

Over the years, Hong Kong has evolved into China's chief source of foreign exchange, funneling an estimated $3 billion annually into Chinese state banks from the sale of food, medicine and other raw material. China also supplies water to Hong Kong, for which it receives about $50 million in fees annually.

For the British, the question of what would happen in 1997 to the last significant vestige of their world empire was a tricky matter to be approached with extreme caution.

They reasoned that since the Communists never had recognized the legitimacy of the Opium War treaties, the lease expiration date on the New Territories might be irrelevant.

At the same time, the British had long assumed Beijing eventually would reclaim Hong Kong, and they weren't prepared to seriously challenge that despite the colony's enormous economic value and its dubious future under the communist flag. Moreover, the British recognized that Kowloon, the New Territories and Hong Kong island had become economically indivisible. They had to be prepared to surrender the entire area.

By the late 1970s the question of 1997, like a slight nagging headache, began to thump a little more doggedly.

It became evident that the question would have to be resolved years before the lease expiration date, simply in order to preserve the colony's stability.

The last thing London wanted was a panic about the future by Hong Kong's 5.5 million residents, 98 percent ethnic Chinese, many of them refugees from the regimentation and political turmoil of mainland life.

China kept its wishes for Hong Kong's future a secret up until 1982. By then, businesses in the colony had started wondering whether they should continue to invest there or consider moving out. The Hong Kong stock market was taking a beating.

That was precisely the kind of situation the British wished to avoid. A business exodus from Hong Kong would sap its lifeblood, billions of dollars in freely moving capital that had made the colony one of the world's leading financial and industrial centers.

Britain began to quietly intimate to China that it wished to discuss Hong Kong's future. Nonetheless, when China finally announced it wanted Hong Kong back upon the expiration of Britain's lease in 1997, the news produced shock waves.

Chinese officials chose the occasion of a visit by British Prime Minister Margaret Thatcher to tell her directly and bluntly what they wanted, after a welcome ceremony in Beijing's Great Hall of the People.

Premier Zhao Ziyang, trying to calm the fears, indicated China wouldn't interfere in Hong Kong's affairs even after Britain's lease expired. "I don't think Hong Kong needs to be concerned about the future," he said. "What does Hong Kong have to worry about?"

Negotiations began immediately on the future of Hong Kong but the atmosphere was tense and uncertain. It was no secret that Mrs. Thatcher and Deng Xiaoping had a sharp exchange on the subject.

Mrs. Thatcher, especially, seemed to touch a raw nerve in Beijing after her visit, when she said the treaties that made Hong Kong a British colony were valid. Deng seethed at this assertion, and the official press called the treaties invalid products of Britain's 19th century "gunboat diplomacy."

Suddenly the possibility of a collapse in Hong Kong confidence seemed much more real, and raised the prospect that China could simply reclaim its sovereignty by force well before 1997.

There would be little Britain could do to stop that. Even Mrs. Thatcher, whose military victory in retaking the disputed Falkland Islands from Argentina had made her enormously popular at home, was not about to engage the Chinese in a similar confrontation.

The prospect of Asia's fattest port, an unrestrained den of capitalism and free enterprise, falling into the hands of the world's largest communist country presented a somber picture after all those years of quiet cooperation and looking the other way.

Many Hong Kong people decided the best option was to emigrate to the United States or another Western country. Visa applications soared, the Hong Kong stock market suffered another tumble and property values sagged.

Part of the fear stemmed from uncertainty over whether the negotiations were making progress, or

even what the agenda was. Neither side was talking and that was viewed as a bad sign.

Deng then proposed an innovative idea that helped ease the growing sense of panic and helplessness in Hong Kong. The idea eventually became the blueprint for a historic handover agreement.

Deng said post-colonial Hong Kong could keep its economic, social and legal structures for at least fifty years as a special administrative region.

It could even issue separate passports and retain autonomous membership in international economic agreements such as the General Agreement on Tariffs and Trade.

But China would appoint a governor, take responsibility for Hong Kong's security and deploy troops there. Hong Kong residents would become citizens of China. Queen Elizabeth's face would no longer adorn the Hong Kong dollar or postage stamp.

On July 1, 1997, the expiration of the Treaty of Nanking, Britain's Union Jack would come down, replaced by China's scarlet hammer and sickle, marking the end of Britain's colonial reign.

Deng called the idea "one country, two systems" and clearly proposed it with Taiwan in mind. Deng envisioned a unified China with the vast majority of the people practicing socialism, and a few special areas practicing capitalism.

He believed the capitalist areas would provide the money, technical knowledge and management skills to help the socialist areas develop more rapidly.

Deng saw no contradiction in this proposal and thought it to be quite a simple solution to what he called "questions left over from history."

Still, it wasn't so easy. The British wanted details of Hong Kong's post-colonial rights and freedoms spelled out in precise detail, while the Chinese preferred to keep them vague. There also were complicated questions about post-1997 land ownership, establishing a system of local elections before the takeover date and the timetable for a transition from British to Chinese administration.

The negotiators were burdened with an additional pressure of completing a draft agreement within two years, a deadline imposed by Deng himself.

He wanted a Hong Kong pact in his hands before October 1, 1984, the thirty-fifth anniversary of the founding of the People's Republic, when the government planned an extravagant celebration. The recovery of Hong Kong was to be a major theme of that event.

Less than a week before, on September 26, British Ambassador Sir Richard Evans and China's Vice Foreign Minister Zhou Nan initialed a pact for post-colonial Hong Kong in the year 1997.

A few days later a humble Mrs. Thatcher returned to Beijing and joined Premier Zhao to formally sign the joint declaration that would surrender Hong Kong to China. Deng, a slight smile on his lips, looked on.

At the obligatory toasts to Sino-British friendship afterward, Deng downed a shot of fiery maotai sorghum liquor and promised to visit Hong Kong for the hand-over ceremony in 1997.

The British, acknowledging they had no choice but to sign, still tried to put the best face on an agreement which they called a triumph of diplomacy.

If successful, the pact would mark the first time that the two major antagonistic political systems of the 20th century, communism and capitalism, would function under one government.

Deng gained an immediate propaganda advantage with the pact and again invited Taiwan to negotiate a similar arrangement.

But the Nationalists denounced the agreement as a fraud and a betrayal that they said doomed Hong Kong to a dismal future. In their own public relations gesture, they even offered Hong Kong residents unlimited visas and home-mortgage loans to resettle on Taiwan. Their only requirement was a loyalty oath.

As for the people of Hong Kong, China's pledge was better than nothing. But it did little to shorten the long lines for emigration visa applications at the American consulate.

It published heroic stories of peasants who toiled to buy their own crop sprayers, trucks and even computers to help them manage their finances. Extraordinary publicity was given to a group of Chinese peasants who toured Japan at their own expense in the summer of 1984, an unprecedented event.

Still, the overwhelming majority of Chinese incomes remained quite low. The publicity given to these newly emerging rich families was meant to inspire others. Much of it was exaggerated and even outright wrong.

The reaction of many Chinese to these Horatio Alger stories was envy and resentment, not only among poor peasants but also the two hundred million people living in the squalid cities. So far, most of the reforms hadn't made an appreciable difference in their take-home pay or any other aspect of their dreary lives.

So by 1984, Deng and his colleagues slightly revised their original strategy. They said not everyone could reap the economic benefits of hard work at the same time.

A Chinese woman tailor, one of nearly seventy who practice their trade on Democracy Street in Lanzhou in 1980, fits a customer for a Western suit.

"Our government promotes the policy that some people get rich first," said Deng's top agricultural theorist, Du Runsheng, an architect of the reform. "Then we'll have the other people get rich. Our final purpose is to have all the people get rich."

The pronouncements from Beijing to be patient for prosperity often went unheeded, however. Stories about harassment of rich peasants began to surface regularly in the state-run press.

They ranged from extortion and assaults on successful families to theft and destruction of their property. Some of the vandals were said to be local Communist Party officials who saw the rich peasants as a threat to their own power.

In one prominent case in Jiangsu province, poor peasants poisoned their rich neighbor's flocks of ducks because they thought he was too rich. In an account of extortion in Henan, a peasant who contracted to grow eight thousand tree saplings was forced by his neighbors to surrender six thousand of them.

Reports from other provinces suggested police and militia units were assigned to protect the property of richer peasants from poorer jealous neighbors. In one country in Hubei province alone, nearly all one hundred and thirty so-called "specialized households" of rich peasants had been victimized by crime.

Undeterred by these disturbing developments, Deng and his proteges, Hu Yaobang and Zhao Ziyang, vowed to press ahead with their reforms.

In their blueprint of the future, the rich peasants would be the catalyst for a vast self-generating sprawl of development in the backward countryside, eventually engrossing half the rural population—four hundred million people—in construction, factory production and service industries.

Still, by the end of 1984, the senior leaders toned down the extravagant propaganda about getting rich. The awards and honors for peasant "millionaires" were quietly dropped. At the same time, new book of speeches by Deng sought to reassure skeptics that China would remain socialist.

"I am afraid that some of our old comrades have this fear: after a generation of socialism and communism, it is unacceptable to sprout some capitalism," he said in one of the speeches. "It cannot harm us, it cannot harm us."

Wooing the Foreign Imperialists

One of Deng's most sensitive and controversial departures from Maoism was the courtship of foreign capitalists, mainly from Japan and the United States.

The days of imperialist plunderers, gunboat diplomacy and colonial enclaves that banned Chinese and dogs were history, but for thirty years the communists had instilled hatred and resentment of foreign exploiters into Chinese society.

Now Deng was inviting the descendants of those foreigners back to China and disbanding another institutionalized Maoist dictum: "Zi li geng sheng," which means "self-reliance."

Deng offered potential foreign investors promises of cheap labor and rent, lush profits and tantalizing access to the world's biggest consumer market if they would invest in Chinese industry and help it modernize with advanced technology and management.

Up to now, about the only significant foreign business window into China had been largely for purchasing Chinese goods, at a twice-annual fair in

Canton with admission by invitation from the Ministry of Foreign Economic Relations and Trade.

Under the communists, the ministry had acted as the country's sole agent for dealing with overseas companies. It authorized deals to sell foreign merchants items such as canned foods, simple machinery, textiles and pottery.

To many Western multinational companies, the prospect of doing business with China on a much broader scale could not be ignored.

The simple arithmetic of selling each Chinese a bar of soap, pair of shoes or a candy bar, not to mention a television, personal computer or car, was

mind-boggling. China's potential for growth dwarfed the prospects of other developing countries.

The Chinese leaders did nothing to dissuade this foreign enthusiasm, which they saw as essential regardless of how unrealistic or overly optimistic it might be.

Presiding over the Third Plenum of the Communist Party's 12th Central Committee meeting in 1984 is (right) Hu Yaobang, with Premier Deng Xiaoping at his side. The session adopted major urban and economic reforms.

In their view, China had to open on an unprecedented scale and they were the cheerleaders.

This reopening began in earnest in 1979 after relations with the United States were normalized. Hundreds of foreign companies sent emissaries on trade and investment tours.

They were welcomed to Beijing by Deng and his economic strategists, who feted them to elaborate banquets at the Great Hall of the People and offered a range of opportunities that illustrated just how behind the country's economy had fallen.

The Chinese wanted foreign help in offshore oil drilling, coalmining, roadbuilding, nuclear power-plant construction and telephone communications.

They were ready to discuss joint ventures in semiconductors with the Japanese, aircraft assembly with the Americans, automobiles with the West Germans and wine-making with the French.

They sought overseas partners for an ambitious plan to build hundreds of modern tourist hotels to replace the ominous, Stalinesque, Soviet-designed structures of the 1950s, which were proving woefully inadequate to handle the enormous leap in tourism, one of China's most promising foreign-exchange earners.

Strained Chinese-Soviet relations benefited from China's opening to the outside world as well. In 1982 both sides resumed regular discussions aimed at promoting normalized ties and improvements in two-way trade.

Bottles of Pepsi Cola go past Chinese inspector in the company's 1982 plant in Shenzhen special economic zone.

Chinese Hotels

The first two big joint ventures with foreigners sanctioned by the central government in 1980 also were the most conspicuous, to foreigners and Chinese alike.

They were swank hotels for overseas tourists, standing out like sore thumbs among the regimented apartment blocks and grim 1940s-vintage brickface factories of eastern Beijing.

The Jianguo ("Build the Nation") hotel opened in 1982, a $22.6 million, four hundred and eighty-room, four-story cream colored stucco structure modeled on a Holiday Inn in Palo Alto, California.

The hotel featured a candle-lit French restaurant with strolling Filipino minstrels, a sushi bar, a disco open until 2 a.m., a pool and a coffee shop that for awhile was the only place in China to get hamburgers and french fries.

The Great Wall Sheraton Hotel opened in 1983, a $75 million, one thousand and seven-room, twenty-two-story glass-and-facade affair that had similar amenities never before seen in China, including twenty-four-hour room service with menu items ranging from turkey clubs to pizza.

In both projects, the majority owner was an entity of the Chinese government and the minority interest was held by an American company.

Despite public displays of cooperation, the relationships between the joint-venture partners often were stormy, frustrating and marred with misunderstandings.

In many ways, the hotels became barometers of the troubles foreigners faced in doing business with the Chinese.

Because of the unavailability or inferior quality of many Chinese building materials, much of the glass, concrete, steel, paint and carpeting in the hotels had to be imported.

By far the most difficulty was faced by the Great Wall Sheraton, which was completed months behind schedule partly because of shoddy workmanship by Chinese carpenters and plumbers.

Many of the bathrooms had to be redone, the pool reportedly leaked and parts of the basement garage were closed because ceiling tiles kept falling off.

But the bigger difficulties lay in the day-to-day management of the hotels, the responsibility of the foreign partners. They confronted the task of training workers who not only were lazy and inefficient, but could not be fired under the Chinese system of guaranteed jobs. After much threatening, the foreigners obtained limited power to discipline slackards or have them transferred.

Like other luxury hotels later built elsewhere in China as joint ventures with foreigners, the Great Wall and Jianguo were expensive. Prices were payable in foreign currency only.

At the insistence of the majority owners, ordinary Chinese often were prevented from entering these gleaming examples of capitalism. This was part of the government's systematic attempt to limit the population's exposure to foreign influences.

Many Chinese privately resented this form of discrimination. Some compared it with the restricted access to the exclusive overseas enclaves and "treaty ports" of pre-revolutionary China, but then it was the foreigners who kept the locals out.

Despite what China called the "three obstacles"— Soviet support for Vietnam, the Soviet occuapion of Afghanistan and the deployment of troops along the Chinese frontier, these negotiations resulted in new cooperation agreements and the first high-level contacts between Moscow and Beijing in fifteen years.

Many Western companies were dazzled by the Chinese eagerness for change and plunged into negotiations, heartened in part by China's passage of a joint venture law in the spring of 1979. But from there, the honeymoon slowly began to fade.

The foreigners soon discovered the maddening problems in doing deals with a xenophobic country isolated by Maoist dogma and convulsions for three decades, victimized by foreigners for centuries and mired in Confucian bureaucracy for two thousand years.

It took almost a year for the central government to sanction the first joint ventures, after protracted negotiations that were reopened several times and occasionally bordered on collapse. All were in Beijing, where top officials could closely scrutinize them.

For their part, the Chinese remained deeply suspicious of foreign motives for wanting to do business in their country, despite the warm smiles, official welcomes and banquet toasts to the principles of equality and mutual benefit.

Many Chinese leaders, even Deng himself, feared they might unleash a new era in foreign exploitation. These leaders also feared what they called the corrupting influence of foreign ideas that their liberalization might bring. The short-lived Democracy Wall movement of 1978-79 was proof enough for them.

For that reason, the government went to extraordinary lengths to limit, control and occasionally frustrate the pace of foreign investment and other overseas business relationships in China.

It banned most ordinary Chinese from the new hotels for foreign tourists and allowed only carefully selected employees to work in them.

It required all foreign companies to hire translators, drivers, clerks, cooks and other local staff through a special government agency, the Foreign Enterprise Service Corporation, which became notorious for exacting wages that were up to ten times what the workers actually received.

The government also established experimental, restricted-access "special economic zones" along the coastal areas for most joint ventures, so their success or failure could be closely scrutinized and the foreign influence confined to a limited area.

Chinese negotiators developed an art form out of exacting as much money as possible from foreign partners in joint ventures and revising terms of their deals after they had been signed, just to make sure the foreigners knew who was the final authority.

The cost to foreign companies doing business in China, originally considered one of the biggest attractions, grew in quantum leaps and led many to reconsider their initial plans.

Over the first few years of Deng's open-door policy, the price of hotel rooms, telex machines and office space was doubled and doubled again. Tariffs on imported items used by foreign businesses were raised from 80 percent to 160 percent. This meant, for example, that a $10,000 Toyota would cost more than $26,000 when the cost of shipping and incidentals was included.

Television sets are checked out in a special economic zone of Shenzhen in 1982.

Shanghai's No. 1 sewing machine factory reported improvements in quality and efficiency after a technical innovations drive among its workers resulted in this automated steamline for processing sewing machines, among other improvements.

By 1983, some multinationals were spending more than $75,000 a month just in rent to keep a one-person office in Beijing and had yet to secure any significant business.

China's capital soon ranked with Tokyo and New York as among the most expensive outposts for foreign firms. The Chinese said this was as it should be; why shouldn't they charge as much?

But there was a big difference. Beijing lacked the facilities and quality of life of other world business capitals. By international standards, the telephone service was sporadic, hotels second rate, air, rail and shipping links atrocious.

Some companies simply decided they'd had enough and moved out of China. Some quietly shifted their important operations to Hong Kong, a model of efficiency with quick access to the mainland.

But others took the long-term view and decided to stay, concluding that China was going through the same kind of growing pains and learning experiences as the Japanese and Koreans had a few decades earlier when they were still developing.

It was worth spending the extra money and enduring the frustrations now for a big payoff in the 21st century, these companies assured themselves.

Besides, many such as American Motors, IBM and McDonnell Douglas already had invested many millions of dollars in China and could not walk away even if they wanted to.

Crackdown on "Spiritual Pollution"

The influx of foreign businesses and tourists that began in 1979 introduced the Chinese to a vast array of previously forbidden cultural novelties long taken for granted in the West.

From disco dancing to Disney characters to abstract art to bluejeans, exotic stimulants poured in and became enormously popular among the young, despite the government's efforts to carefully filter out what it deemed "unhealthy influences."

The prolonged deprivation made almost anything foreign a status symbol. Foreign insignias on clothes and watches were immensely valuable. Urban "liu mang"—hoodlums—roamed the streets wearing sunglasses emblazoned with foreign emblems. Foreign cigarettes were so treasured they often were used as barter or even an alternate form of money.

Many Chinese adolescents yearned to emulate the affluent lives of their counterparts in Taiwan, Hong Kong and America. It was a trend that disturbed the Communist leaders, but short of draconian restrictions there was little they could do about it.

Besides, many had urged young Chinese to study English, Japanese and other alien tongues. Some had even sent their children abroad to study and they modeled foreign influences themselves.

Premier Zhao Ziyang, for example, usually wore Western clothes, sported trendy eyeglasses and was chauffered about in a gleaming Mercedes. Party General Secretary Hu Yaobang preferred Western suits and liked forks and knives at the dinner table.

Nonetheless, more conservative and older members of the party leadership were growing alarmed. They believed the relaxation had opened the intake valve for evil ideas and ideologies with suspicious names like humanism, individualism and existentialism.

Many were particularly upset over a soaring demand for literature and art with apolitical themes and a black market that sprouted in foreign pornographic magazines, books and videotapes.

They argued that such influences subverted the value of China's opening to the outside world and ultimately threatened the socialist system and the party's monopoly on power.

Tolerance, they said, would only encourage the kind of Western decadence and corruption that the communists claimed to have erased through three decades of hard work.

In their view, the only way to combat it was through an intense political shock treatment of propaganda and education to remind Chinese that they must follow the socialist road and reject decadent Western values.

So was born the first big political campaign since the Cultural Revolution. Party propagandists called it a drive to crush "spiritual pollution."

By the fall of 1983, the phrase "spiritual pollution" began to appear regularly in the state-run press, spearheaded by an article in the party's theoretical journal *Red Flag*.

"Spiritual pollution in the ideological field has become so shocking that it is intolerable," the journal proclaimed. "This is by no means much ado about nothing. Like atmospheric pollution in the physical world, spiritual pollution in society should also be regarded as a public health hazard to be wiped out."

To the Chinese population at large, this type of ferocious language signaled a strong and frightening crackdown on art, literature, drama, fashion and

China's Airline

Perhaps no other state-run business was more ripe for revamping under China's economic reforms than CAAC, the national airline that had become renowned for surly service, unexplained flight delays, dirty planes and questionable safety.

CAAC is the acronym for Civil Aviation Administration of China. But a standing joke among Chinese and foreign passengers is that the initials mean "China's Airline, Always Canceled."

Under the old centralized system, CAAC had a monopoly on domestic routes and was China's only international airline. CAAC also was self-regulating since it was part of the government.

The reforms called for the breakup of CAAC into regional competitive domestic airlines, at least one international carrier and a separate regulatory unit, functioning much like the Federal Aviation Administration in the United States.

CAAC's service was so unpredictable and frustrating that even high-ranking Communist Party officials complained to foreigners about it without fear of retribution.

At CAAC's main headquarters in Beijing, passengers had to buy tickets at a grimy sales counter with sour-faced clerks. For many years the airline would not take reservations by phone.

Even passengers lucky enough to buy tickets weren't necessarily going anywhere. The airline frequently scrapped flights at the last moment without explanation.

Sometimes the delays became so maddening that passengers revolted. In one case reported in Canton, ticketholders stranded for two days cornered the regional CAAC manager, who promised them refunds and lodging, an unusual concession.

Although the pilots were qualified air force veterans, they often paid little attention to passenger comfort, bucking turbulence without changing to calmer altitudes and coming in for landings as though they were flying divebombers, riders complained.

In the late 1970s, the airline took a few fundamental steps toward improvement. It expanded the fleet of aging Russian prop planes and fuel-guzzling, cramped Ilyushin jets with modern Boeings and McDonnell Douglas models. But even the newer planes quickly acquired an aged look because they weren't routinely cleaned.

Under one of the first Sino-foreign joint ventures started in 1980, a special CAAC catering service was established in Beijing to prepare on-board meals. Before that, about the only CAAC in-flight ameneties were chewing gum, stale candies and key chains.

CAAC also established computer reservation links with foreign carriers and modernized its flight-attendant uniforms, shifting from shapeless military fatigues to stylish blue suits and caps.

Still, some resident foreigners in China simply refused to fly CAAC, including a few of the aviation consultants retained by the airline to help train its staff in modern airline management.

CAAC machinists have been seen washing out and reinstalling engine filters that should have been discarded, in order to save money. They often seemed to neglect regular checks of landing gear tires, which would become dangerously treadbare.

Unlike safety practices on other airlines, CAAC crews evidently had orders to resist hijackers with force if necessary. When five Chinese commandeered a CAAC jet in 1982, the flight attendants ambushed and subdued them with brooms and bottles, but not before one hijacker exploded a bomb. The aircraft still managed to land safely and the crew was decorated for bravery.

"If death will come whether you fight or just wait, why not strike one last time?," one of the stewardess heroines said.

foreign contacts.

In some ways, it was reminiscent of the Cultural Revolution era that Deng Xiaoping himself had vowed would never happen in China again. The reaction among China's intellectuals was panic.

In universities across the nation, classics by Western philosophers ranging from Jean Paul-Sartre to Bertrand Russell, introduced only a few years earlier, suddenly disappeared from libraries, removed by party functionaries or nervous educators.

The campaign quickly grew in scope. Short stories and novels were scrutinized for spiritual pollution, which included romance, beauty, admiration of Western culture and critical references to socialism and communism. Some authors were sharply rebuked, though none were known to be imprisoned.

Provincial and local party functionaries took the ideological campaign a step further, using it to attack rich peasants and petty entrepreneurs at free markets from Canton to Inner Mongolia. They seized bootlegged tapes of Taiwanese pop stars, copycat bluejeans and other foreign reminders, even makeup and lipstick.

In the capital, Chinese who had developed friendships with foreigners over the previous few years of liberalization suddenly wished they hadn't because it could be a black mark against them.

Many stopped seeing their foreign colleagues and didn't return telephone calls. Some foreign businessmen negotiating deals with the Chinese found their counterparts abruptly unavailable, which they attributed to fears about the spiritual pollution campaign.

To the outside world, the campaign had the markings of a dangerous slide into the past.

Negative foreign reaction was compounded by a sudden police crackdown on violent crime in China, which resulted in the summary executions of thousands of alleged murderers and rapists.

The ferocity of the anti-crime drive raised questions about China's commitment to the rule of law and due process. It seemed for a while as if the government was alarmed about its ability to rule.

Ironically, the spiritual pollution campaign's creator was a victim of past political excesses himself, party propaganda chief Deng Liqun, former secretary to the late President Liu Shaoqi and a vice chairman of the prestigious Academy of Social Sciences.

Like many other senior party leaders, Deng Liqun had been purged during the Cultural Revolution as a "capitalist roader." After he was rehabilitated, he reportedly drafted the formal document that repudiated much of Mao's philosophy in 1981.

Deng Liqun did not want a return to the political extremism and anti-foreignism of the Mao years. But his failure to control the direction of the "spiritual pollution" crusade at a time when China was desperately seeking foreign help for its economy got him into trouble with other senior leaders including Deng Xiaoping.

In the spring of 1984, the "spiritual pollution" campaign was effectively scrapped when the party announced it applied only to ideology, not literature, art and culture—and certainly not the flow of Western technology and management expertise the Chinese hungered for. Deng Liqun disappeared in disgrace and didn't resurface until nearly a year later.

The demise of the spiritual pollution crackdown was like the end of a pendulum swing toward conservatism and caution for the Communist Party and marked a victory for its liberal wing, led by Zhao Ziyang and Hu Yaobang, who wanted to open China's doors wide. It signaled the start of more flexibility, greatly expanded contacts with the outside world, the elevation of more reformers to high-level positions and a bold advance toward a market-oriented economy and away from rigid central planning.

Despite occasional harangues against what the government called "unhealthy tendencies" such as a resurgence in gambling and pornography, the next two years marked one of the most relaxed periods of Communist China's history.

For the first time, China hosted an international car rally, held a national beauty pageant, showed U.S. football on TV and invited the first big-name foreign rock band to do a tour. The British duo Wham! played to sellout crowds in Beijing and Canton.

Writers and artists, once again emboldened to speak out, called on the communists to reject past restrictions on creative freedom and restore China's image as a center of world culture.

Economists starting talking about capitalist innovations ranging from credit cards to reviving the closed Shanghai stock market, ideas that would have been branded as heretical departures from Marxism only months earlier.

Tourist officials disclosed plans for a Disney-type amusement park, a racetrack and even a golf course adjacent to the fabled Ming Tombs outside Beijing.

"What we are doing today is audacious," Deng told Japanese visitors. "However if we do not do it, our future will be difficult."

Even President Reagan, who once had decried the normalization with China as a betrayal of Taiwan, was so impressed with the pace of reform and enthusiasm of the Chinese when he visited the country in May 1984 he described them as "so-called communists."

With proof that the reforms in the countryside were enormously successful by multiplying peasant incomes and productivity, the leaders prepared to start economic restructuring in the cities.

They formally presented their vision of the urban economy's future at a party Central Committee session in October 1984, which promised some of the most drastic and wrenching changes yet.

The reforms would relax party control over factories and other state-run businesses, compel them to compete with each other, replace unqualified managers and give diligent workers wage hikes.

In perhaps the most explosive reform, the leaders pledged to dismantle the complex system of subsidies that had kept most prices artificially low for more than thirty years. They vowed to let the laws of supply and demand determine prices.

Reforming this system worried the party the most, because it raised the possibility of unrest over rising prices, a problem the Communists claimed to have solved after they took power.

That solution had come at a heavy cost, however, in the form of chronic shortages, inefficiency and waste. By some reckonings, at least half the state budget was used for price subsidies and keeping moneylosing industries afloat. That money could have been spent on contruction, education or national defense.

The pricing system itself was a hodge-podge of rationing and bureacracy that even party conservatives acknowledged was incomprehensible. It meant, for example, that a bag of coal cost less than a bag of sand, and a few eggs cost more than a

Western influence is seen in outlying areas, too, as this young Khazak herdsman carries a tape cassette player as he rides to meet friends in the remote Xinjiang region in northwest China.

chicken. Workers in Beijing spent less than $1.20 a month on rent and less than a dime for a bowl of steamed dumplings. But a winter coat could cost them $40 or more than two months' wages.

Party officials promised price reform would be gradual, but many skeptical consumers were worried and immediately began to hoard goods, fearing they would become too expensive later. For awhile, panic buying gripped cities all over China.

The concept of competition, meanwhile, baffled and worried many state-run business managers, used to a risk-free life of fulfilling low state quotas with shoddy merchandise and service. Most thought competition was unique to capitalism. They often didn't know or care if their operations were profitable.

But in the future, the party's economic reformers decreed, all businesses would be "put to the test of direct judgment by consumers in the markeplace so that only the best survive."

Chinese consumers applauded this decree, hoping it would make managers more accountable and end the notoriously rude and undependable performances in a range of state-run businesses, from department stores to restaurants to the national airline. One of the most visible responses to the loosening of economic control was enormous growth in consumerism and small-scale private businesses. This is exactly what the reformers wanted, hoping the hunger for a better life would make people more productive.

Increased popularity of things Western in 1984 is apparent here as Chinese crowd the counter where Western-style suits are sold.

Shopper demand soared for goods ranging from clothes to household appliances. Millions of Chinese were on waiting lists for "the five new desirables"—televisions, refrigerators, washing machines, electric fans and radio recorders.

State factories could not supply even a fraction of the demand for these items and the government spent billions of dollars importing them, mostly from Japan.

Although a revision in the 1982 constitution formally had restored the right of individuals to engage in private entrepreneurship, doubts about whether this policy would last deterred the spread of these individual capitalists until 1984.

But by early 1985, there were more than nine million private businesses in China. They ranged from taxi services and freight haulers to clothing factories and coal mines. The press even told of a woman who operated a private telephone company and peasants who had pooled their money to build a resort hotel.

The new reforms allowed some individuals to run larger businesses formerly managed by the state. They also freed many factories to directly negotiate deals with foreigners, spend foreign exchange as

An increasingly common sight in the 1980s: a blue jean-clad Chinese biker and his Japanese-made motorcycle in Canton.

they deemed fit and borrow enormous sums of money from banks, presumably to upgrade equipment and operations.

The loosening of controls infused China with a new burst of energy, making it seem that Deng Xiaoping's vision of quadrupling national output by the end of the century was quite possible.

But the reforms also sowed the seeds for unprecedented corruption and a staggering inflation spiral. These were problems that would later grow to epidemic scale and play an important role in reviving the debate over which direction China was heading.

Before long, the reformers again found themselves fending off criticism that the changes they had introduced undermined communist discipline and amounted to a resurrection of capitalism.

The scandals increasingly centered on the special economic zones, established by Deng Xiaoping in 1979 to accelerate the pace of foreign investment.

So far, however, the number of overseas businesses to set up shop in the zones had been disap-

Young Chinese woman enjoys "wild celebration" cocktail in a Beijing hotel lounge that may have been China's first such watering hole for Chinese, opened in 1986.

The Hainan scandal seemed to mark the height of China's decentralization for awhile. It was obvious by then that the government was urgently re-evaluating the pace of reform and wanted to slow things down.

Spending had gotten out of control, consumerism had reached a feverish pitch and China's trade deficit was rising at an alarming rate, especially with Japan.

The Japanese had rushed to exploit China's willingness to spend its meager foreign reserves on consumer goods, without necessarily considering the long-term implications.

China's $6 billion deficit with Japan in 1985, triple the level of 1984, aroused latent feelings of resentment and hostility among the Chinese, who felt they had been victimized once again by their old wartime nemesis.

Suddenly, senior leaders began finding fault with Japan. They criticized what they called Japanese schemes to sell China shoddy goods. They denounced Prime Minister Yasuhiro Nakasone for plans to visit a Buddhist shrine in Japan that exalted its wartime heros, calling the visit an example of reborn Japanese militarism.

By late 1985, Chinese leaders were openly discouraging consumers from buying Japanese products. Some began to talk of Japan's "economic invasion" of China and labeled it a new form of imperialism. Another swing of the pendulum was at hand.

Corruption Grows to "Evil Wind"

The written Chinese character for corruption is a pictograph of meat putrefying in a storehouse. By 1985, the stench of rotting meat was becoming dangerously strong.

Tales of brazen bribery, embezzlement, misuse of funds, price gouging, smuggling, counterfeiting, pilfering and profiteering were the main stories in the state-run press almost every day. Many of these scams were directly blamed on a breakdown in discipline caused by the decentralization of economic control.

"These unhealthy tendencies violate the Central Committee's policies, create confusion in the reform, sabotage the state plan and normal economic life, posing a great danger," the *Peoples Daily* decreed in a Chinese New Year's editorial.

pointing. They seemed primarily to be breeding grounds for smuggling and other forms of malfeasance.

The worst scandal of the year concerned backward Hainan Island, a special economic zone that the Chinese had hoped to turn into a second Hong Kong.

In June the press reported a multimillion dollar scheme by officials on the island to import foreign cars, TVs and other luxury goods and resell them for huge profits on the mainland.

Even Chinese navy and air force units were involved, helping to ferry the contraband. The boldness of this scheme suggested that the level of corruption in other zones probably was just as bad.

Particularly alarming to top leaders was a wave of unauthorized selling of goods by local officials, party members and even army officers out to make money for themselves.

Many ignored directives banning them from going into business, giving rise to a cynical slogan: "You have your policy, I have my counter-policy."

Foreign tourists and business people noticed the change from several years earlier, when Chinese were models of honesty, known to return discarded razor blades to hotel guests.

Now the foreigners often had to contend with money-grubbing taxi drivers, chambermaids who rifled their luggage and a new breed of petty criminals known as the "money changers."

These young unemployed men often lurked outside hotels and restaurants, cajoling tourists to trade illegally in the special foreign currency notes usually

Policeman walks amid demonstrators at City Hall in Beijing as an April 1985 sit-in continued. Hundreds of Chinese sent to the provinces during the Cultural Revolution were seeking permission to resume legal residence in Beijing.

required to buy luxury imported goods unavailable to most Chinese.

Since their introduction in the late 1970s, these notes had become a black-market currency, worth many times the value of the domestic money known as renminbi.

The money changers often would use the foreign certificates to buy TVs, stereos or other coveted merchandise in one of the "special economic zones" for foreign investment that dotted the Chinese coast, then sell them back home at vastly inflated prices.

In an attempt to discourage official corruption, the press often exposed local functionaries who threw extravagant parties at state expense, gave gifts to themselves, extorted grease money from private entrepreneurs and demanded bribes from foreign businessmen.

Many transgressors were ordered to study the "three do nots: Do not stretch out your hands for gifts, do not accept gifts, do not use public money for big banquets."

More serious cases were treated with greater severity. Occasionally the press would disclose a staggering scandal in which officials were sentenced to prison or death.

IX

Road to Tiananmen

China has only about two million university students—one for every five hundred citizens. Yet this small minority traditionally has been the standard bearer of political change and the voice of social discontent.

Students, particularly those of prestigious Beijing University, have played a key role in every major upheaval of the 20th century. Students were at the forefront of the May 4th Movement of 1919, China's first real popular appeal for democratic reform, and the anti-Japanese campaigns of the 1930s. The Cultural Revolution got its start on university campuses, and students were among the most deeply affected by that convulsive decade. Many of China's Communist leaders started their revolutionary careers as campus radicals.

Thus, when one thousand student protesters marched through Tiananmen Square on September 18, 1985, the Beijing leadership, committed to maintaining the status quo and perpetuating Communist rule, reacted swiftly and firmly.

The demonstration, marking the 54th anniversary of the Japanese invasion of northeast China, was ostensibly to protest a resurgence of Japanese militarism and Japan's economic invasion of China. Much of what the students were shouting echoed government statements protesting a visit by Japanese Prime Minister Yasuhiro Nakasone to a war shrine, and complaining about Japan's growing trade surplus with China.

But the rally was the first in the square, China's symbolic political center, since April 5, 1976, when thousands of people rioted against the radical leftists then in power. It was also the biggest spontaneous protest to be staged since the Democracy Wall movement of 1978-79. Protests quickly spread to other cities, including Xian, Lanzhou, Wuhan and Chengdu.

The authorities were also aware that the anti-Japanese slogan-shouting was a thin cover for student grievances against their own government. One poster that appeared at Beijing University at the time demanded "freedom and democracy." Another apologized to those who sacrificed their lives in the war against Japan and said: "What has all our sacrificed blood given us? Police and refrigerators." It referred to senior leader Deng Xiaoping's policy of maintaining tight political and security controls while trying to keep people happy by increasing their material possessions.

Some of the students were protesting over little more than poor campus conditions. They complained of their unheated, overcrowded dormitories, early lights-out regulations and bad food in campus canteens. But other far-reaching themes—themes which were to be repeated in 1989—also surfaced in the fall of 1985. Students expressed outrage at official corruption and nepotism, and deplored a system whereby university graduates had little choice in where they would work and received salaries often far lower than the earnings of semi-literate peddlers in the local free markets.

The government concern that the protests could quickly get out of hand was indicated in a strong editorial appearing in the English-language *China Daily* on October 15: "It is wrong for anyone to try to get rid of the (Communist) party's leadership or negate the policy of opening to the outside world under the pretext of democracy and legality."

Government officials, including Beijing Mayor Chen Xitong, flocked to campuses to admonish students about acting outside proper channels and to assure them that those in authority were listening to

Chinese policeman clears Tiananmen Square of passersby on the New Year's morning 1987, after students threatened another pro-democracy demonstration.

their complaints about rising prices and low wages. Beijing Communist Party Secretary Li Ximing spoke out against the "Four Bigs"—speaking out freely, airing views fully, holding great debates and writing wall posters. The "Four Bigs," a slogan from the Cultural Revolution that became associated with the excesses of Mao Tse-tung's Red Guards, "would be harmful to unity and stability," Li said.

Vice Premier Li Peng, who would later be promoted to premier and play a leading role in the military crackdown at Tiananmen, delivered a stern lecture to several hundred students summoned to a secret session at Zhongnanhai, the heavily-guarded Communist Party compound in central Beijing. Li, flanked by Politburo member Hu Qili and hardline party propagandist Deng Liqun, presented an argument that was to be heard repeatedly during the coming years—the students were patriotic in their sentiments but had "gone overboard" because they lacked full understanding of the realities of China. Any future demonstrations and wall posters would be investigated and those found responsible could be charged with counter-revolutionary crimes.

Li, who met the students in his capacity as head of the State Education Commission, even then was taking a tough stance toward the students that appeared to put him at odds with his later rival Zhao Ziyang. Then-Premier Zhao, speaking on October 21 at an airport news conference before departing on a trip to a United Nations session in New York, told foreign reporters that the demonstrations "might be, as you say, a reflection of democracy in China."

Zhao said the government did not support the demonstrations, but neither did it prohibit them. Legally he was right. China's constitution guarantees citizens "freedom of speech, of the press, of assembly of association, of procession and of demonstration."

But the party also would not tolerate further public dissent.

Through propaganda and veiled threats, the authorities managed to keep students from taking to the streets again on December 9. Instead, four thousand school children were herded onto Tiananmen Square on that day to pledge their loyalty to the Communist Youth League and the party.

But the rumblings on campus were far from settled. On December 11 more than a thousand students at Beijing's Agriculture University staged an on-campus protest against poor living conditions and the army's occupation of more than half their campus since 1968.

The next day, student unrest broke out in the very different setting of Urumqi, the provincial capital of

Xinjiang Uighur Autonomous Region in the vast deserts of far-western China. About one thousand students, mostly Moslem Uighurs, staged China's first anti-nuclear rally, demanding a halt to nuclear tests at China's Lop Nor facility in Xinjiang. On December 22 about two hundred Uighurs from the National Minorities Institute in Beijing marched to Tiananmen Square to demand that the government end the testing and exempt Uighurs from China's strict family planning regulations. A few days later a similar protest rally was held in Shanghai's riverside business district.

China's fifty-five ethnic minority groups comprise only 6 percent of the population, but many, like the Moslems of western China, live in isolated but highly strategic border regions. Since the Cultural Revolution, the Beijing government has sought to prevent unrest by encouraging the maintenance of traditional lifestyles and allowing a measure of self-autonomy. The government stressed that the Lop Nor tests in no way endangered the health of Xinjiang residents, and managed to keep a lid on the Uighur unrest.

But civil disobedience in China was just getting started. The Uighur protests were a mild precursor of the violent riots that were to break out two years later in Tibet. And the students who went back to class after staging their minor disturbances over Japan's war record and exports of TV sets were only planning for far greater things to come.

1986—The Reformists Take Charge

In 1986, one decade after the cataclysmic changes that brought an end to the Cultural Revolution, China appeared to be heading with certainty and unity toward a more peaceful and prosperous future.

Support for Deng's economic reforms was nearly universal, and there was growing momentum for political reforms that would make China a more democratic and more tolerant society. Life had improved dramatically for millions of Chinese since 1976—the year both Chou En-lai and Mao Tse-tung died, Deng was purged yet again by Mao's wife Jiang Qing, her leftist "Gang of Four" was arrested and a massive earthquake killed two hundred and forty thousand people in the northeast city of Tangshan. No one wanted to return to those days of gnawing poverty and never-ending cycles of political upheaval.

The nation of one billion still faced daunting problems. More than twenty percent of the nation was illiterate and sixty million people in the countryside were living under what one of the world's poorest countries considered its poverty line.

In the cities, many salaried workers were hit hard by inflation, an unknown phenomenon in the pre-Deng days of rigid central planning. Housing remained a serious problem, with each urban resident occupying only 6.3 square meters in apartments often lacking private toilets and baths.

There were more than twenty million redundant workers in Chinese factories who spent their days playing cards, smoking cigarettes or napping in the sun. Experiments were being conducted in closing down money-losing factories and making managers and workers responsible for turning out profits, but large-scale unemployment was still an unacceptable alternative in socialist China.

Crime in China's more open society was increasing at an alarming rate despite the execution of an estimated ten thousand convicted criminals since an anti-crime campaign began in 1983. The older generation viewed with horror young people's attraction to flashy and expensive clothes, discos and Hong Kong kung fu movies, and decried the rise in

Zhao Ziyang (l.) and Chen Yun at the 12th National Party Congress in 1982.

premarital sex and pornography.

But people's lives had improved markedly in the decade since 1976. More than 93 percent of urban families had televisions and half had cassette tape recorders. More than one-third owned washing machines. Consumption of pork, China's favorite meat, had doubled from the end of the 1970s.

More than fifty thousand free markets had sprung up around the country, and there were seventeen million self-employed people, a hundred times greater than in 1976. City residents who once could buy little except cabbage in state-run food shops during the winter months now could go to the free markets to pick from a far wider, if more expensive, variety of vegetables and meat. For the Chinese economy, 1986 was on the whole a propitious year. The government, after two years of excessive growth in 1984 and 1985, put the squeeze on credit and tried, with only partial success, to curtail public spending. The austerity program put a crimp on individuals seeking loans for new businesses, but did manage to cool off the economy and slow down inflation. Capital investment during the year rose only 8 percent, to $31.3 billion, down from 44.6 percent growth in 1985, and industrial output rose by a healthy 9.2 percent. Grain production increased

to 390 million tons, up more than ten million tons from a disastrous harvest in 1985. The number of rural enterprises reached twelve million, employing more than fifty million people and alleviating the problem of surplus labor in the countryside, where 80 percent of China's one billion people live. For the first time, rural industrial output value surpassed that of agricultural output.

With the economy going along at a relatively smooth pace, Beijing's economic planners felt emboldened to move ahead with new reforms. One of the most radical breaks with socialist traditions was the decision that state-run and collective factories should be declared bankrupt if they consistently lost money. More than 20 percent of the nation's state-run enterprises are perennial money-losers, a result of poor management, lack of worker incentive, outdated equipment, disregard of market trends and rising costs of raw materials coupled with arbitrarily

"Private" tailors line up at their portable sewing machine workplaces on West Democracy Street in Lanzhou, west of Beijing, waiting for customers.

The Talien rolling stock plant in the coastal industrial city of Luta was revised to produce internal combustion locomotives. Formerly, it could only repair steam locomotives.

low state-set prices for finished goods. The government annually spends around $10.8 billion to subsidize unprofitable enterprises, about one-sixth of the entire budget.

In August 1986, the Shenyang Explosion-Proof Equipment Factory, a collective with seventy employees, had the dubious honor of becoming the nation's first enterprise to be declared bankrupt. The factory had lost money for six straight years, had accumulated debts of $75,000 and had ignored previous orders to put its house in order. Other factories in Shenyang, an industrial city in northeast China, were given a year to turn around their losses. The cities of Wuhan, Chungking, and Taiyuan were also chosen as pioneers in experimenting in bankruptcy to set the stage for the drafting of a national bankruptcy law.

"Why should we protect those enterprises which cannot keep on going because their equipment and technology are completely out of date?" the normally conservative government spokesman Yuan Mu said in a statement that in the old days would have branded him as a heartless capitalist.

On the more positive side, China in 1986 sanctioned the use of stocks and bonds to attract funds for economic development. Shenyang again led the way by opening the nation's first bond market in August. In the same month the People's Construction Bank of China made the first issuance of bonds for a key state project, $145 million for an ethylene plant in Shanghai. In September came the heralded opening in Shanghai of China's first post-revolution stock market. The Shanghai bourse was hardly a threat to Wall Street. Although fourteen hundred Shanghai companies had issued stock, the People's Bank of China allowed only two to be listed on the exchange. All shares—in essence, bonds—were bought up within hours and afterward trading virtually stopped because there were no sellers. Still, share-issuing experiments spread quickly across the country, providing factories with new capital and giving shareholding workers an initiative to work harder.

Worker initiative was also at the heart of a labor

Crowds mill around China's first securities market, which opened in Shenyang in 1986.

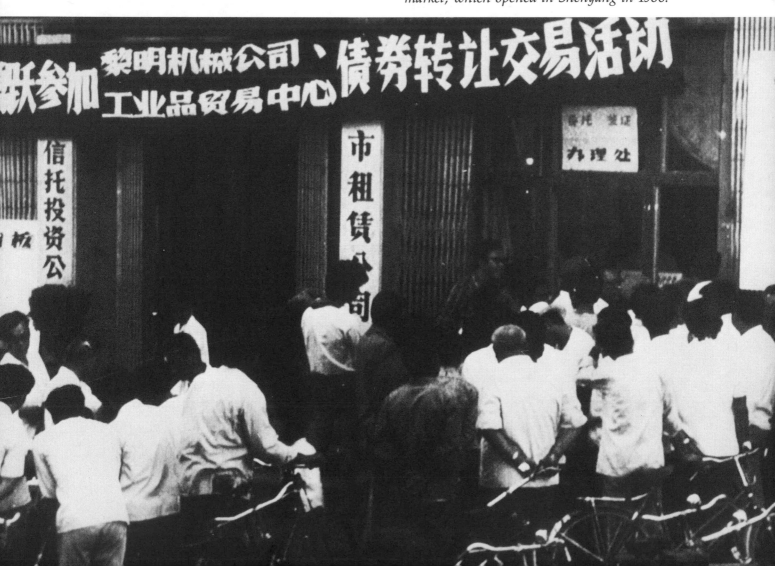

contract system that went into effect on October 1, National Day. It stipulated that all those employed by state-run factories in the future would sign contracts for a specific period of time. At the end of that period the worker could leave for another job or the factory, if it had just cause, could reassign him to a different job or request his transfer. The government hoped the new system would help bring an end to the embedded customs of lifetime employment and "eating from the same big pot," regardless of job performance.

Experiments also continued in the factory responsibility system, giving factory managers greater authority over their operations while making them

Restaurateur La Shanqin, his wife and other members of his small restaurant staff pose at the door of their privately-run diner in Lanzhou, capital of Gansu province. His wife wears a hood in compliance with Moslem traditions.

The owner of a private restaurant shows off a plate of steamed bread stuffed with meat.

responsible for their profits and losses. Some managers signed contracts with the state that linked the earnings of both management and workers to the profits of the operation.

Implementation of the system was hampered, however, by the government's reluctance to move ahead with price reforms to end artificially low prices set by the state on many goods. Many managers found it impossible to make profits when they had to turn to the expensive free markets to obtain scarce raw materials but couldn't sell their products at their real market value. The notion that party secretaries, traditionally the real power in factories, should step aside and let better-trained managers make the key decisions on day-to-day operations

also met strong resistance from officials fearing loss of personal influence.

Finally, in October the government published a twenty-two-article document designed to eliminate problems faced by foreign investors. As of 1986 foreign businessmen had invested $4.8 billion in two

Young Chinese man pedals slowly down a Beijing street in 1987 with more than seven hundred boxes balanced precariously on the back of his pedicab.

A workshop of the Shanghai Diesel Engine Plant was expanded in 1973 to produce large-sized diesel engines for shipbuilding.

thousand joint ventures, providing a crucial source of hard currency and technology for China's modernization drive. However, new investment was down 20 percent in the first half of 1986, partly the result of recurring complaints about high taxes, arbitrary fees, lack of freedom to hire and fire workers and inability to repatriate profits. One of the largest Sino-U.S. joint ventures, the $50 million Beijing Jeep Corporation financed by American Motors Corporation, nearly collapsed earlier in 1986 when the factory was unable to come up with the foreign currency needed to import assembly kits and was forced to stop production. The Beijing government, seeking to avoid a major embarrassment, bailed out the ailing enterprise.

Another important legislative act of 1986 was the declaration of compulsory education through the ninth grade. Education officials acknowledged they were fighting an uphill battle in their campaign to provide a good education for all its citizens. Educational facilities in many remote rural areas were woefully inadequate and underfunded. In addition, reforms in the countryside were contributing to a high dropout rate: with the return of family farms and the rapid growth of sideline industries, farmers needed the extra hands of their children and saw few benefits in keeping their children in a school system where only a tiny percentage of rural children advanced to higher education. Educators estimated it would be at least the year 2000 before the

One of the many women who work as machinists in this precision valve factory in Wuzhong in northwest China. Despite improvements, women in China still faced difficulties at all levels.

goal of compulsory education could be reached.

China made substantial advances in 1986 in the diplomatic sphere. In July, Soviet leader Mikhail Gorbachev gave a speech in Vladivostok in which he offered compromises on long-standing Sino-Soviet border disputes and called for an end to the hostilities that had divided the two Asian powers for more than a quarter-century. Deng, in a September television interview with CBS, said he would be willing to travel anywhere in the Soviet Union to meet Gorbachev, but the Soviet Union must first take steps to remove the "three obstacles"—Soviet support of Vietnam's invasion of Cambodia, the Soviet occupation of Afghanistan, and the heavy deployment of Soviet troops on the Sino-Soviet border. Deng emphasized that Cambodia in particular blocked the normalization of Sino-Soviet ties.

But China was ready to restore long-severed ties with the Soviet bloc in Eastern Europe. Between the fall of 1986 and early 1987 the leaders of five East Bloc nations, Poland, East Germany, Czechoslovakia, Bulgaria and Hungary, trooped to Beijing to meet Deng and revive government and party relations frozen by the 1960 Sino-Soviet split.

Deng, meanwhile, confirmed the strength of Sino-U.S. ties in an October meeting with U.S. Secretary of Defense Caspar Weinberger. The Pentagon chief in turn announced the first port call by U.S. warships to China since the Communist takeover in 1949. The three American Navy vessels arrived at the port city of Qingdao in November, with a band aboard one of the vessels playing "Happy Days Are Here Again."

The reformists in 1986 made some of their most exciting advances, at least in theory, in the area of political reform. Deng, whose basic premise was that political reforms must follow, and not accompany economic progress, appeared to have reached the conclusion that China was now ready for a modicum of liberalization. Political reform, the patriarch said, was "urgent and necessary."

The political reform fervor began to build after an August speech by Vice Premier Wan Li at a soft science symposium where he stressed that scientific advances can only come if the political environment is characterized by democracy, equality and consultation. The state-run press, picking up the cue, began to run articles from leading academics about the need for political reform. The weekly *Liaowang* *(Outlook)* quoted Beijing University Professor Gong Xiangrui as saying China was burdened with a "patriarchal system" characterized by autocracy, bureaucracy, abuse of power and overconcentration of power in the party. Fei Xiaotong, a well-known

sociologist and prominent victim of Mao Tse-tung's "anti-rightist" crackdown in 1957, called the political system "an unwieldy, overlapping, inflexible and inefficient administrative organization" where "division of duties is excessive and redundant."

Some of the sharpest comments came from the *Guangming Daily*, an official nationally circulated paper aimed at intellectuals. The rigid pursuit of communism, it said on November 1, "was really a narrow-minded view that scared those patriots who wanted to make contributions to the country." China's goal, it said, should be to "ecome a more democratic, prosperous and civilized country, with a better economy and higher living standard." The same daily, in a commentary three weeks later, said Asian countries cannot modernize without becoming highly Westernized. It said, approvingly, that "of the Eastern countries that have modernized, there is not one that has not linked up closely with Western culture."

Among the intellectuals who spoke out in 1986 were those who were later to be victims in the 1989 crackdown on political dissent. Yan Jiaqi, director of the Institute of Political Science under the Chinese Academy of Social Sciences, who was to flee the country and be branded a counter-revolutionary for his pro-democracy statements, gained prominence for his outspoken opinions. "A country that lacks democracy may achieve a temporary economic miracle, but its long-term development will unavoidably be hindered," Yan was quoted by the China Daily as saying in September.

Li Honglin, president of the Academy of Social Sciences in Fujian province, in that same month told *Shanghai's World Economic Herald:* "If a high degree of democracy is not attained, if people are not given a say in economics, politics and culture, no matter how powerful the incentives offered by the central leadership, maximum productivity and economic benefits will be hard to achieve."

Li is believed to have been detained in June 1989. *The World Economic Herald,* a liberal weekly, was accused of encouraging anti-government activities and closed down for revamping.

The Communist Party, in acknowledging the need for political reform, never suggested China was heading toward a Western-style multi-party system of government. The dominant role of the party in all aspects of Chinese political life was not to be questioned. The concept of "checks and balances" did crop up, in the sense that largely powerless legislative bodies and mass organizations should have more input in formulating and revising government policies. But ultimate authority in determining policy and personnel, from the county to the national level, continued to rest solely with the party.

There were some cosmetic steps toward more popular participation in government. Amendments to the election law passed in early December stipulated that the number of candidates must exceed the number of seats by a certain percentage in district, county and village elections. The rules said that at the county and village level, there must be 33 to 100 percent more candidates than the number of seats. It is only at this lowest level of government that Chinese citizens have a direct vote for their lawmakers. At all other levels up to National People's Congress, deputies are chosen by the next-lower level people's congress. The reforms also said anyone with the backing of ten people could be nominated for a preliminary list of candidates for office at the grass roots level, although the final list would be announced only after "discussions," meaning approval by the local Communist Party office.

Otherwise, when Deng and other leaders spoke of "political reform," they generally referred to the need to ease aging revolutionaries out of office, streamline the inefficient and overstaffed bureaucracy and formulate a system of law that would define the rights and responsibilities of citizens and give a legal framework to a heretofore arbitrary pattern of decision-making.

Reformers also talked of separating the functions of the party and the government, confining party officials to ideological matters and leaving affairs of state to trained managers. This idea was met with resistance and engendered heated ideological debate.

Finally, 1986 was a year of some creativity and general optimism in the arts. It was the thirtieth anniversary of Mao's "Hundred Flowers" policy, his 1956 pronouncement that urged artists and intellectuals to "let one hundred flowers bloom, let one hundred schools of thought contend." Mao's invitation—many say lure—for people to express themselves was followed within months by a cruel "anti-rightist" campaign in which thousands of people who spoke out about problems in China were persecuted, expelled from their posts and shipped off for "reform through labor."

Intellectuals in 1986 were certain the repression of the past would not be repeated. "Writers today are more confident and more courageous. They don't believe that what happened thirty years ago will happen again," said Yuan Ying, writer, head of the Literature and Arts Department of the Communist Party's *People's Daily*, and a victim of the 1957 anti-rightist campaign.

The year was marked by the popular success of several works that challenged the outer limits of political acceptabilty.

Zhang Xianliang's "Half of Man Is Woman" touched on two volatile themes—political oppression and human sexuality. The re-emergence of Chinese film was led by "Black Cannon Incident," a cutting portrayal of bureaucratic meddling, incompetent officials and anti-intellectualism in China that was also based on a Zhang Xianliang story.

On stage, the play "WM" drew large audiences with its story of young people whose lives were disrupted by the Cultural Revolution. The play was inexplicably closed by authorities in Beijing, but continued to be shown in Shanghai.

It was this government ambiguity that Zhu Hoze, director of the party Propaganda Department, referred to when he spoke of "ripples" in literature and art. "As regards literary and artistic creation as a whole," Zhu said, "everyone is in a good mood and the situation is better than during any period in the past. Writers and artists now have more opportunities to display their abilities. There are favorable conditions for blazing new trails and for the prosperity of literature and art. Under such an extensive environment, however, there are still some ripples and aftershocks."

Student Demonstrations— The Winter of Discontent

The trouble began as early as mid-November, 1986. Students at one Shanghai university put up posters complaining about mandatory morning exercises, while students in the northern cities of Taiyuan and Jinan boycotted school cafeterias or staged hunger strikes to protest poor-quality food.

The student unrest first took on political coloration—and became known to the outside world—when students took to the streets on December 5 in the unlikely place of Hefei, provincial capital of Anhui province.

Anhui, skirting the Yangtze River in east-central China, is a largely rural province known mostly for its poverty. But Hefei is also home to the China Science and Technology University, one of the nation's top technical schools. Its vice president was astrophysicist Fang Lizhi, a man about to rocket to national fame and notoriety.

About one thousand students staged a demonstration on December 5 to protest what they charged were unfair practices in the choosing of delegates for the local legislature. Students said they were given no voice in the process of naming candidates to represent the school in the local people's congress. Students succeeded in getting the election, set for December 8, postponed until December 29, and received promises that student leaders could stand as candidates. But on December 9 an even larger gathering, up to three thousand, rallied for political reforms. Students were "rushing off campus into society to strive for democracy" was how one university official described the event.

On the same day, an estimated five thousand students marched on the train station and government offices in Wuhan, another provincial capital, one hundred sixty-eight miles west of Hefei. The marchers, peaceful and unhindered by police, chanted slogans for democracy and freedom.

The demonstrations next moved onto their main stage, Shanghai. Despite a news blackout on the student unrest in the official press, Shanghai students knew of the events in Hefei and Wuhan. Word travels quickly in China through the unofficial avenues of telephone and travel, and Western radio broadcasts, particularly the Voice of America and the British Broadcasting Corporation, are popular sources of news not carried in the Chinese media. Shanghai students were also upset by an incident in early December when police beat several students who climbed on stage and started dancing during a concert by the American rock group Jan and Dean.

But the government put much of the blame for the Shanghai outbreak on Fang Lizhi, who gave impassioned speeches for democratic reform at several Shanghai campuses in November.

Fang, born the son of a postal clerk in Hangzhou, near Shanghai, in 1936, entered Beijing University at age sixteen to study theoretical physics and nuclear physics and went on to become one of China's pioneer researchers in laser theory. His studies in cosmology and black hole physics were to win him international acclaim. Like Andrei Sakharov, the Soviet scientist and dissident to whom he was often compared, Fang used his international reputation as a platform and a shield to present his increasingly provocative views on the need for rapid democratic reform in China. Yet unlike Sakharov, the university vice president from Hefei was virtually unknown outside scientific circles until the students went into the streets that December.

Fang gave a speech at Shanghai's Jiaotong University on November 15 in which he said that "students are a progressive force for democratization.

This has been the case in all past eras. . . . Chinese intellectuals should demonstrate their own strength. In fact, they already have this strength, but they are not conscious of it or have not dared to demonstrate it. If only they dare to stir up trouble, the impact will be very great."

Three days later, Fang spoke at Tongji, another major university in Shanghai. "When viewed as a socialist system, I think what we have done in the last thirty years is a failure. The result of the pursuit of orthodox socialism by Marx, Lenin, Stalin and Mao Tse-tung and what we pursue today is actually a failure."

On December 10, the first posters went up at Jiaotong University. As on other campuses, many of the issues raised on the posters concerned poor living conditions and other minor student grievances. But as the week progressed, the posters took up more substantial questions of democracy and personal freedom in China. Students spilled out of classrooms to debate the issues and demand action to compel the government to bring about rapid political reform. Deng Xiaoping was generally popular among the students for initiating economic reforms that had brought prosperity to millions of Chinese. But Deng had said it would take ten years to carry out his modest program of political reform, and another twenty to thirty years before China would be ready for national elections. For the students, this bordered on foot-dragging. They wanted change now.

On December 18, Shanghai Mayor Jiang Zemin went to Jiaotong University to persuade the students to cease their political activities and go back to class. Jiang was a cosmopolitan former engineer who graduated from Jiaotong. Since becoming mayor in 1985, he had been at the center of efforts to bring economic reforms and modern technology to the city of twelve million, but was regarded as cautious toward political reform.

Months later, Jiang told several Western reporters that when he went to the campus he saw a poster with Chinese-language excerpts from Lincoln's Gettysburg Address, and surprised students by reciting from the speech, in English. But he said he told students they only knew the words and not the essence of the American president's speech. He said he told them the government shared their concerns about democracy, reform and school life, and they had the constitutional right to demonstrate. But he called on them to refrain because they would disrupt yearend efforts to reach production goals, tie up the city's normally clogged transportation system, discourage foreign businessmen from investing in Shanghai, attract criminal elements and allow old leftist followers of the "Gang of Four" to take advantage of the situation.

Jiang described the meeting as "chaotic," with some students shouting him down. The next day, the demonstrations began in earnest.

On December 19, up to ten thousand students, led by those from Jiaotong, took to the streets, marching to People's Square, a large plaza in the center of the city facing the Shanghai People's Congress building. The next day their numbers grew to an estimated thirty thousand banner-waving people. It was the largest spontaneous demonstration in China since the Tiananmen Incident of April 1976, when some one hundred thousand poured onto the square to mourn Chou En-lai and criticize the "Gang of Four." Waving banners reading "Long Live Democracy" and "Give Us Freedom," the Shanghai students marched from the square down Nanjing Road, the main commercial avenue, to the Bund, the riverside business district. The crowds, swelled to perhaps seventy thousand by the curious and other bystanders, finally proceeded to the City

Hall before breaking up, some returning to the square for an all-night vigil. About one thousand police guarded City Hall and other buildings along the mile-long route. Students broke through some barricades along the way, but there were no serious confrontations with the security forces. Students handed out leaflets saying two hundred of their classmates had been detained during the previous night's rally, but government officials denied any arrests were made.

The next day, Sunday, tens of thousands of students, waving banners from a dozen local universities, again congregated on the square. Many students carried banners advocating democracy and saying "we want law, not authoritarianism." At City

Students in Shanghai in 1986 marched carrying banners demanding democracy, despite notices banning assemblies without a permit.

Young man who contends his talents aren't recognized displays banner saying, "No road to heaven, no door to earth" for the talented.

Hall, a crowd of about thirty thousand watched five thousand students demand that Mayor Jiang appear and give a public accounting of their demands. He didn't come out, and by evening the crowds were dispersing. About ten thousand students, braving frigid weather, huddled in a cordoned-off area of the square, but many talked of returning to class the next day.

The demonstrations continued for two more days, but the numbers were far smaller and the government, its patience apparently at an end, was getting tough. On Monday, the 22nd, the city government announced a ban on all unauthorized demonstrations. People were forbidden from "insulting government cadres, policemen and other state functionaries . . . and strictly forbidden from barging into factories, schools and scientific institutes to agitate people into making trouble and disrupting order in production, classes and scientific research."

On the 23rd, about two thousand students set out from Tongji University, one carrying a sign reading "(Deng) Xiaoping, Where Are You?" But they were turned back by police before reaching City Hall. The city announced it had arrested three workers for damaging cars and soliciting money during the disturbances. It also accused demonstrators of beating thirty-one police and breaking into the People's Congress building, claims the students denied.

Workers and other non-students who followed the processions were generally sympathetic, but few joined in the protests and there were no attempts, either by students or workers, to organize non-student support. During nearly forty years of Communist rule, workers had learned to stay clear of political struggles, and realized they had far more to lose than students when the political crackdown came. "It's not just the students who want democracy," one Nanjing worker said later in the month as he watched a student rally in that city. "Workers and peasants want it too, but we have families to support and it would be difficult if we lose our jobs."

If the students wanted democracy, they were not always clear on exactly what that might entail. Unlike during the demonstrations of 1989, there was little criticism of specific government leaders and only isolated suggestions that China would be better off with an end to one-party Communist rule and the establishment of a Western-style multi-party system. The large majority expressed support for Deng Xiaoping and his reforms, questioning only the pace, and not the goals, of the reforms. Better representation on local legislatures was an issue on several campuses, and some students called for universal suffrage.

But the students in general saw "democracy" in terms of a fairer and more liberal, open society. That meant less bureaucracy, less official corruption, a more independent press and less controls over their lives. In particular, students wanted the right to choose their own jobs and place of residence. The feelings of many of the protesters was probably summed up by one student who said, "democracy is whatever benefits the people."He mentioned better housing, lower consumer prices and better salaries as objectives that would make China more democratic.

One reason for the lack of ideological clarity was the relative youth of the demonstrators. A surprisingly large number were freshmen and sophomores. Asked why more upperclassmen were not among the marchers, students said those nearing graduation had to think about job placements, and didn't want any black marks on their records that might mean ending up in an unpleasant job.

Many students referred to the May 4th Movement as a model. On May 4, 1919, students in Beijing gathered at Tiananmen to protest the Versailles Treaty ending World War I that gave large concessions in eastern China to Japan. The movement is regarded as the beginning of Chinese nationalism. Communist historians mark it as setting the stage for the birth of the Communist Party two years later. The student implication that they, like their counterparts of 1919, were revolutionaries fighting against social injustice was sharply rejected by the government, which stressed that the revolution had been won and the student's place was in the classroom, not on the streets.

There was also a strongly pro-Western, particularly pro-American flavor to the demonstrations, indicated by the Gettysburg Address posters and banners depicting the Statue of Liberty. Students admired the openness, the rights of expression, the mobility and the material wealth of the West. Moreover, they were part of a generation that eagerly followed, if at some distance, the latest in Western pop tunes, movies, books and clothes fashions. There was an English-language craze among young Chinese, as thousands strove for the ultimate goal of a scholarship to study in the United States or another Western country.

The students also looked to the West to aid their cause by encouraging the Beijing government to carry out democratic reform and by helping spread the pro-democracy message to other Chinese and the rest of the world. Police in Shanghai barricaded the entrance to the American consulate after demonstrators tried to march there to make their demands known to the world. One American reporter from VOA was nearly crushed by friendly demonstrators, and finally had to take refuge behind police lines.

Despite the news blackout on the Shanghai demonstrations—the first report in a Chinese paper didn't appear until December 22—word of the disturbances was reaching other cities and other students were taking to the streets. On December 16 up to five thousand students rallied in Kunming, the capital of southern Yunnan province, demanding more say in local elections. Around the same time, more than one thousand marched in Shenzhen, the freewheeling special economic zone adjacent to Hong Kong, to protest planned tuition hikes. In the eastern city of Nanjing, crowds of up to ten thousand for six straight nights from December 22 gathered around the Drum Tower, a landmark in the city of three million, to argue about democracy, econom-

ic reform, population problems and other pressing issues of the day. The speakers were vague about their goals, but said they wanted less authoritarianism, less bureaucracy and more democracy and freedom. Another major march was staged on December 23 by Nankai University students in the northeastern port city of Tianjin. In all, demonstrations and protests were confirmed in at least a dozen Chinese cities that month.

Beijing, meanwhile, remained surprisingly quiet. Beijing students, particularly those from prestigious Beijing University, prided themselves as being China's vanguards of political activism. After all, it was Beijing students who initiated the May 4th movement and the various anti-Japanese campaigns of the 1930s. It was on Beijing campuses that the radi-

University students in Beijing pro-democracy rally at the end of 1986.

cal leftism and Red Guard agitation of the Cultural Revolution found form. This time, however, Shanghai, that crass center of commercialism, had stolen the limelight.

Posters went up at Beijing University and other campuses around December 12, many of them voicing support for the goals of their fellow students in Shanghai. The posters quickly became the focus of campus activity. Students read their contents into tape recorders, or recited them at night by candlelight. Impromptu debating sessions went on for hours in the small square at Beijing University in front of the poster billboards. Some students left for Shanghai to join the marches there.

On December 22, conservative Mayor Chen Xitong was asked why the response in Beijing to the student movement had been so subdued. "The students here are willing to support our policies because they know they are correct," he said. "Demonstrations are useless. Workers do not support them. Peasants do not support them."

The next day, the students took to the streets. About four thousand students from Qinghua University gathered in the evening to sing the Interna-

tionale and the national anthem and make speeches saying the student union and the Communist Youth League did not represent them. About one thousand then marched to nearby Beijing University and other campuses in the academic area of northwest Beijing, chanting "Long Live Democracy" and "We Demand Freedom."

On December 29, several hundred students from Beijing Normal University, angered when a pro-democracy poster was torn down, marched out of the campus at 1 a.m. and set off for other campuses, picking up a crowd of several thousand before the

rally ended at Qinghua University five hours later. Despite a new city ordinance banning unauthorized marches, police made no attempt to interfere.

On the morning of January 1, Chinese police, alerted by posters on several campuses calling for a march on Tiananmen Square, sealed off the one hundred-acre square, and sprayed water over large sections, creating hazardous patches of ice. Shortly after noon, a crowd of students and onlookers that quickly grew to about a thousand marched from the national history museum on the east side of the square for several blocks up Changan Avenue. The crowd then headed back toward the square and plunged through a gap in the police lines, bursting into the empty plaza. Police charged the demonstrators and violent shoving matches ensued with several dozen people detained. The students, who had been carrying banners reading "Support the Reforms" and "Support Deng Xiaoping," were heard shouting "they're trying to make Tiananmen a political forbidden city," referring to the old imperial palace on the north end of the square which once was off-limits to ordinary people.

That night, some five thousand students from Beijing University and other schools set off on a ten-mile trek through snow-filled streets to Tiananmen to demand the release of twenty-four students they claimed were detained during the protest earlier in the day. Police set up roadblocks and linked arms across intersections to impede their path, but gave way when the students shoved through and made no real attempt to stop them. University officials caught up with them along the way to announce that the detained students had been released and plead with them to return to their schools. Many did, but about a thousand eventually completed the five-hour march, reaching the Martyr's Monument on the deserted square and staging a one-hour sit-in before agreeing to board buses provided by police for the ride home.

On December 26, Beijing also banned unauthorized rallies, and on December 29 the *People's Daily* stepped up the rhetoric, saying "a small handful of people with ulterior motives" was using current difficulties "to resort to fabrications, rumor-mongering and vilification in an attempt to debase the party leadership and socialist system and confuse and poison people's minds."

On the same day, two aging revolutionaries, both

Chinese university students wave V-for-victory sign after being told classmates arrested in New Year's Eve 1986 demonstrations had been freed by police.

ideological hardliners, raised the alarm on "bourgeois liberalization," contamination by Western ideas and customs, and gave the first hints of a political purge in the offing. Some people, said Central Advisory Commission Vice Chairman Wang Zhen, are "spreading national nihilism, denigrating China and advocating all-round Westernization." Former Politburo member Bo Yibo said "the fallacy that everything foreign is better than China's and even the moon over foreign countries is fuller than that over China is a betrayal of the cultural traditions of China."

The next day, December 30, national television news showed film from Shanghai of uprooted trees, wrecked cars, bikes strewn across streets and buses stuck in great waves of marchers, and intoned warnings about the dire consequences of social unrest. Vice Education Ministry He Dongchang acknowledged that "God allows young people to make mistakes," but the government will not abide those mistaken into thinking they can overthrow the Communist system.

By the beginning of the new year, as the demonstrations tapered off, it became increasingly clear that the government and party were gearing up for a full-fledged political campaign against bourgeois liberalization. As is often the case, the *People's Daily* gave one of the clearest indications of the new political line. The demonstrations, it said on January 6, "are the outcome of several years of an unbridled ideological trend of bourgeois liberalism and of the failure on the part of some of our comrades to take a clear-cut stand and resolute attitude toward it." Liberalism, it said, "is poisoning our youth, jeopardizing social stability and unity, interfering with our reforms and open policy and hindering the process of our modernization. How can we remain indifferent anymore?"

The harshness of the rhetoric seemed out of synch with the extent of the demonstrations. After all, Vice Minister He had emphasized that only 2 percent of China's two million university students had joined marches, and participation of non-students was nearly nonexistent. The protestors, peaceful and moderate in their demands, had generally returned to their campuses without the government having to resort to force. But for the party hardliners, the aging ideologues who had been shunted to the side while China became immersed in Western-style markets and ideas, the demonstrations were an opportunity to regain lost ground and strike against political rivals they saw as undermining China's revolutionary traditions.

On the top of the hit list was the head of the Communist Party, Hu Yaobang.

The conquest of Tiananmen was a symbolic victory of sorts for the students, but the movement was quickly losing momentum. Student leaders were disorganized and had few concrete goals. The propaganda campaign being waged by the government against them was becoming increasingly threatening and students were under strong pressure from their schools and their parents to end the agitation. End-of-semester exams were coming up, and the frigid weather was hardly conducive to sit-ins and other street action.

There was one last act of defiance. On January 5, about five hundred students gathered at Beijing University to burn copies of the Beijing Daily after it carried a particularly vitriolic attack on the students. Students threw hundreds of copies of the daily, the propaganda arm of the city government, out of dormitory windows as cheering crowds tossed them into a bonfire.

But by this point it was the protests which were burning themselves out, setting the stage for a long winter of political backlash.

The government, ill-prepared for the first substantial outbreak of political unrest since the Cultural Revolution, showed some hesitation before finally coming down hard with an anti-liberal, anti-demonstration policy.

Initially, the government sought to head off the students by praising their patriotic spirit and saying the leadership agreed with their goals. Senior officials such as Shanghai Mayor Jiang Zemin and Beijing Mayor Chen Xitong, in visits to campuses, told students the government was listening to their demands, and urged them to work with the party rather resort to impetuous and ineffective demonstrations.

The official Xinhua news agency quoted on unidentified senior education official as saying, "It is understandable that college students should be concerned about the restructuring of the political system and hope to express their views on these issues." The official acknowledged that students have a constitutional right to demonstrate, although he reminded them that "big character posters," one of the primary vehicles for defaming people and spreading political agitation during the Cultural Revolution, were now illegal.

Police, obviously under orders to avoid violence, showed remarkable restraint throughout the protests in Shanghai and Beijing. Police frequently set up roadblocks in attempts to stop marches, but, except for Tiananmen on New Year's Day, quickly gave way when the students began to push through. On People's Square in Shanghai, police eventually roped off the area and allowed only students inside, so the political protests could proceed without the risk of non-student mobs causing trouble. More than a dozen people were arrested during the various protests, but almost all were non-students accused of vandalism and inciting riots, not student activists.

But the government attitude toward the protests took a quick turn when the Shanghai rallies began to attract tens of thousands. On December 22 Shanghai banned all demonstrations that did not have the prior approval of police. The next day the *People's Daily*, the mouthpiece of the party, warned that "actions of students may even be used by a few people who have ulterior motives and who want to see the world plunged into chaos." This theme, that "a small handful of people with ulterior motives" was trying to manipulate the students, was to be played again and again and would be amplified during the 1989 demonstrations.

The press also began to accuse the students of reviving the dreaded days of the Cultural Revolution, when millions of young Red Guards took to the streets to persecute individuals, destroy private property and disrupt government and business operations. Xinhua quoted one unidentified Shanghai bystander as saying, "we have just gained some peace after the Cultural Revolution and is the suffering brought about by the Cultural Revolution not enough?" Student leaders strongly denied the comparison, saying their movement was peaceful, non-vindictive, not anti-government and not, as in 1966, part of a campaign inspired by top leadership to eradicate political adversaries. Nevertheless, memories of the Cultural Revolution certainly was a factor in the lack of popular support for the students. Many people expressed agreement with the students' aims but added that they never wanted to return to the turmoil of the Cultural Revolution.

Bourgeois Liberalization— A Campaign Contained

Communist Party General Secretary Hu Yaobang's failure to make any public appearances in the crucial first weeks of January was a telling sign that he was in political trouble. On January 11, Noboru Takeshita, then secretary general of Japan's Liberal Democratic Party, was told upon his arrival that Hu would be unable to meet with him because he was "too exhausted from overwork."

But Hu would not be the first to lose his job. On January 12, Anhui provincial party boss Li Guixian, a man rising in the party hierarchy, announced that Fang Lizhi had been fired as vice president of the Science and Technology Institute for slandering socialism. The president of the institution, Guan Weiyan, was also dismissed.

Li, later named to head China's central bank, "advocated bourgeois liberalization, defamed the party's leadership and party officials, negated the achievements of the party over the past decades, and slandered the socialist system. He also sowed discord among the party and the intellectuals, especially the young intellectuals." Although dismissed and reviled in the weeks to come in the official propaganda campaign, Fang was not arrested or exiled, the certain fate of victims of China's past political campaigns. Like others named as culprits in the anti-bourgeois liberalization campaign, he continued to lead a more or less normal life, in his case as a researcher at the Beijing Observatory.

On January 13, Deng Xiaoping told Takeshita that intellectuals, not students, were the cause of the unrest and named three people—Fang, journalist Liu Binyan and writer Wang Ruowang—as among the most egregious offenders.

The next day, the Shanghai Communist Party announced that Wang had been expelled from its ranks, saying he instigated students and other youths to follow the "road to liberalization." He was a curious choice to be singled out as a target of the campaign. The elderly Wang had been an outspoken advocate of freedom in the arts, but he was semi-retired from writing and had not become involved in the student movement. However, he apparently had long been on Deng's sack list because of a run-in between the two in the past. Now, Deng had found his opportunity to settle old scores.

On January 16, the evening television news flashed that Hu Yaobang, seventy-one-year-old head of the Communist Party for almost seven years and heir-apparent to Deng Xiaoping, had resigned after acknowledging serious mistakes in his handling of party affairs. An enlarged meeting of the Central Committee Politburo, in accepting his resignation, "gave Comrade Hu Yaobang a serious and comradely criticism and at the same time acknowledged his achievements." Premier Zhao Ziyang was named acting party chief and Hu, in line with the policy of leniency toward wrongdoers, was allowed to retain his posts on the Politburo and its important Standing Committee.

Hu Yaobang

Hu Yaobang, the bubbly and bold Communist Party general secretary and one-time heir apparent to Deng Xiaoping, had a history of sometimes reckless utterances that landed him in embarrassing trouble a number of times before his demise in 1987.

His gaffes touched topics ranging from China's unsanitary eating habits to the questionable value of worshipping Karl Marx and V.I. Lenin, still revered icons of orthodox communism.

Foreign diplomats and correspondents in China learned to always scrutinize Hu's remarks with extra caution because they might not reflect Chinese government and party policy.

In October 1984, while Hu was making one of his periodic tours of the countryside, he abruptly advocated that China embrace the Western dining concept of individual plates and silverware and forsake the use of chopsticks.

"We should stop unhealthy eating practices," Hu told peasants and local communist functionaries. "Encourage dividing up food, put out a few knives, forks, buy a few plates, eat Chinese food in the Western style. In this way we can avoid contagious diseases."

His exhortation received widespread publicity abroad as an example of how China was trying to Westernize. But it went virtually unheeded in China, where using chopsticks and communal plates for food are an ingrained part of culture.

Hu's frankness on the shortcomings of the most senior Chinese in the leadership sometimes was too revealing and may have offended what later became known as the "Gang of Elders." While feting Burma's visiting president San Yu in November of 1984, Hu told him, "We are trying to solve the problem of senility among our cadres." Later that same year, a front-page *People's Daily* newspaper commentary reportedly written by Hu declared that Marxism-Leninism was largely an outdated philosophy.

"Marx died a hundred and one years ago. His works are more than a century old," the commentary stated. "We cannot depend on the works of Marx and Lenin to solve our modern-day questions."

That commentary also aroused considerable interest abroad and reinforced the impression that China was abandoning rigid devotion to communist ideals and moving toward something more flexible.

Deng Xiaoping was said to be so upset about the implications of the commentary that the next day the newspaper printed a highly unusual cor-

The party accused Hu of mistakes on "major issues of political principles in violation of the party's principle of collective leadership." More specifically, secret party documents said Hu sought to protect advocates of bourgeois liberalism and was guilty of leading a struggle against leftist but not rightist ideas. He was charged with promoting dangerously high growth rates and promoting consumption ahead of production. He was also charged with ignoring party and government directives and failing to consult with party leaders before making statements on both domestic and diplomatic policy. Obviously, opposition to the outspoken reformer predated the student unrest by years. Conservatives suspected him because of his unabashed support of reforms and his criticisms of Mao's Cultural Revolution. The military reportedly was unhappy with the idea of him succeeding Deng. And apparently Deng became disenchanted with the little man from Hunan because of Hu's tendency to speak off-the-cuff and ignore the party elders, including Deng, when making decisions. On January 19, the official press reported that Fang had been expelled from the party. Among his transgressions, reports said, were his inciting people to change the true colors of the party and negate its leading role and saying that Marxism no longer had meaning as a science.

The campaign, now in full swing, began to cast a long shadow over writers and artists. The *Guangming Daily* said on the 21st that party members in art and literary circles must "stand at the forefront of the struggle" against those who deny the superiority of socialism and practice bourgeois liberalism. Wang Meng, the liberal novelist who had been named Culture Minister the previous June and was now reportedly in danger of losing his job, told provincial culture officials that their major task of the year was to educate writers and artists to fight anti-socialist trends.

Peng Zhen, a crusty conservative who chaired the

rection, stating that Marxism-Leninism could not "solve all of our modern-day questions."

On another occasion, just before American warships were to pay the first port call to China since 1949, Hu declared that nuclear-armed vessels would never dock in a Chinese harbor, regardless of U.S. Navy secrecy over whether its ships carry atomic weapons.

Hu's remark delayed the port call, much to the embarassment and annoyance of U.S. and Chinese military officials who had negotiated the symbolic event by getting around the sensitive nuclear weapons question.

His effusive praise of Japan was sometimes another source of embarassment to the Chinese, especially older revolutionaries who had lived through the brutal Japanese occupation of the 1930s and 1940s and remained highly suspect of Tokyo's intentions toward closer ties.

On more than one occasion, when Hu was greeting Japanese youth delegations, he urged the young people of both countries to forge a friendship that would "last for centuries."

Hu's warmth toward Japan would become an element in his dismissal in January 1987, when the Politburo blamed him for encouraging the "bourgeois liberalization" that had led to an outpouring of student pro-democracy demonstrations.

The party's official criticism of Hu included charges that he had "mishandled" relations with

Japan, meaning he had allowed the Japanese to exploit China economically.

Hu Yaobang, in 1982.

National People's Congress, dredged up a 1942 manifesto by Mao in which he had told writers and artists that their main function was to learn from the masses and advance the cause of socialism. "Art for art's sake" was strictly a frivolous notion of the decadent West.

On January 24, it was reported that Liu Binyan, one of China's best-known writers and journalists, had been expelled from the party for vilifying the party and attacking Marxism. Liu, a senior writer for the *People's Daily* and a fearless chronicler of official corruption, was accused of "fabricating facts to attack the party and confound readers unaware of the truth."

Hu Yaobang, who hadn't been seen for months after his ouster as Chinese Communist Party general secretary, reappeared at the March 1987 National People's Congress.

229

During the 1956 "Hundred Flowers" movement, Liu wrote "Bridge Worksite," in which he criticized a group of bureaucrats, and a novel, "News Behind the News," on ideological struggles and politics in a provincial newspaper office. Both works were branded as "poisonous weeds" in the anti-rightist crackdown that began the next year and Liu was forced to stop writing and sent to do physical labor. He came back more than twenty years later with the same crusading spirit, writing the sensational semi-documentary "Between Men and Monsters," about a county party secretary who amassed a fortune by taking bribes and using her power to extort money from subordinates.

Unlike Fang, however, Liu saw hope for the Communist system and felt he had a role in making it work by exposing its weak points. Despite the growing list of party leaders who objected to his probes, he said in 1985 that "the days when writers, as the voice of the people, were subjected to persecution and exile are gone for good." Like many Chinese intellectuals who had survived years of persecution, Liu was an optimist. Once again they had been sadly mistaken.

By the end of the month, the entire nation was caught up in the propaganda campaign. People around China were listening to reports such as one from Henan provincial radio which chanted, "Socialism is good, socialism is good, let us sing the

Zhao Ziyang, premier of the State Council, at a National People's Congress in 1986.

glorious battle song still more resoundingly." Others were trying to outdo each other in the fierceness of their tone. "Bad people who have wormed their way among the students to incite them to make trouble and carry out acts of sabotage must be exposed resolutely and dealt blows the moment they are discovered," said the radio in remote Gansu province.

Yet by the end of January, it was also apparent that Zhao Ziyang, Hu Yaobang's partner in reforms, was moving to keep the campaign within bounds. At a Chinese New Year gathering on January 29 he made it clear that the struggle against bourgeois liberalization was to be limited to party members and was to be confined mainly to the ideological field. In a meeting with the president of Gabon several weeks later, Zhao also stressed that the political campaign would not affect China's economic reforms or policy of opening to the outside world.

Zhao was largely successful in this effort. Other intellectuals were publicly criticized and several of Hu Yaobang's proteges were transfered from politically sensitive jobs. They included Public Security Minister Ruan Chongwu and party propaganda chief Zhu Houze. But compared to previous campaigns, personal suffering was kept to a minimum.

Except for being subjected to more hours of political education, most people's lives were unaffected. Textile Minister Wu Wenying said that producing, and presumably wearing, fashionable clothing should not be confused with bourgeois liberalization. Japan's Shiseido opened a Chinese-run factory in Beijing to produce lipstick and other make-up for the nation's fashion-conscious young women. There were no incidents, such as during the "spiritual pollution" campaign of 1983, of overzealous cadres cutting off women's long hair or snipping off their high heels. Mickey Mouse and Donald Duck cartoons, started the previous December, continued to be shown on television every Sunday night, to large and enthusiastic audiences.

But the ideological pulse was still beating strong. In mid- February, Vice Premier Li Peng, the head of the State Education Commission, told a national education conference that the student demonstrations "resulted from years of vague and wavering attitudes toward the trend of bourgeois liberalization. They were wrong and had bad social effects, no matter what motives the students involved had." Li went on to bring up the old debate about whether intellectuals should be "well read" or "very red." "Only those who have both ability and political integrity are to be regarded as qualified students needed in socialist construction," he said.

During March, the ghost of Lei Feng was exhumed. Lei Feng was a foot soldier who died at the age of twenty-two in 1962 when his truck ran into a telephone pole. After his death, readings of his diary and investigation of his life found Lei to have been a selfless person who secretly did chores and good deeds for his fellow soldiers and the masses and who was fanatically devoted to serving the party. The party resurrected him, with some embellishment, as a heroic Communist and a model to all young people in danger of straying from the socialist path.

"The spirit of Lei Feng is the spirit of communism," said Politburo member Yu Qiuli at one of the many Lei Feng seminars that month. "It is the spirit of serving the people with all of one's heart and mind. It is the spirit of ardently loving the party, ardently loving the motherland, ocvercoming, learning, arduously struggling, selflessness and living to make people happy."

On the other side was the decadence of Jean-Paul Sartre's existential philosophy, a favorite target during anti-Western campaigns. Canton's *Yangcheng Evening News* said "Sartre's theory of absolute freedom is the philosophical foundation of anarchism." Fang Lizhi, it said, had been "egging on" students with such existential ideas.

The press also carried out a daily campaign to expose the problems and weak points of capitalism. American democracy, it stressed, was a plaything for the rich, and only those with money could run for public office. Hu Sheng, head of the Chinese Academy of Social Sciences, wrote in the *People's Daily* that "if a country this huge with an extremely backward economic and cultural base had hobbled down the capitalist road, one can imagine how many soical contradictions and class conflicts would have arisen, and what cost in suffering and bloodshed the people would have paid."

By the end of March, it appeared the campaign was winding down. Zhao, in a carefully worded speech on March 25 to the annual session of the National People's Congress, China's parliament, said China's ideological task is to uphold socialism. "But this must not interfere with economic reform or lead to a hunt for the ideologically suspect." Zhao went on: "Without reform and China's policy of opening to the outside world, socialism would come to a standstill and become ossified. . . . Under no circumstance is it permissible to stifle democracy on the pretext of opposing bourgeois liberalization or to resist and even crack down upon the justified criticisms of error and mistakes in our practical work."

As late as May Chinese cadres were being told

that the two books that were required reading that year were "Build Socialism with Chinese Characteristics" and "Uphold the Four Basic Principles, Oppose Bourgeois Liberalism."

But Deng, in a June 4 meeting with a Japanese politician, made it clear that the campaign was over when he said the nation faces greater political obstacles from the left—meaning the old hardliners—than the right and needs to bring in younger leaders to steady the nation's political course.

The *People's Daily* on June 10 parroted his views: "It is also completely wrong to look at the reforms from the point of view of ossification and wonder whether reform means pursuing capitalism."

By the summer of 1987, the days of many of China's "ossified" leaders were numbered.

Chinese tot and his father model Disney souvenirs, a Mickey Mouse beachball and a Donald Duck badge.

The Old Guard Retreats

With all the political posturing of the first half of the year, 1987 was not memorable for its advancements in economic reforms.

The most widely discussed reform idea of the year was the contract-management system, in which an enterprise signed a contract with the state to provide a certain amount of goods or profit. The enterprise was responsible for losses and stood to gain if it exceeded its production quota and sold goods on the more lucrative free markets. The system was designed to give workers an incentive to work harder and produce more, but the government found most companies were putting increased revenues into bigger bonuses and other short-term benefits. Little was going into investments for plant improvements or research.

Banned during the Cultural Revolution, beauty parlors like this one in Fuzhou were doing a brisk business in 1987.

Plant managers were also hamstrung by the pricing system that often made it virtually impossible to come up with the profits they now were under pressure to produce. Many manufacturers had to compete on the free markets for scarce and increasingly expensive raw materials, but were forced to sell their goods to the state at irrationally low prices. Some economists warned that the economic reforms were heading for a dead end without comprehensive price reform, but the government, fearing inflation, went the other direction and imposed price controls on a new range of goods.

With the rise in wages surging well ahead of productivity gains, a nationwide boom in capital construction projects, the chronic shortage of raw materials and energy and the government policy of shoving billions of newly printed yuan bills into circulation, inflation was inevitable. In 1987 the price index was up more than 10 percent in some cities, and there were incidents of panic buying of salt, matches, sugar and other products. Many developing countries would welcome an inflation rate in the 10 percent range, but for China, which had kept prices basically frozen for three decades following 1949, double-digit inflation was regarded as dangerously high.

Other reforms, in stock ownership, bankruptcy and financial markets, were also stalled, first by the political uncertainties fostered by the hardliners' power play in the first half of the year and then by growing doubts within the government about whether the economy, freed by the reforms from excessive state supervision, was now running out of control.

China also was rocked by demonstrations in Tibet, in one of the most violent outbreaks of minority unrest in Communist China's history. The protests began on September 27 in the Tibetan capital of Lhasa, when several dozen people, mostly Buddhist monks from the Sera Monastery, staged a rally to call for Tibetan independence and the return of their exiled spiritual leader, the Dalai Lama. Their rally was in part inspired by a visit by the Dalai Lama to Washington, where he appealed for Tibetan independence in a meeting with members of the U.S. Congress.

Lhasa residents, angered when police arrested some of the demonstrators, exploded on October 1, China's National Day. Up to two thousand people stormed the square around the Jokhang, Tibetan Buddhism's holiest temple. The crowd stoned and beat police officers and burned a police station in front of the temple. The Chinese side said six policemen were killed in the riot; Western and Tibetan witnesses said at least eight Tibetans were killed, mostly by police gunshot.

More than a thousand security forces were moved into the city of one hundred and thirty thousand, setting up roadblocks around Buddhist monasteries and rounding up dozens of monks, who were blamed for instigating the riots. When about sixty people, believed to be young monks in civilian clothes, marched to the government office on October 6 chanting the Dalai Lama's name, police moved in quickly to arrest them. On October 8 local authorities expelled fifteen Western journalists who had come to cover the demonstrations, giving them forty-eight hours to leave Tibet. Tourist officials also put restrictions on travel by individual foreigners to Tibet as the government moved to impose a news blackout on the remote Himalayan area.

The Dalai Lama, who fled to exile in India following a failed uprising in 1959, was calling for Tibetan self-autonomy, with the Beijing government to be granted sovereignty over foreign policy and defense. But China, which claimed Tibet had been a part of Chinese territory for seven hundred years, would broach no idea that might stir up nationalist sentiments among its other ethnic minorities.

The nation's minority groups make up only 6 percent of China's population, but many live in sparsely populated, resource-rich and strategic regions along China's borders with the Soviet Union, Vietnam, Burma and India. Particularly sensitive areas are Tibet and Xinjiang, home to millions of Moslems with an affinity with fellow believers across the Soviet border in central Siberia. Although in recent years China has encouraged ethnic minorities to retain their traditions and cultures and exempted them from the one-child policy, strong resentments remain going back at least to the Cultural Revolution when leftist Red Guards smashed their temples and banned religious worship.

China was also undergoing rough times with its two biggest trading partners outside Hong Kong, Japan and the United States. High duties placed on Japanese goods such as automobiles and televisions following the September 1985 demonstrations had helped reduce imports from Japan and bring trade figures more in balance. But political friction rose over Japan's decision to let the defense budget go over 1 percent of gross national product. China claimed that decision, and the activities of right-wing fringe groups, raised the specter of a resurgence of Japanese militarism.

China also chose to make a major issue out of an Osaka court decision to award a student dormitory in Kyoto to the Nationalist government on Taiwan.

The Tokyo government insisted the court case was a legal matter in which it could not interfere, but China charged that Japan was abrogating on its commitment to a one-China policy.

China and the United States came to diplomatic blows over both Iran and Tibet. The United States claimed China was selling $1 billion a year in arms to Iran for use in its war against Iraq. Of particular concern to Washington was the alleged sale of Silkworm missiles which were being used against commercial shipping in the Persian Gulf. In October the State Department canceled a meeting on further liberalization of high technology sales to China following Silkworm attacks that damaged a U.S.-flagged

Beijing policeman directing traffic in front of China's new Kentucky Fried Chicken restaurant.

oil tanker and an oil loading platform in Kuwaiti waters.

China denied selling any arms to the two sides in the Iran-Iraq war, although it acknowledged that Chinese arms might make their way to the Mideast through international arms markets.

China reacted even more strongly to U.S. congressional resolutions and statements concerning Tibet. In June, before the fall uprisings, Xinhua said Senate demands that China improve its human rights record in Tibet "betrayed that its authors were a group of people ignorant of the fundamental norms of international relations and knew nothing about the need to respect other countries' sovereignty." In November the Foreign Ministry on several occasions expressed "strong dissatisfaction" with U.S. comments on events in Tibet and said they

could seriously affect bilateral relations.

One bright spot toward the end of the year was Taiwan's decision to relax a thirty-eight-year-old ban on travel to the mainland. Since the beginning of the decade, China had been pushing the Nationalist government in Taipei to allow non-official contacts in such areas as post, communications and visits as a first step toward easing tensions across the Taiwan Straits and moving toward eventual reunification. After China's 1984 agreement with Britain on the return of Hong Kong, China proposed that the same formula of "one country two systems" be applied to Taiwan. The Beijing government went further, suggesting that the Taiwan government and defense apparatus could be retained after reunification with the mainland.

Since losing the civil war to the Communists and fleeing to Taiwan in 1949, the Nationalist government had stuck rigidly to its "three nos" policy of "no contact, no negotiation, no compromise." But younger leaders and opposition parties in Taiwan were beginning to call for greater flexibility to reflect the changing political situation of the 1980s when the threat of military attack from the mainland had waned, China was taking a conciliatory position, and China had risen to be one of the leading nations of the world.

In September, two young reporters from Taiwan's *Independence Evening News* defied the government ban on travel to the mainland for the first openly acknowledged visit across the Taiwan Straits. "We have no biases of any kind. We will be fair-minded and objective in reporting what we see, what we hear and what we learn," said Lee Yung-der. Lee and Hsu Lu were given a warm welcome by the Chinese side, which agreed to most of their re-

Followers of Confucius, wearing traditional gowns, commemorate his 2,536th birthday in 1986 at a ceremony in downtown Taipei, Taiwan.

quests, including an interview with Fang Lizhi. Lee commented candidly that Beijing was "twenty to thirty years behind" Taipei, and noted how poor the housing was in a city with luxury hotels more posh than those found in Taiwan. Freedom of speech, Lee said, "was not very abundant."

Lee and Hsu were prosecuted on their return to Taiwan for providing false information on their travel documents but the charges were eventually dismissed. At the end of October, Pi Chieh-hsing, deputy editor of Taiwan's *World News Service*, became the first Taiwan reporter to cover a Communist Party Congress. At the end of that congress, new Party General Secretary Zhao Ziyang stepped over to Pi, welcomed him to China and said: "It's true that we have made some progress in the last eight years. But there are also some things that are very backward. You should not only see the good things but also the bad things."

On October 31, the Nationalist government lifted the ban on travel to the mainland for family reunions. Military servicemen and public servants were still not allowed to go, but otherwise the response was overwhelming. Tens of thousands of people applied for visits, and by the end of the year at least ten thousand had made the trip, usually through Hong Kong or Tokyo. Many did go looking for relatives they had not seen or heard from for more than forty years. An equal number were simply tourists, eager for a look at the cultural homeland which had been forbidden ground for so many years. Taiwan businessmen flocked to the coastal provinces of Fujian, Guangdong and Zhejiang looking for partners in joint ventures and contracts with Chinese producers. Indirect trade climbed from $1.5 billion in 1987 to $2.4 billion in 1988.

Taiwan would later further relax restrictions on contacts. Academics were allowed to attend conferences and athletes were sent to meets on the mainland. Indirect trade was recognized. A limited number of mainlanders were permitted to visit relatives in Taiwan. By mid-1989, the number of Taiwan residents who had traveled to the mainland had reached 600,000.

The 13th Communist Party Congress, which convened in the Great Hall of the People on October 25, was a dramatic climax to an eventful political year. For foreign China watchers, it was proof that Zhao Ziyang and his reformists had triumphed and were now in firm control over the nation's political and economic destiny. For the Chinese leadership, the congress was one of the most important events in recent party history, rivaling the Third Plenum of the 11th Central Committee of December 1978 when

Deng consolidated his power and decreed that "practice," not ideology and class struggle, must be China's guiding principle. Nine years later, the 13th Party Congress was to give party endorsement to reform and the open door policy and affirm that China would not veer from this course for decades to come.

The meeting also appeared to officially sanction the first peaceful succession of power in Communist China's history. Deng Xiaoping, after years of threatening to leave the political scene, retired from most of his party posts, pulling with him into retirement many of the old revolutionaries who had become a serious drag on his reform programs. Younger, better educated and more progressive leaders took their place, assuring a new era of common purpose toward a modernized and more open China.

The passage of power to younger officials who support Deng's reforms guaranteed "China's stability and continuing reforms for a fairly long period to come," the *China Daily* prophesized.

Less than two years later, much that was accomplished at the 13th Party Congress has been reversed or cast in doubt. Zhao Ziyang has been drummed from the party and his supporters purged from power for many of the ideas he espoused at the party congress in 1987. The party elders who supposedly stepped graciously off the political stage returned with a vengeance to oversee the anti-liberal campaign.

But on October 25, when nearly two thousand delegates gathered at the Great Hall, the first party congress in five years appeared to mark the triumphal retirement of Deng Xiaoping and the new era of Zhao Ziyang. Deng, looking tanned and healthy and wearing a well-tailored gray Mao suit, led the procession of leaders onto the dais, to the loud applause of the delegates. Zhao quickly followed, a contrast with his dark Western shirt, blue shirt and red tie. Zhao stepped to the podium, and with Deng, the central leadership and a huge hammer and sickle at his back, launched into a two-and-a-half hour speech outlining the present ideals and future goals of the party and the nation.

Zhao spoke of his mentor Deng in words of praise for an individual seldom heard since the days of Mao. Deng, he said, has made great contributions to political history "with his courage in developing Marxist theory, his realistic approach, his rich experience and his foresight and sagacity." The past nine years of economic reform had given the nation sustained growth, secured adequate food and clothing for almost all China's one billion people, created millions of job opportunities and ended long-lasting shortages of consumer goods.

Speaking at the 8th Party Congress in 1956, Mao Tse-tung's designated successor Liu Shaoqi had proclaimed that China had entered an "advanced" stage of socialism. Now, thirty-one years later, Zhao stressed that China would be in the "primary stage of socialism" through the middle of the 21st century. Party ideologues who had spent nearly a decade stumped by how to incorporate market-oriented reforms into socialist theory were delighted—they proclaimed the "primary stage" idea a major ideological breakthrough that would be the basis of China's modernization drive over the coming decades.

Foreign observers saw the idea more as a matter of expedience than philosophy. By effectively declaring that anything that contributes to China's modernization will be acceptable during the primary stage, Zhao was giving a "socialist" endorsement to his plans for stock issues, more reliance on private enterprise, the right of the successful to get rich,

A vehicle decorated as a dragon puffs smoke during a parade in Taipei, Taiwan, in 1985, to celebrate Nationalist China's National Day.

private housing and the diminishing of party powers in the factory.

Zhao tried to soothe the nerves of more orthodox socialists by saying that "the capitalist road is a blind alley for China." But he added that radical socialism doesn't work in a country where seven hundred million peasants still use hand tools to make a living and many industries are "even a century behind present-day standards." He called for the creation of Communist China's first civil service system in which bureaucrats would be chosen on the basis of merit and fair competition rather than personal contacts and seniority.

Zhao also made an aggressive appeal for political reform, emphasizing to the aging revolutionaries, now fading from the scene, that "our current political structure, taking shape during the revolutionary war years . . . no longer conforms with our drive for modernization . . . under conditions of peace." Echoing words that Mikhail Gorbachev was using in Moscow, Zhao said, "without reform of the political structure, reform of the economic structure cannot succeed."

Zhao made only four brief references to "bourgeois liberalization," an idea now firmly out of favor, and stressed that China's main task is to avoid "ossified" thinking.

As the week-long session of closed meetings neared an end, it became clear that Deng Xiaoping's name was not on a preliminary list of candidates for the Communist Party Central Committee. China's supreme leader, it appeared, was living up to his promise to resign from his top posts.

Deng was lionized in the official press for his contributions to the nation. "He stands taller and sees farther than we," the *People's Daily* wrote of the 4-foot-11-inch Deng. "Several comrades shed tears," it said of delegates who heard Deng was stepping down.

But the "great man" was also leaving one important foot in the door. He was re-elected during the Congress as chairman of the Central Military Commission, a key post in a nation where the voice of the army carries considerable weight. Zhao Ziyang was appointed first vice chairman of the commission, a move obviously made to ensure Zhao would be acceptable to the military when he succeeded Deng as supreme leader.

Other names missing from the new Central Committee list included National People's Congress Chairman Peng Zhen, eighty-five years old, President Li Xiannian, eighty-two, and former Vice Premier Bo Yibo, seventy-nine, people who had played a role in the founding of the People's Republic but who were now aging voices of caution in a nation trying to move boldly into the future.

In a gesture to prove that China's political process was becoming more democratic, the delegates were finally given a list of one hundred and eighty-five candidates for the one hundred and seventy-five

seats on the Central Committee, the body that meets once a year or more to approve party decisions when the full congress is not in session. Out of 1,950 votes cast, Zhao Ziyang was named by 1,943, second only to Beijing party chief Li Ximing, who polled 1,944. Ousted party leader Hu Yaobang was

The new standing committee of China's Communist Party after 1987 election by ruling Politburo in Beijing (l. to r.): Party General Secretary Zhao Ziyang, Li Peng, Vice Premier Qiao Shi, Hu Qili, and Vice Premier Yao Yilin.

also re-elected with a high number of votes, and Hua Guofeng, the man who succeeded Mao but was sent into political oblivion by Deng, retained his seat.

Among the ten who were defeated was Deng Liqun, a hardline Communist theoretician and ideologue who was held responsible for the 1983 campaign against "spiritual pollution."

The Central Committee was reduced in size from two hundred and nine to one hundred and seventy-five, and there were only one hundred and twelve holdovers from the old body. The newcomers included close associates of Zhao such as Chen Junsheng, secretary general of the State Council and Bao Tong, Zhao's political secretary and head of the Research Center for Reform of the Political Structure.

On November 2, the day after the congress closed, the new Central Committee convened to name a new Politburo and Politburo Standing Committee, the two core groups which are ultimately responsible for deciding party policies. Once again there was a dramatic switch toward younger, better-educated people. The average age of the seventeen-member Politburo dropped from seventy-seven to sixty-four. Octogenarians such as Deng, conservative economist Chen Yun, Peng Zhen and Li Xiannian were replaced with younger technocrats such as Shanghai Mayor Jiang Zemin, Tianjin Mayor Li Ruihuan, Vice Premier Tian Jiyun and Foreign Minister Wu Xueqian. Hu Yaobang retained his seat, another indication of his continued support among party progressives despite his disgrace of the previous January.

The Standing Committee was also revamped, with only Zhao Ziyang retaining his seat. Deng, in giving up his spot on the body, crafted the new membership so that no one faction would dominate. The reformists were represented by Zhao and party Secretariat member Hu Qili. Balancing them out were two relatively conservative vice premiers: Li Peng, the Soviet-trained engineer widely expected to succeed Zhao as premier, and Yao Yilin, an economist who generally took a go-slow approach to market-oriented reforms. The fifth seat went to Qiao Shi, another member of the Secretariat or administrative office of the party. Qiao's background was mainly in legal and security matters and his stance toward reforms was less clear. Qiao, foreign analysts speculated, would be the swing vote on the committee.

The impression that the 13th Congress had ushered in a new era in Chinese politics was bolstered by a remarkable news gathering on the final day of the conclave. Eschewing the traditional press conference, rare enough among Chinese leaders, Zhao and the other four members of the new Politburo Standing Committee made a surprise appearance at a reception. Glasses in hand, the five circled the room to exchange toasts and, led by Zhao, answer questions thrown at them by journalists. All five were in well-tailored Western suits, and Zhao urged journalists to tell the world that his was made in China.

The self-assured new party chief assured the foreign reporters that persistent rumors of factional fighting within the leadership were unfounded. "All those who base their analyses of China on this idea will make one mistake after another." Zhao acknowledged that "I cannot say there is not one single person opposed to reform," but added that "different points of view . . . will encourage democratization and ensure that we don't make mistakes."

Following up on the need for greater freedom of expression, Zhao said that "in the past some people abroad criticized us for treating the National People's Congress as a rubber stamp. But we are going to change this. We are going to treat the NPC with more respect." He said, "There is some freedom of dissent in China but not absolute freedom. No country in the world has absolute freedom."

Zhao was also quick to defend China's human rights policy in Tibet, which China stresses was rescued from a system of cruel serfdom when the Communists took over. "Why do some people in the U.S. Congress . . . support the restoration of serfdom in Tibet? Does serfdom accord with human rights?"

Many delegates left the congress confident of quick implementation of bold reforms now that the party was squarely behind the new leadership. After all, Zhao himself promised that the proportion of China's economy controlled by central planning would fall from 50 to 30 percent in the next two or three years. Another Zhao associate, Rural Policy Research Office head Du Runsheng, told reporters that the government was ready to move ahead with plans to let farmers transfer land utilization rights, giving peasants greater mobility and loosening their age-old bonds to the land.

But not all shared the aura of good feelings. "There may be some changes," said one twenty-two-year-old Beijing worker when asked about what the 13th Congress would mean for China. "But the changes will not meet our demands because we have high demands. We look forward to high consumption but for now this demand can't be met."

Setbacks for Reform

The mood of reform generated by the 13th Congress carried through the first half of 1988. The phrase of the day became "emancipate your minds," and officials at all levels were told that the time had come to abandon the old and adjust to new and different ways of doing things. "Why is it that many comrades have not fully emancipated their minds?" the weekly party magazine *Liaowang* (Outlook) asked. It's because they have failed to translate the new theories of reform into actual experience, the journal said. "Only when there is such a leap in our understanding will our minds catch up with the pace of reform and opening up to the world."

"We should realize that some of Lenin's conclusions, like those in the 'Manifesto' by Marx and Engels, were erroneous and should be corrected," wrote the Guangming Daily, China's paper for intellectuals. "For example, he held that as capitalism reached the stage of monopoly, it would vanish very soon."

Capitalism, it said, has greatly changed since the middle of the 20th century. "This is manifested in the relatively faster speed of its economic development and the universal improvement in the material and cultural life of the society as a whole."

Led by Zhao, the first halting efforts were being made to separate the functions of party and government and reduce or eliminate the powers of party cells in government offices and businesses. As the Beijing Daily said in January, China had backed itself into a situation where "without the approval of party secretaries, the heads of government departments could not make any important decisions or handle important matters. This stifled the creativity and enthusiasm of the government organizations."

Zhao, in what appeared to be a strategic move to keep the reform campaign on center stage, delivered a major speech on reforms just days before the March opening of the annual National People's Congress, where conservative NPC Chairman Peng Zhen and cautious acting Premier Li Peng would be in the spotlight.

Zhao urged increasing incentives to foreign businesses to trade and invest in China, a thorough shakeup of the sluggish government bureaucracy, more competition among factories and more openness in party and state affairs. He gave another strong plug for his controversial plan to pour money into already relatively well-off coastal areas to turn them into export-producing centers capable of absorbing advanced technology. The coastal development plan was opposed by some who feared it would only widen the already considerable income gaps between coastal and interior provinces. Zhao stressed the plan would "bring along the development of inland areas."

At the NPC, Song Ping, state councillor and head of the party Organization Department, announced a major overhaul of the State Council that would reduce the number of organs in China's cabinet from forty-five to forty and cut the number of staffers from fifty thousand to forty thousand.

Song also said the government would no longer manage enterprises directly, as it had under Soviet-style central planning, but instead would be responsible for general planning, finances, supervision and regulation.

The two-week NPC session has hailed as the most democratic ever. Major policy-making and personnel matters remained firmly in the hands of the party, with administrative assistance from the State Council. But the NPC, previously restricted to mechanically approving legislation and other decisions hoisted upon it from above, was gaining some status as a forum where issues could be debated and a minor amount of dissent was allowed. The nearly three thousand delegates raised such problems as inflation, lack of money for education, the need for roads in their home regions and official corruption. "It is pleasing to note that virtually no motion was passed by a unanimous show of hands, customary at previous legislatures," the *China Daily* wrote. "The debates now heard from the Great Hall of the People should go on across the country, so as to channel more constructive opinions and innovative experiences to the national leadership."

Newly chosen NPC Chairman Wan Li used the word "democracy" seventeen times in his ten-minute address to the body. But the road to democratic process was not easy. In one slightly embarrassing incident, presiding official Xi Zhongxun introduced a measure for passage and asked for comments. When there was none, he called out "approved" even before the usual hand vote could be taken. Laughs were heard among the delegates. "Habit," commented one Chinese reporter.

The first session of the 7th NPC, which convenes once a year with a five-year term for its delegates, as expected named Li Peng premier and appointed three vice premiers; the conservative economist Yao Yilin, the more reformist Tian Jiyun and former Foreign Minister Wu Quexian. Two Deng allies, eighty-one-year-old General Yang Shangkun and outgoing Vice Premier Wan Li, succeeded two hardliners, Li

Xiannian, seventy-eight, and eighty-five-year-old Peng Zhen, in the posts of president of the PRC and chairman of the National People's Congress.

A new State Council, or Cabinet, was named, although many of the ministers either retained their posts or turned them over to bureaucrats within the system. Xinhua described the new government as "a group of technocrats who are younger in age, pragmatic and enthusiastic in the reform."

The twenty-day session also approved laws promising company managers and foreign joint ventures freedom from government interference in their business affairs and voted to make the southern island of Hainan China's newest province. Hainan was also named a special economic zone as part of Zhao's vision of coastal development that would introduce foreign-funded, high-tech, export-oriented industry to China's eastern seaboard.

Li's keynote speech on the opening day of the session was in general a strong endorsement of reform. He expressed support of Zhao's coastal development plan and for the first time in public said he backed gradual decontrol of prices long distorted by state subsidies. "We should continue to put reform at the center of all our undertakings," Li said. "It has become an irreversible trend for the masses and cadres alike to take an active part in the reform."

But as Zhao and Deng, sitting behind the speaker, listened on, Li also injected some cautionary notes. "We must not rush headlong into mass action, issue arbitrary orders and spoil things by excessive enthusiasm," Li warned. "We cannot succeed if we are too impatient for quick results." He also named inflation, which approached 20 percent in some cities the previous year, as the nation's top economic problem.

Several weeks later, at a news conference at the end of the session, Li again denied that he and Zhao were at odds over policy matters. "There is some comment in the foreign press that Zhao favors reform . . . and I'm in favor of stabilizing the economy. They somehow pit these two views against each other. This is a misunderstanding," he said, arguing that steady economic growth and the reforms were compatible.

The key question in the first half of 1988 was how to proceed with price reforms—bringing prices of commodities in line with their real market values—without adding to the serious problem of inflation and further angering an urban population already resentful over living costs outstripping wage increases.

The government was forced to take a step backward at the end of 1987 by re-introducing, for the first time in decades, pork rationing in Beijing in other Chinese cities. The shortages in pork, the favorite meat of Chinese, was a typical result of the problems caused by China's two-tiered pricing system in which prices were at times set by the state and at other times determined by market demand. Pig farmers were being hit by sharply rising costs of feed, often available only on the free markets, and the low price the government paid them for their animals. Unable to make a profit, farmers began culling their stocks, and pork supplies plummeted.

The government agreed to raise its buying prices to encourage production, but said there was little it could do about rising feed prices when grain production was stagnating and the amount of feed available for livestock was limited. Zhao even proposed to the NPC that the Chinese try to control their craving for meat and eat more vegetables.

The government was clearly caught between its desire to cool growing public discontent over rising prices and its need to press ahead with price reform.

In February, signalling a dramatic step away from the government goal of gradually ending price controls, Li Peng said the State Council was considering ways to expand its price subsidy programs. Li emphasized that price stability was essential to the success of the reforms.

Food prices in particular were going up at an alarming rate. Retail prices in urban areas were up 13.4 percent in the first quarter of 1988 compared to the same period in 1987, while food prices jumped 17.9 percent and vegetable prices were up by 48.7 percent.

In Shanghai, vegetables were 89 percent more costly than a year before, while in Nanjing state-owned stores were running out of fresh produce because farmers were refusing to sell for the low payments being offered and consumers were forced to pay far higher prices on the free market.

Beijing and other cities in May pushed ahead with price hikes for pork, eggs, vegetables and sugar in hopes of inducing growers to produce more and end shortages. Each employee in the city was provided with a $2.70 monthly subsidy to help ease the pain of the larger food bill.

In July the government dealt another blow to consumers by raising the price of name-brand cigarettes by up to 290 percent and multiplying the price of some of China's favorite liquors. A bottle of "maotai," the nation's most famous and sought-after spirit, went up in price from $5.40 to $32.40.

The Politburo in June announced that a three-to-five year plan to decontrol prices was being drawn up, but after the cigarette and liquor increases State

Council spokesman Yuan Mu told the disgruntled public there would be no more price hikes for the rest of the year.

Many Chinese didn't believe him. In August, fed by rumors of a major new round of price hikes, people across the nation set off a serious wave of panic-buying and runs on banks. Long lines formed in front of banks as people feared that their savings would be made worthless by rising prices. In Shanghai, $27 million was withdrawn in a two-week period.

People were taking their money and buying up whatever they could find on the store racks, from matches to television sets. Poor quality goods which had sat on shelves for years were snatched up. One store in Wuhan which normally sold five or six washing machines a day was selling one hundred and couldn't keep up with demand. People were carting off spittoons, refrigerators and large chunks

of salt. The *China Daily* cited the case of one old man who joined a line outside an electrical appliance store and told the sales clerk he would buy whatever everyone else was buying. He went home with two stereo systems costing $675.

Meanwhile, other aspects of the economy were careening out of control. Despite repeated pronouncements by Beijing that headlong spending on new projects had to stop, investment in capital construction was up 45 percent and industrial growth was charging upward at an unsustainable 20 percent. With the nation's inefficient coal and oil industries expanding production by only 4 or 5 percent a

Delivery cyclist pedals by the Great Hall of the People, his cart laden with the bounty from the Chinese government's policies of economic reform and growth: Japanese freezers and TVs.

year, the nation's energy shortages were getting progressively worse. Many factories, particularly the booming rural and township enterprises that did not have guaranteed power supplies, had to shut down two and three days a week because of power shortages.

Beijing appeared to have lost control of banking. Money supply jumped an astonishing 40 percent in the year ending in June 1988, assuring that credit was available for new investors and defeating the government goal of holding down capital construction. Rural banks, which were funnelling all their money into expansion of local industries, got caught short and didn't have enough money to pay farmers for their grain. A highly volatile situation developed where farmers, already bitter over the low sums they received for their crops, were getting paid with IOUs. Corruption was rife, especially among local officials taking advantage of the two-tiered pricing system. The common ploy was to buy up hard-to-get materials at low, state-set prices and then resell them for large profits on the free or black markets.

The state budget deficit, like inflation and foreign debt an inconceivable concept before the reforms began, had grown to $2.2 billion a year, because of the spending boom and the heavy burden of subsidizing money-losing state enterprises. Western economists noted that if foreign loans and treasury bond sales were included in the budget figures, the deficit would be more in the range of $6.5 billion.

The Communist Party, at a critical meeting of its Central Committee in late September, in effect put economic reforms on hold and clearly indicated that Li Peng had eclipsed Zhao Ziyang as the spokesman for the nation's economic policy. The committee approved in principle a five-year plan committing the country to eventual price and wage reforms but promised no new price hikes for a two-year period so the government can "put an end to confusion" in the economy.

Li acknowledged that the two-tiered pricing system was not to be tampered with for the time being. "We recognize it has a lot of shortcomings, but it also has advantages. We will have to keep it for quite a long time. At present we cannot get rid of it," he said.

The retrenchment policy also shelved plans to decontrol steel prices, tightened price regulations and control over fertilizer, pesticides and other items prized by speculators and froze new loans to construction projects outside the state plan. Capital construction outlays were to be cut by $13.5 billion, about one-fifth of planned 1988-89 spending.

Investigations were to be launched into the thou-

sands of trade and finance companies, many with direct ties to senior party and government officials, that were closely linked to illegal profiteering rackets. A two-to-three year ban was imposed on the construction of office buildings, auditoriums and hotels not approved by Beijing and steep surcharges were levied on public offices buying imported cars and televisions and holding lavish banquets with public funds. The government set up twenty-seven special teams to mount a nationwide four-month campaign on cheating, tax evasion, profiteering and illegal payment of bonuses.

"Orders must be obeyed and prohibitions observed," Premier Li said in a stern speech on September 30. "It is absolutely impermissible for each to go his own way."

Shanghai's liberal World Economic Herald warned that "mayors and party committee secretaries are again herding groups of officials to check commodity prices on the streets. . . . It is necessary to prevent the old system from staging a comeback. Even during the period of stabilization, it is necessary to find new ways to meet the need of future reforms on an even larger scale."

Foreign policy, at least, went relatively smoothly for China in 1988. U.S. Defense Secretary Frank Carlucci came out of September talks in Beijing saying he was "fully satisfied" with Chinese explanations it would exercise prudence in its sales of arms, particularly missiles, to the Middle East. Although it was not clear whether China had in any way shifted its arms export policies, Carlucci's statement in effect ended the contentious issue of the Chinese connection in the Iran-Iraq war.

Apparently in reward, Washington announced during Carlucci's visit that the United States would permit China to launch American-made satellites. China was eager to start its own commercial launching service, and had tentative contracts with Australian and Hong Kong firms, but had needed to overcome Washington's concern about safeguarding technology on American-made satellites and preventing the Chinese from pricing American competitors out of the market.

China was also pleased about George Bush's victory in the November presidential election. Bush headed the U.S. liaison office in Beijing in 1974-75 and was regarded as an "old friend" of China. Deng, in an unusual endorsement by a foreign leader, told Carlucci in September that he knew Bush well and "I hope he'll win the election."

An August visit by Japan's Prime Minister Noboru Takeshita provided a respite for the chronic bouts of friction between the two countries. Take-

China and Tibet

When Deng Xiaoping eased the ban on religion imposed by his radical predecessors, it was too late to salvage most of Tibet, the isolated former Buddhist kingdom in the strategic Himalayas where Chinese occupiers systematically looted, vandalized or destroyed practically every important spiritual symbol.

Despite carefully chaperoned tours by the Chinese, foreign visitors to Tibet have concluded to their horror that the devastation amounted to a near annihilation of a deeply religious culture that had thrived for more than two thousand years.

Almost all of Tibet's twenty-seven hundred temples and monasteries were dynamited or pillaged after China took over in 1950. Of the one hundred and ten thousand monks who once lived in them, only a few thousand remained.

Radical Red Guards who journeyed to Tibet on Mao Tse-tung's orders to "storm the heavens" during the Cultural Revolution went on a plundering terror spree that the religious revival of the late 1970s could never erase.

Tibetan refugees estimate tens of thousands of people were killed or imprisoned during that period. The Dalai Lama, Tibet's spiritual leader-in-exile, has estimated 1.2 million have died at the hands of the Chinese occupiers he fled from in 1959.

In their worst excesses, the Chinese outlawed all expressions of Tibetan art, language and music. They forbid the recruitment of monks and made most work at menial labor.

The Chinese wrecked the lines of "chorten" prayer flags that adorn Tibetan valleys and ridges, leveled the piles of "mani" prayer stones outside towns, and sloshed the sides of mountains with the characters, "Long Live Chairman Mao."

They decreed the traditional two-story Tibetan home a "bourgeois excess" and ordered the second floors razed. They exterminated large numbers of Lhasa apsos, the ubiquitous pet dogs that many Tibetan families keep.

They cut the long plaits of hair worn by Tibetan adults, calling them "dirty black tails of serfdom."

In the face of the most devastating repression seen anywhere during Mao's rule, most Tibetans remained shamelessly religious, much to the exasperation and astonishment of the Chinese.

Under Deng, the Chinese have reluctantly admitted they made mistakes in Tibet, still the poorest region under their control and the only one practically 100 percent subsidized by the government.

By late 1979, Beijing had begun to drastically rethink its entire approach to Tibet's development, and in the early 1980s relaxed nearly all religious controls.

It even invited special emissaries of the Dalai Lama to visit Tibet, part of an overture toward the spiritual leader for a possible reconciliation.

The envoys were mobbed by ecstatic Tibetans and became a source of embarrassment to the Chinese, who have since turned cooler toward the Dalai Lama and taken a hard line on Tibetan autonomy.

Beijing reportedly has deployed more than a hundred thousand troops around the Tibetan plateau because of a stubborn underground independence movement and a tense frontier with India, home of the Dalai Lama's kingdom in exile.

---

shita helped keep the summit harmonious by announcing plans to provide China with $6 billion in government credit and soft loans for some forty infrastructure projects in the 1990-95 period. The two sides also signed an investment protection agreement that China hoped would cure the reluctance of Japanese businessmen to invest in the country. Leaders of the two countries spoke of a "new era" of good relations.

China scored two diplomatic breakthroughs in December of that year. First, Qian Qichen became the first Chinese foreign minister to travel to Moscow in thirty-one years. The visit was an indication of the rapidly improving relations between Beijing and Moscow, an outgrowth of the Soviet troop withdrawal from Afghanistan, an easing of tensions along the Sino-Soviet border and the general international trend toward detente. China still regarded Soviet aid for Vietnam's military adventure in Cambodia as a major obstacle to normalization of Sino-

Soviet relations, but the Qian visit moved a Deng-Gorbachev summit meeting one step closer to realization.

Later that month, Rajiv Gandhi became the first Indian leader to visit Beijing in thirty-four years. The world's two most populous nations were still split by border disputes dating back to their 1962 frontier clashes. But with the Gandhi visit, the two sides agreed to put aside their differences.

The Dalai Lama's supporters in Tibet, meanwhile, continued their resistance against Chinese authorities. On March 5, on the final day of a ten-prayer festival in Lhasa that the Chinese authorities had sanctioned as a way of showing that all was back to normal in the Tibetan capital, a monk stood up and started shouting pro-independence slogans. Other monks began throwing stones, and police fought back with their own stones, clubs, tear gas and finally bullets. Monks set up barricades in the Barkhor marketplace around the Jokhang Temple, lit bonfires and attacked the vans of Chinese television crews filming the five-hundred-year-old festival. One policeman was fatally stabbed and thrown from a window. The rioting continued the next day, with the death toll, according to unofficial estimates, rising to twenty-one Tibetans and three policemen. Tibetans said police rounded up hundreds of people in door-to-door searches, and spoke of a "reign of terror" in the city.

Violence broke out again in December when a small group of demonstrators marched into the Barkhor square led by a monk carrying Tibet's banned snow lion flag. Foreign witnesses said police opened fire without warning—the Chinese said they fired warning shots into the air—killing two people and injuring a dozen others. Troops fired on fleeing Tibetans and used tear gas to break up crowds. Large military convoys moved into the city as a warning against any further resistance.

Public protest took a very different turn that same month when anti-black racial incidents flared in four Chinese cities. The trouble started with a Christmas Eve brawl in Nanjing between African students trying to bring Chinese girlfriends to a school dance and Chinese school workers and students. Chinese later stoned the Africans' dormitory and marched through Nanjing streets over the next few days shouting "kill the black devils" and demanding Africans involved in the fight be punished.

The Nanjing Africans, contending they were subject to constant abuse and discrimination and their lives were threatened, tried to leave the city for Beijing in hopes of returning home, but were detained and held by police. Anti-black incidents also broke out in Wuhan and Hangzhou and five hundred foreign students began boycotting classes at the Beijing Languages Institute to demand protection for Africans after Chinese students distributed anti-African leaflets.

The Chinese government, which had long fostered Third World solidarity with African nations and supported about fifteen hundred African students in China, was embarrassed by the incidents and strongly denied the existence of racism in China. But Africans complained of constant harassment, particularly if they tried to date Chinese women.

With the anti-bourgeois liberalization campaign of the first half of 1987 fading into the past, artists once again were working with confidence and occasionally toying with subjects of a controversial nature.

The film "A Small Town Called Hibiscus," an eloquent depiction of the suffering caused by the Cultural Revolution, won the Golden Rooster, China's top film award. Granting of the prize had been delayed since the past spring because some senior officials had objected to the movie's characterization of party cadres as narrow-minded and power-seeking.

The film "Old Well," a graphic account of poverty and backwardness in rural China, also opened in Chinese theaters. Perhaps because of its sensitive subject matter and its—for Western audiences—tame love scenes, it was only after the film had won several international prizes that the decision was made to let Chinese audiences see it.

"Old Well" and other prize-winning movies were coming from the unlikely direction of the Xian Film Studio in the ancient capital of central China. Far from the censorious eyes of Beijing's culture czars, the studio was also producing such films as "Black Cannon Incident" and "The Horse Thief," which was never shown to general Chinese audiences because of its depiction of poverty among Tibetan horsemen. Wu Tianming, director of the studio, told The Associated Press in February that the atmosphere in the art world had improved since the 13th Party Congress of the previous fall. "If I had criticized high cadres several years ago, I would have been in trouble. But right now I think it can't be."

That summer, thought-provoking art found its way to an even more unlikely medium, China's tightly controlled state-run television. Five young writers, led by Su Xiaokang, produced the six-part documentary "He Shang" ("River Elegy"), with its theme of China's cultural rigidity and obsession with the past, and concluded that the nation's infatuation with its cultural uniqueness made it incapable of dealing with the future. The series, which focused on the Yellow River, the Great Wall and other monuments that epitomized China's culture, was strongly condemned by some Chinese leaders, but was generally welcomed as a work that compelled the Chinese to seriously reflect on their past and future.

"It is a major breakthrough in the traditional making of TV series," the *China Daily* wrote. "The fresh evaluation of the Yellow River and the success of 'He Shang' also reflect the prevailing social trends in China."

A rare sight in a public exhibit in China, nude photographs entitled "Human History" are displayed in a Beijing Museum in 1988.

Debate about the role of the arts in socialist China was a main topic when fifteen hundred writers and artists gathered in November for the first national conference of the China Federation of Literary and Art Circles in nine years.

Presenting the government view was Politburo Standing Committee member Hu Qili, the party's top commissar for culture and propaganda. Hu, regarded as being in the reformist camp, reminded the artists that their main task was to "help boost the morale of the nation, improve the overall quality of the people and unite, encourage and inspire them with literary and art works." But he added that the "Hundred Flowers" concept of freedom of expression was now a reality, and "the party must not interfere arbitrarily." In handling controversial subjects, "administrative orders should be avoided

whenever possible and at no time should such questions be handled by launching a political movement."

Artists at the meeting were more forthright about the need for the government to stop defining cultural and artistic values. Xia Yan, a leading leftist dramatist since the 1930s, said abandonment of the slogan "Literature and Art is Subordinate to Politics" was a big step in the "emancipation of the mind." Wu Zuguang, a playwright who was openly criticized during the anti-bourgeois liberalization campaign of the previous year, stressed that interference and meddling in the arts must be brought to an end. "Interference should not be allowed because literature and art works are intended for readers and audiences. They are the only ones who have the right to make suggestions."

The Voice of Dissent

The close of the writers and artists conclave was followed by a burst of artistic activity, some of it challenging the outer limits of censors' tolerance. In late December China's first exhibition of nude art opened to huge crowds at the prestigious China Art Gallery. The show, featuring realistic, abstract and expressionist depictions of nudes, contained one hundred and twenty-eight paintings by twenty-one artists. It was unique in that the organizers had raised their own money to finance the exhibition, and were entitled to a good share of the profits.

"We're making money. And that, for artists in China, is a rare thing. I don't care about the rest," said Ge Pengren, the assistant professor at the Central Academy of Fine Arts and organizer of the show, when asked about criticisms it was too commercial.

The sponsors charged up to ten times the usual entrance fee for art shows at state galleries, but still drew more than two hundred thousand people in the half-month the exhibit was open. Art fans also bought up a book with glossy photos of the works on display and postcards featuring the paintings. Some art critics grumbled about the money-making aspects of the show and there was some criticism that a heavy percentage of the viewers were leering juveniles, but on the whole critics praised the exhibit for breaking new ground in China's constricted art environment and contributing to a more relaxed and mature attitude toward human nudity.

The exhibit's one sour note came when six wom-en who had modelled for paintings in the show went on strike and threatened to sue the Central Academy of Fine Arts for publishing the book of paintings and the postcard without their knowledge and permission. Nude modeling in state art academies had been revived in 1984, but many Chinese still regarded such work as licentious, and many models concealed the nature of their well-paying jobs from families and husbands. Two women finally went to court, one saying she had been driven from her home and her husband was divorcing her after they learned of her nude modeling. "Society considers me worse than a prostitute because I've done in the open what those women do in the dark," the other model said. "I can't even go to the public baths because other women point at me and laugh."

China's first "sex movie" opened in Beijing in January, but "Widows' Village," a story of frustrated love in a taboo-dominated Chinese fishing village in the 1940s, proved a disappointment for viewers who had come to be titillated. Scalpers were drawing in crowds with lurid suggestions of sex on the screen, but the love scenes from the unexpurgated version shown outside China fell victim to the censors' scissors.

Art and free expression aside, various activities that many older Chinese still considered to be steeped in Western decadence were flourishing.

Private bars, many of a decidedly seedy nature, were springing up in Shanghai, Canton and to a lesser extent Beijing. The authorities periodically raided and closed the more unsavory ones, but others soon took their place. Discos became a favorite place for young women to meet well-heeled young men—often taxi drivers and private entrepreneurs with lots of cash.

The revealing styles shown off at myriad fashion shows spilled out onto the streets, where young women sported miniskirts and high heels and glamorized themselves with the new brands of makeup advertised every day on television. Pool became the rage, with shaky-legged tables appearing on sidewalks throughout the cities and alongside rice paddies in the countryside. Young men spent hours around the tables, usually with an American cigarette dangling from their lips.

The official press had begun issuing alarums about the growing problem of prostitution, not only among women lured by the possibilities of quick

A trio of Chinese models, wearing Scandinavian furs as part of a promotion program, pose with a traffic policeman.

Marriage and Romance

One subtle but devastating result of the Cultural Revolution was its creation of a generation of Chinese, most of them women, condemned to live out their lives lonely, single and childless.

Millions of youthful Chinese, exiled to the countryside to labor in the fields or study the thoughts of Chairman Mao during the political campaign, had no time or inclination for romance.

When Mao's pragmatic successors allowed them to return home, many already had surpassed thirty years of age, traditionally considered past the window of marriageability in China, especially for women. They became known as "da qingnian" or "older youths." Sometimes the women were called "lao guniang" or "old maids."

Their plight was aggravated by the historical lack of privacy in China and the absence of places for people of the opposite sex to socialize. About the only way to meet potential companions was through introductions at work or school.

The problem of China's lonely heart generation became so severe that in the early 1980s Chinese leaders organized mass matchmaking drives in cities throughout the country.

Through the All China Women's Federation, singles were encouraged to register and state their preference for the kind of mate they wanted. The federation sponsored dances, picnics, even a computer dating service in Beijing.

Whether this effort reduced the number of singles older than thirty has never been disclosed, although the press occasionally has publicized a few mass marriage ceremonies of partners who found their lovers through state-run matchmakers. The government's Cupid role also has faced a persistent problem: picky mates. Despite vastly increased opportunities for unwed people to find love and romance, many sought perfect partners who simply didn't exist.

"Men's and women's criteria for selecting mates are not practical. This situation is unsettling," the party mouthpiece People's Daily once complained.

"Women want a man who is well-built, well-educated, talented and has a good profession," it said. "Men want a woman with the face of an actress, body of an athlete, manner of a servant and cooking skill of a chef. This can be found only in fairyland."

CHINA

riches by propositioning a foreign businessmen, but also involving only Chinese. Hundreds of massage parlors opened for business in southern cities around Canton, and many were closed for selling sex. Cases of venereal disease, which China claimed to have eliminated in the 1950s, were doubling and tripling every year and the government put out dire warnings about the dangers of AIDS, although only a few isolated cases, mostly involving foreigners, had been discovered in China.

The government was also increasingly concerned about pornography as publishing houses, now required to turn a profit, rejected more serious fare for books filled with sex and violence. Bookstalls did a steady business in postcards and picture books offering soft-core pornography.

On February 5, the nude art exhibit was followed by an even more controversial show, the largest exhibition of avant-garde art in China's history. The show, at the same China Art Gallery, was closed within hours when a women artist, defying a ban on performance art, shot her own model of a phone booth with a BB gun. The woman, who served a three-day jail term with her boyfriend accomplice, said she had wanted to add a destructive element to her work. There were other performers on the opening day, including a man selling shrimp to protest the commercialization of art and an artist who tossed handfuls of condoms and money on the floor. Near the entrance was a black coffin on top of which was written, "This exhibition is in honor of all the Chinese artists who gave their lives for modern art." The show reopened five days later, and thousands flocked to see the state of avant-garde art in China, which included surrealist paintings, abstract sculpture and such oddities as a waterbed filled with dead fish and three huge balloons shaped like breasts.

Beyond such public spectacles, musicians, poets and writers were beginning to form their own salons where they could openly discuss new trends in their fields and express their frustrations about past strictures. "None of us knows how long this will last," a self-described "free" artist said. "But it's a good time to be creating."

For the government, a far more worrisome development was the opening of political discussion salons, where students, teachers and other concerned people, including party members, gathered to exchange ideas on how to bring about democratic reform in China.

They attracted people like Su Shaozhi, former head of the Research Institute of Marxism-Leninism-Mao Tse-tung Thought in the Academy of Social Sciences. "China is in crisis—political, economic and cultural," the outspoken Su said. "We need to democratize this society to allow the people to supervise the party and the government."

The recognized leader of the reform movement was astrophysicist Fang Lizhi. Fang had been working at the Beijing Observatory at Beijing University since being fired as vice president of the Science and Technology University in Hefei and expelled from the party in January 1987 for stirring up pro-democracy sentiments among students. He was allowed to continue his research work unimpeded, and, although he was prevented from accepting invitations to visit the United States and Britain, was given approval for trips to Italy and Australia for academic conferences. The official press wrote in glowing terms of how he was publishing books and actively pursuing his scientific career. The obvious point, made with some truth, was that intellectuals who clashed with the party might suffer some political repercussions, but unlike in the past would not be ostracized or jailed and would be encouraged to play a positive role in society.

Fang, however, would not mildly retreat behind his telescope. Protected in part by his newly won international reputation as the voice of Chinese dissent, Fang spoke out against the system with increasing boldness in interviews and speeches both at home and abroad. He said Marxism was outdated, urged that one-party rule be ended and criticized China's human rights record. "I'm a soldier who already crossed the river," he said when asked if he was afraid of being arrested. "There's no way to turn back."

In January, Fang made the audacious move of writing an open letter to Deng Xiaoping, urging him to declare a general amnesty for political prisoners to mark the fortieth anniversary in 1989 of the founding of the People's Republic. Fang in particular singled out Wei Jingsheng, a leading activist in the Democracy Wall movement of the late 1970s who was in the tenth year of a fifteen-year prison term for counter-revolutionary activities. Wei, China's most famous political prisoner, had disappeared in the Chinese gulag. People who had passed through the prison system said he was alive but may have gone insane from the long years of harsh treatment and solitude. Chinese authorities insisted he was in good health.

Fang, in speeches that January, stressed the time had come to form pressure groups to force the government to change. He emphasized, however, that "this pressure is not intended to overthrow anybody. We only want to pressure people to go in the

252

*Astrophysicist Fang Lizhi, a leading voice in sup-
port of democratic reform, in front of a picture of
Albert Einstein.*

right direction." On February 4, Fang stood up at a lunar new year's tea party attended by local celebrities in the arts, science and trade and urged them to do their part for human rights in China. "Some people think China doesn't need democracy, but I think human rights is basic."

That same month, thirty-three well-known intellectuals followed Fang's lead and wrote a second letter, this one to the National People's Congress, urging an amnesty of political prisoners. The letter, the first of its kind by intellectuals, said an amnesty "would be beneficial to the atmosphere of reform and in accordance with the increasing respect for human rights which is a pervasive trend in the world today." Among the signatories were Bing Xin, eighty-seven, one of China's most respected women writers; poet Bei Dao; Marxist theorist Su Shaozhi; writer Wu Zuguang; former *People's Daily* editor Wang Ruoshui and novelist Zhang Jie.

The question in everyone's minds was how long the government would tolerate this current outbreak of free expression. Many believed the government, using a method that had trapped its critics several times in the past, would give the intellectuals their opportunity to speak out and then, when they went beyond proper bounds, crack down hard.

Some expressed optimism that this time things were different. The theory that the conservatives were waiting to ensnare liberal thinkers "doesn't take into account that the Chinese have changed," said Hou Hanru, a philosopher at the Fine Arts Academy. "The people aren't listening to the government anymore. If it yells again, nobody will follow."

Even the official press was emboldened to speak out on the issue of human rights. In January the *People's Daily* reported that there had been more than eleven thousand cases of human rights violations in China in 1988, including torture, illegal arrests and unwarranted search and seizure. Also in January, the lively daily *China Youth News* reported an incident in Chengdu, Sichuan, where members of the official Youth League who tried to set up a street sale of scarce goods were beaten and shocked with electric truncheons by government thugs.

Fang offered what was probably one of the most telling factors behind the government's benign neglect of dissent—that China's leaders were far too busy dealing with the nation's worsening economic situation. "The government right now is very weak due to economic problems," he said. "Even inside the party they can't agree on things."

The austerity policy announced by Premier Li in September had yet to show positive results. Con-

sumer prices at the end of 1988 were up by as much as 36 percent over a year earlier. Industrial output fell 10.9 percent in January from December—a good sign as the government tried to slow growth—but in the wrong areas of energy, steel and raw materials. The energy crisis was becoming more serious, with millions of workers idled every day because their factories lacked power and raw materials.

The government reported that losses incurred by state-run enterprises jumped 26.6 percent in 1988 and that one out of four central-government run plants were losing money. Subsidies to prop up inefficient, money-losing operations were draining the national budget of about $10.8 billion a year.

In the cities more than one-third of residents saw their real incomes decline in 1988 as a result of rising prices. Panic-buying of grain, soap, toothpaste and other items, sparked by rumors of price hikes, was reported in some cities.

The grain harvest in 1988 was disappointing for the fourth straight year, due in part to farmers' reluctance to grow grain at the low state-set prices. *The Peasants Daily* said in January that hundreds of farmers in rural Anhui province were making dangerous midnight truck runs through checkpoints along the provincial border in order to reach richer neighboring provinces where grain commanded a higher price on the free market. At least one young driver was killed as he tried to crash through a border guardpost.

The fast-growing rural and township enterprises that had provided work for about eighty million people in the countryside were facing tough times because the state was depriving them of energy and materials and restricting credit. The Agricultural Bank of China said credit for rural industry would be cut from $4 billion in 1988 to $1.9 billion in 1989 so more money could go to agricultural production. Many of the seventeen million rural and township enterprises, which grossed $5.7 billion in profits in 1988, had to scale down operations or go out of business. Some consolidation was needed—many of the rural factories were polluting energy-wasters using outdated equipment and producing low-quality goods. But the loss of jobs in the countryside resulted in millions of transients drifting into Beijing, Canton and other cities looking for construction work and other manual labor jobs, creating a whole new set of social problems.

Li Peng, in his work report to the National People's Congress in March, stressed that "both government and people should be mentally prepared for a few years of austerity. . . . If we set a good example and explain clearly to the people the need for tight-

ening our belts, they will surely understand and support it." Li also made veiled criticisms of Zhao Ziyang's advocacy of a fast pace in adopting new economic reforms. "We . . . did not pay sufficient attention to taking comprehenisve and coordinated measures and failed to tighten control and supervision at the right moment. We were too optimistic."

Some young economists, meanwhile, were saying that China needed to go faster, not slower, in dismantling state controls and incorporating more private enterprise in the economy. Several economists

A Chinese success story of the '80s pictured here, with Xu Kaye (left), his wife and son, and their family car, a rare and valuable commodity. Xu, a former peasant and assembly line worker, owns a television parts factory in Ningbo.

at the Chinese Academy of Social Sciences, taking advantage of the current tolerance toward controversial opinions, called for China to abandon public ownership. Others proposed allowing workers and

Li Peng Emerges

The Standing Committee of the National People's Congress, China's legislature, on November 24, 1987, convened to name Vice Premier Li Peng, a fifty-nine-year-old technocrat, China's acting premier. Li succeeded Zhao Ziyang as head of government following Zhao's appointment as general secretary of the Communist Party.

Li was for many a political enigma, a man who pledged allegiance to the reforms and open door policy but who could not shake the widely held view that he was a "conservative" who preferred central planning to a more market-oriented economy.

The conservative label was in part born of his past association with the Soviet Union. He studied at the Moscow Electrodynamics Academy from 1948 to 1954 and was said to speak good Russian. Li also had spent most of his career in China working in departments concerned with heavy industry, areas where central planning came more prominently into play. He was chief engineer of the country's largest hydroelectric complex in Jilin province and head of the Beijing Power Supply Bureau before becoming minister of Power Industry in 1979. He was named vice premier in 1983 and head of the State Education Commission in 1985.

A strong advocate of nuclear power and development of China's high technology industries, Li said China must introduce more Western technology and "adopt some useful and good methods practiced in capitalist society." He told foreign reporters that his conservative label was a "misunderstanding" and that he fully cooperated with Zhao and other leaders in promoting reform.

Yet Li also made clear that the reforms should be confined to well-defined socialist parameters. "We cannot implement the capitalist economic and political system, and cannot implement the capitalist concept of values or the decadent way of life because our socialist system runs counter to it," he told students in late 1985. "To allow bourgeois freedoms would only make our country's affairs chaotic."

Foreign visitors who met with Li were impressed by his no-nonsense style, his command of facts and his attention to detail. Some Chinese, however, described him as a plodder who owed his rise to the top to his connections with senior leaders. At age three, following the execution of his father by the Nationalists, Li became one of several dozen orphans taken under the wing of Chou En-lai and his wife Deng Yingchao. He was said to have a close relationship with Deng, who, like her late husband, was one of China's most beloved people.

---

institutions to trade their shares in their companies on a national stock exchange.

Soviet Foreign Minister Eduard Shevardnadze, returning Qian Qichen's visit to Moscow in December, arrived in Beijing in early February to finalize plans for the first Sino-Soviet summit since an acrimonious meeting between Mao Tse-tung and Nikita Khrushchev in Beijing in 1959, the year before the Sino-Soviet split. On February 4, after a meeting with Deng Xiaoping, Shevardnadze announced that Mikhail Gorbachev would come to Beijing in mid-May. He added that the two sides had agreed to work toward reducing offensive forces and easing tensions along the Sino-Soviet border. Shevardnadze also claimed that broad agreement had been reached on the need for the two countries to work toward ending the conflict in Cambodia, the issue China insisted was the key to normal relations between Moscow and Beijing.

The second major diplomatic event of February, a visit by President George Bush, started out in mutual harmony but ended in discord, embroiled in China's increasingly volatile political situation.

Bush had been in office only a month, and there were no major bilateral issues that had to be dealt with. But the new president, in Asia for the funeral of Japan's Emperor Hirohito, decided to make a quick trip to Beijing to renew old acquaintances going back to his days as U.S. liaison officer in the capital and reinforce the two nations' strong ties before the Gorbachev visit. Much of it was pure theater of political good will—a stop to meet the people in Tiananmen Square, attending church services, receiving bicycles from Premier Li and being granted the first live interview by a foreign dignitary on Chinese television.

But the Chinese obviously had dissidents on their mind and were waiting to make clear their unhappiness over U.S. support for China's pro-democracy forces. Deng's message to Bush, that China needed political stability to advance its economic reforms, was of a subtle kind, but Zhao, in a lengthy discourse, came right to the point. A few people "blame the difficulties in the reform of the economic system on political reasons. They call for the introduction of multiparty politics and the parliament politics of the Western countries," Zhao said. Such people are trying "to stir up social disorder. . . . Largely speaking they will make the reform fail." Zhao added that "some personages in American

An enterprising photographer with a set up business on the Great Wall of China at Badaling, selling instant snapshots of Chinese and Western tourists.

A Chinese couple carries a new TV set home in Beijing in 1988, as a decade of reform led to increased consumerism. (In 1981, less than 1 percent of urban families owned a color set; in 1988, it was more than 30 percent.)

society who support those people who are dissatisfied with the Chinese government will not contribute to the stability of China's political situation and the undergoing of the reform, nor will it be conducive to the friendship between China and the United States."

The leadership's annoyance over U.S. support for political reform came as no surprise, although it was noteworthy that Zhao, regarded as China's most liberal leader, had delivered the harsh lecture to the U.S. President. It may be that Zhao, already in retreat because of the problems plaguing his economic reforms, was trying to defend himself from the increasingly vocal conservatives by showing a more hardline position toward political dissent.

On February 26, China provoked a diplomatic incident by mobilizing police to prevent Fang Lizhi from attending a barbecue hosted by Bush for Chinese leaders and well-known figures. Two other political critics, Su Shaozhi and Wu Zuguang, attended the party at the Sheraton Great Wall Hotel without any problem, but police barred Fang and his wife Li Shuxian from the door and then harassed them as they tried to contact American officials and reach the U.S. Embassy.

Bush expressed regret over the mistreatment of the invited guest, and Chinese activists said they were outraged. "I was ready to go back to my work and forget about politics," said poet Bei Dao. "But if this is how they are openly interfering in human rights, then I must fight back." Journalist Dai Qing said the methods used to strike at Fang were "neolithic. Our government has changed so much for the better, it was pitiful for them to do this now."

The government, however, was unapologetic. The Foreign Ministry, in a statement, said the invitation for Fang to attend a dinner held in honor of Chinese leaders "can only be interpreted as a support to this kind of people and disrespect for the host country." It added that China was "surprised at the irresponsible remarks" made by the United States concerning the incident and "express our deep regret."

In general the government was becoming more strident in its criticisms of political activism. The Justice Ministry, responding to the petitions by intellectuals for an amnesty of political prisoners stated that "it is against China's legal principles to stir up public opinion in an attempt to overturn independent jurisdiction by soliciting signatures." Government spokesman Yuan Mu, at a March 14 news conference, said China was "not happy" about the activities of dissidents, who he said were "relying on foreign forces." He stressed that "no one is allowed to infringe upon the interests of the state, society or other citizens."

Premier Li, in his work report to the NPC on March 20, also made clear that opposition to government policies would not be tolerated. "All social unrest and turmoil, without exception, hamper construction and reform, to the extreme detriment of the fundamental interests of the people."

The intellectuals, however, showed little signs of being intimidated. At the end of February a group of journalists, engineers and other intellectuals banded together to oppose the Three Gorges hydroelectric project, a massive dam project on the Yangtze River that had been under consideration for decades. Critics claimed the damming of the river would displace millions of people and cause incalculable environmental damage. Never before, however, had intellectuals joined together to form a united front to oppose the government over an environmental issue. "Since the 1949 revolution, my country has undertaken thousands of mistaken projects," said journalist Dai Qing. "You would think that in a planned economy things would be carried out scientifically. That's not the case in China."

In early March, forty-two prominent scientists signed an open letter urging China's top leaders to guarantee freedom of speech, publication and information. They asked for the release of "all young people who were convicted and sentenced to labor reform because of ideological problems."

Later that month, forty-three more intellectuals signed a petition urging the NPC "to release a large number of detained prisoners . . . as the country prepares to celebrate its fortieth anniversary."

The petitions for the release of political prisoners—China consistently denied there were any political prisoners in its jails—was gaining wide publicity and support outside the country. On March 29 a group of Hong Kong activists arrived in Beijing to present the NPC with a similar appeal for an amnesty signed by twenty-four thousand people. They were stopped by customs agents and their documents were confiscated.

Chinese authorities, ever sensitive about upsetting Hong Kong's fragile confidence in the Sino-British decision to return the colony to Chinese sovereignty in 1997, were embarrassed by the storm raised by the Hong Kong group. The next day, the overzealous customs officials returned the documents, and a low-ranking NPC official was produced to receive the petition from the Hong Kong compatriots.

But Wang Hanbin, vice chairman of the NPC, also made clear at a news conference that there was neither need nor plans for an amnesty for Wei Jing-sheng and others convicted of counter-revolutionary crimes. And on April 3, at another NPC news conference, Premier Li warned that democratic reform, if "carried out in haste or an excessive extent, . . . will certainly affect the situation of unity and stability, and if the stable situation is undermined then it won't make our work of construction of reform smooth."

The annual session of the NPC ended the next day after the nearly three thousand delegates passed laws giving citizens limited rights to sue the government and delineating the powers of the Communist Party- dominated NPC. On the whole the session had been more conservative than the 1988 NPC plenum, with less talk of political reform and a far more sober evaluation of the problems arising from economic reform. Ironically, the NPC's fledgling effort to become a more democratic body was best demonstrated by conservative opposition to a bill giving the freewheeling special economic zone of Shenzhen in southern China the power to

enact its own laws. Two hundred and seventy-four deputies voted against the bill, and eight hundred and five abstained in the most opposition the NPC had ever shown to a bill given to the body for approval.

Meanwhile the Beijing government, distracted by political dissent close to home, had to deal with the worst outbreak yet of violence in Tibet. The troubles began on March 5, the anniversary of the 1988 riots, when thirteen Buddhist monks and nuns began an illegal march through central Lhasa, waving banners and shouting "Independence for Tibet." They were soon joined by a crowd of hundreds that began throwing stones at police and smashing windows. The melee quickly spread throughout the central

A Chinese man admires an instant self-portrait at the Great Wall of China near Beijing. In 1980, color pictures, much less instant ones, were almost unknown among Chinese amateur photographers.

city, with Tibetans trashing the stores and restaurants of Chinese and attacking the government and Communist Party headquarters. The riots continued into the next day, with thousands hurling stones and throwing goods from Chinese stores onto bonfires. The government claimed twelve people were killed while Tibetan sources put the death toll as high as one hundred. Foreign travelers in Lhasa estimated that twenty to thirty lost their lives. On March 7 Beijing announced that martial law would go into effect in Lhasa at midnight and began door-to-door searches for participants in the riots.

It was the first time martial law was imposed in China since the chaotic days of the Cultural Revolution. Foreign tourists were ordered out of the city—foreign journalists were already banned from entering—and the remote mountain capital again became

nearly inaccessible to the outside world.

In Beijing, with the coming of warmer spring weather, political activism began to move from the salons and discussion groups out onto the campuses. On April 3 a small wall poster went up at Beijing University signed by sixty graduate and undergraduate students and demanding the school "protect our rights of freedom of speech and association." The message protested "lawless" university regulations prohibiting students from meeting to

A few Chinese economists proposed the establishment of a nationwide stock exchange on the American model, a radical break with socialist ideology, but these two bond clerks at Beijing's Finance Market had few customers and little to do in 1989.

discuss democracy and political change.

The poster was written by twenty-year-old history major Wang Dan, a name that was to become known to students throughout China in the coming weeks of the democracy movement.

Two days later about two hundred and fifty students at Beijing University defied the school prohibition against public gatherings and met for two hours on campus grounds to discuss politics and listen to Fang Lizhi's wife Li Shuxian, a professor of physics and like her husband an eloquent voice for democratic reform. Wang Dan, who attended the meeting, said, "School officials accuse us of having a special goal, but really we don't. We're just trying to create an atmosphere where people can discover things."

Others in the crowd, while responding to the appeals for democracy, were wary about getting involved in the movement. Older students noted that job assignments were coming up, and they didn't want to do anything that would jeopardize their chances for a good placement. Some expressed pessimism that students could in any way affect the course of the nation. "It's not so much fear that I feel," said one student. "It's just hopelessness. Our leaders don't listen to the people. They never will."

That same day several hundred police moved onto Tiananmen Square and sealed off about three-fourths of the square to prevent rumored demonstrations to commemorate the April 5, 1976, incident when tens of thousands of people spontaneously converged on the square to mourn Premier Chou En-lai, who had died in January, and criticize the leftists who controlled the government.

In Shanghai that day, police detained Chen Jun, the part-owner of a private bar in Beijing with ties to the Chinese pro-democracy movement abroad who had played an active role in organizing the first amnesty petition. Two days later Chen was put on a plane for Hong Kong and then onward to the United States, where he held a green card entitling him to permanent residence.

But government attempts to stifle dissent collapsed on April 15 when Hu Yaobang, the reformist leader who was ousted as party chief in January 1987 for failing to stop student demonstrations, died of heart failure at age seventy-three. Within hours of the announcement of his death, new posters went up at Beijing University praising the man students felt had been victimized because of his dedication to reform.

"Those who should not die have died, but those who should die . . . " read one poster making an apparent reference to the aging conservatives who continued to wield power in the party. Hundreds of students gathered around to read the posters and mourn the man who, more in death than in life, was to become their hero. "Now there is only Zhao," said one student.

"It's not Hu Yaobang we miss," said another, reflecting how Hu was about to become a symbol that would give life to a nationwide movement.

"It's democracy we miss."

Old and new in China, as a young Chinese woman drives a two-horse coach in front of the World Center Building under construction in Beijing. Skyscraper building was a boom although many foreign companies reduced business in China after the Tiananmen bloodshed.

Mao, Revised

Mao Tse-tung's flashes of genius and monstrous mistakes have been well documented. But With each passing year since his death, new revelations have redefined "the Great Helmsman" in a much more critical light. They suggest he was startlingly mercurial and contradictory, obsessed with personal comfort and dangerously naive about what was happening in China and the world.

Some of the most damaging post-mortem information on Mao is a recent compilation of previously uncirculated talks, letters and other writings by the chairman in the late 1950s.

Titled "The Secret Speeches of Chairman Mao," translated by a team of Harvard scholars, the collection shows Mao had little understanding about farming despite his peasant background;insisted China had no population problem, and believed the Western embargo of the country in the 1950s was good because it promoted a crisis atmosphere that would mobilize the Chinese to leap ahead.

At the communist hierarchy's retreat in the seaside resort of Beidaihe in 1957, for example, shortly before Mao decreed the "Great Leap Forward" campaign, he instructed subordinates to enforce close planting for fruit trees because "when they all grow together, they will be comfortable." The directive was disastrous.

Likewise, he rejected the idea that scientific breeding of super-hardy crops would work, despite its enormous success in the United States and other advanced countries.

At the same time, Mao predicted that China's labor-intensive communes would one day produce so much grain they would distribute it free to other countries. Under Mao, grain production stalled.

Up to now, evidence had suggested Mao grudgingly accepted responsibility for the catastrophe caused by the Great Leap Forward, his effort to mobilize China's masses to overtake developed capitalist countries within a few years.

In a 1959 speech, for example, Mao criticized himself for exhorting peasants to build backyard steel furnaces, which resulted in brittle, useless scrap iron and enormous waste. "You should blame me because there are heaps of things I didn't attend to," he said.

Yet other evidence suggests Mao flip-flopped on responsibility for the Great Leap Forward and continued to relish the heaven-moving spirit of such mass campaigns, even if they ended in disaster. When Defense Minister Peng Dehuai criticized Mao for the Great Leap in 1959, Mao dismissed him.

New information about Mao also suggests he had no idea how to spend money or take care of himself, leaving those tasks to his personal secretary, his succession of four wives and a retinue of attractive young women.

Like many other elderly Chinese male leaders, Mao seemed to have a fondness for surrounding himself with nubile members of the opposite sex, such as his Brooklyn-born English interpreter Nancy Tang and a pretty young literary assistant, Wang Hairong.

He also had a penchant for fatty pork, and often gorged himself despite warnings from his doctors. By the time Mao was in his sixties, he was obese and rasped for breath.

Memoirs by a former Mao bodyguard show that Mao never ate, slept or exercised regularly, despite the image of health he promoted by his famous swim across the Yangtze.

He was a sleeping pill addict and would down them after three or four days without rest. He sucked on tea leaves to avoid constipation and puffed so many cigarettes his bodyguards got sick from the smoke.

Mao's crudeness and hostility toward intellectuals have been well documented by foreign scholars, though these parts of his personality aren't widely evident from his works still available in China.

In a 1965 directive on public health, for example, Mao complained that state medical workers were treating only a fraction of the people who needed attention, concentrating their work on research and shunning the peasants, who needed medicine the most.

"Medical education should be reformed. There's no need to read so many books," he said. "The more books one reads the more stupid one gets."

He also ordered medical staff to stop wearing

masks when working because "this creates distance betweeen doctor and patient from the start."

The post-Mao Chinese government's effort to demystify the cult of the chairman proceeded slowly and deliberately, beginning with his famous little red book of quotations.

That revolutionary classic is now a collector's item because most copies were confiscated or destroyed after Mao died. Chinese smokers have used the pages for cigarette paper.

By the early 1980s, Mao's moderate successors blamed him for many of China's calamities. They were uncompromisingly blunt about it in a now-famous twenty-thousand-word document released in 1981, which called the Cultural Revolution a "long drawn-out and grave blunder. Nonetheless, they tempered this criticism with his good work and far-sighted vision as a young revolutionary guerrilla.

The Chairman Mao Memorial Hall, as the mausoleum in central Beijing is named, has been mostly closed since its completion in 1977. That is largely because it's considered an embarrassment, many Chinese have said.

Deng Xiaoping reportedly has considered tearing it down, but that would be a highly sensitive move that could arouse a backlash. So Deng has done what some Mao critics have called the next best thing: allowed the first Kentucky Fried Chicken restaurant in China to open up across the street.

On the 90th anniversary of Mao's birth, Dec. 26, 1983, the Deng regime used the occasion to transform the Mao mausoleum into a revolutionary hall of fame, with prominent attention devoted to other heros of the Chinese revolution including Liu Shaoqi, Mao's old nemesis hounded to death by the chairman as an "imperialist lackey" during the Cultural Revolution.

A biography in the room dedicated to Liu asserts he was "incorrectly criticized" in 1967 and died two years later, but it never mentions who did the criticizing.

Mao has his own memorabilia room as well, adjoining the air-conditioned vault where his preserved cadaver lies in a sealed glass tomb with a red flag draped over it.

But the Mao chronology in his room never mentions the Great Leap or spiteful "anti-rightist" campaigns meant to flush out critics of his policies in the 1950s.

Nor does it play up Mao's relationship with his last wife, Jiang Qing, ringleader of the notorious "Gang of Four" radicals blamed for the Cultural Revolution and its aftermath.

For visitors lucky enough to tour the mausoleum, the best attraction is a souvenir stand that sells Chairman Mao chopsticks, thermometers, combs and jasmine teabags. All are inscribed with the words, "Chairman Mao Memorial Hall, Souvenir of Reverence."

Mao Tse-tung leading victorious Communist troops into Beijing in 1949.

X

Blood of Tiananmen

Hu's death came at a decidedly bad time for the Chinese authorities. Student activism was already at a high level in response to the general mood of openness in the first months of 1989 and the appeals for democratic reform being made by Fang Lizhi and other leading intellectuals.

Students were also beginning to focus on the seventieth anniversary of the May 4th Movement, China's most famous student-led drive for democracy. The 1919 movement, led by Beijing University students, began as a protest against Japanese colonization of Chinese territory but developed into a campaign for democratic and scientific reform. The Communist Party, which also embraces the movement as a starting point for its leftist revolution, warned the students that rebellion against the authorities was fine in the past, but was no longer permitted.

The first march came on April 17, with thousands of students in Beijing and Shanghai taking to the streets. Students from Beijing's Political Science and Law College led the way, laying wreathes in Hu's honor at the base of a monument to Communist martyrs in Tiananmen Square. They sang the Internationale and chanted slogans for about thirty minutes before dispersing. Groups from other schools soon followed. Many of the students said they were participating to honor Hu, and not to make a political statement, but students cheered when one person climbed onto the monument and demanded the resignation of the Politburo. They also cheered a call for Chinese leaders to reassess Hu's place in history and apologize for unspecified past mistakes.

The next day there was a steady stream of march-ers arriving at the square to lay wreaths on the monument. Meanwhile, hundreds of students staged a day-long sit-in in front of the Great Hall of the People, the seat of government located on the west side of the square, demanding freedom of speech and press and public disclosures of the incomes of officials. Later that evening a crowd that swelled to ten thousand with onlookers marched around the square and then headed for Zhongnan-hai, the red wall-enclosed Communist Party compound west of the square.

About 3,000 students milled around the red-lac-quered gate of the party headquarters and shouted slogans, but repeated efforts by some students to push their way into the compound were stopped by plainclothes police. Shortly before dawn, more than five hundred police peacefully dislodged the demonstrators from the gate and sent them on their way home. The students, while accomplishing little, were taken with their own audacity. Not since the Cultural Revolution, when leftist Red Guard youths tried to storm Zhongnanhai to drag out "capitalist roaders" among the party leadership, had students taken their cause to the threshold of power in China.

"This is the most serious demonstration in the past ten years," one student said.

About six thousand students marched on Zhong-nanhai again on the night of the 19th, and for the first time the rallies turned violent. The students

A replica of the Statue of Liberty in front of city government offices in Shanghai, where students demonstrated.

chanted for Premier Li to come out and yelled slogans for democracy and an end to corruption until about midnight, when authorities cordoned off nearby intersections and peacefully split the crowd in two. But about four hours later, with about three thousand protesters still on the main Changan Avenue, police charged, beating and kicking several young people who failed to flee in time. About one hundred and fifty students were dragged away from Zhongnanhai and detained for a short time. Some protesters threw bottles at police and Xinhua said four officers were hurt by flying bottles and bricks.

Some students deliberately smashed soft drink bottles in a political gesture of clear intent. The word for "small bottle" in Chinese—xiaoping—sounds like the name of senior leader Deng Xiaoping, although it is written in different characters.

On April 20 the Beijing city government warned

President Yang Shangkun (at microphones) presides at funeral service for Hu Yaobang. From left to right: Wan Li, Yang, Zhao Ziyang, Deng Xiaoping, Li Peng.

that future demonstrators would be "dealt with severely according to the law," and only about fifteen hundred students braved a heavy downpour and slogged their way to the square. But it was only a temporary respite.

Similar demonstrations mourning Hu and demanding democratic reform were taking place in Shanghai, Nanjing, Tianjin, Wuhan, Hefei and other cities. And on April 21 an estimated one hundred thousand students, workers and peasants gathered on Tiananmen Square to hear speeches and lay wreaths in what may have been the biggest spontaneous rally in China since 1949.

The government announced that on Saturday, when official mourning ceremonies for Hu would be held in the Great Hall, access to streets around the square and the Great Hall would be limited. But as dawn broke, and forty thousand students remained on the square, the government caved in and said they would not stop students from congregating on Tiananmen for their own memorials to the fallen leader.

Up to a hundred-and-fifty thousand came, with

people shouting "Long Live Freedom" and "Down With Dictatorship, Down With Corruption,"and waving colored pro-democracy banners during fifteen hours of demonstrations. More than thirty universities in Beijing and other universities elsewhere were represented. Within shouting distance, inside the Great Hall, about four thousand officials gathered in the morning to pay their last respects to Hu. Zhao, in a short speech, praised Hu as a man "brave enough to admit his mistakes and to insist upon what he thought right. He never tried to hold back his opinions."

Some officials, upon entering or leaving the hall, stopped momentarily behind the protection of three lines of police to gaze out at the great masses of students and other citizens who had come to honor a man they felt had been wronged by the system and tell the Communist Party it had lost the support of the people.

The Tiananmen demonstration ended peacefully, as did rallies in Shanghai, Nanjing, Tianjin and other cities. But riots broke out in the ancient capital of Xian, when non-student mobs shouting anti-government slogans tried to break into the provincial government compound. According to Xinhua, the rioters burned about twenty buildings and ten vehicles and injured one hundred and thirty security forces. Eighteen were arrested. The southern city of Changsha was also hit by rioting the next day, when unruly crowds following a student march began smashing shop and car windows. Ninety-eight people, including six students, were arrested.

That Sunday, April 23, the *Science and Technology Daily* failed to appear until the afternoon because editors and reporters had been locked in an all-night debate over how to portray the Tiananmen rally. The reporters finally won, and the daily came out with a sympathetic but carefully worded account of the gathering, the first such objective description of the student demonstrations in the official press. Students also were collecting funds on street corners to start their own newspaper to present what they said would be an accurate account of the student movement.

The next day, April 24, tens of thousands of students in Beijing universities began a class boycott to press their demands for democracy, human rights and a free press. Posters went up on campuses demanding the resignation of Premier Li and saying Deng Xiaoping was too old and should withdraw from politics. Students held meetings, some under the aegis of newly formed independent student unions, to discuss their next moves. Student leaders stressed they wanted their protest to be peaceful

and legal, and that they were not trying to overthrow the government or the Communist Party.

Some said more than ten thousand soldiers from outlying counties were moved into Beijing over the weekend to prepare for an eventual crackdown.

The students, wavering over whether to proceed with their protests, were galvanized by a harsh editorial in the April 26 *People's Daily* that called the democracy movement "a planned conspiracy which . . . aims at negating the leadership of the party and the socialist system." The daily said the students were trying to "throw society into chaos and destroy the peaceful united political system."

"We must firmly stop such riots," Beijing's Communist Party chief Li Ximing told ten thousand city party officials. Beijing police banned collecting donations, handing out leaflets, giving speeches and public gatherings. But the students, saying the *People's Daily* slander must be answered, massed in the streets on April 27. More than one hundred and fifty thousand students and supporters burst past a police line on the square and temporarily occupied Tiananmen during a fifteen-hour walk around the city.

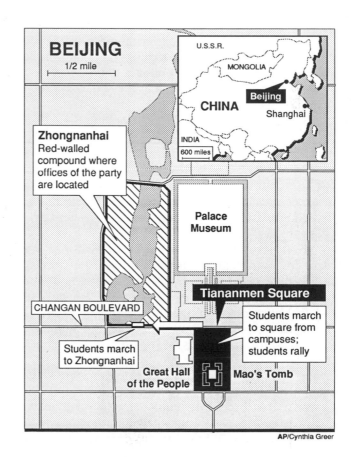

AP/Cynthia Greer

267

Tiananmen Square

Through triumph and turmoil, Tiananmen Square has served as the symbolic heart of political power in Beijing and the site of riveting moments in China's history.

For demonstrations and declarations, celebrations and Sunday outings, the Chinese head to the vast central square in the congested capital city. They mark momentous occasions and they leisurely pass their time at Tiananmen Square. They mourn there, think there, protest there and stroll there.

On one side stands Tiananmen, or the "Gate of Heavenly Peace," which is the main entrance to China's former imperial palace—the Forbidden City. Now, a huge portrait of Mao Tse-tung looks down on the square from the majestic structure once home to emperors and center of regal intrigue.

In 1949, Mao proclaimed the birth of the People's Republic of China from Tiananmen. The new Chinese flag with the hammer and sickle symbol of the Communist Party was raised as throngs of people celebrated the revolution that toppled the Nationalist government.

During the radical leftist campaign marking the 1966-76 Cultural Revolution, a million people were said to have gathered at the square on several occasions.

From a reviewing stand overlooking the square, Mao watched and offered inspiration to thousands of parading Red Guards, the Chinese youth who zealously struck out against Western influences, dissent and intellectual development as part of their leader's Great Proletarian Cultural Revolution.

The square was also the scene of a huge protest in 1976 that signaled the end of the chaotic Cultural Revolution.

The square was the site of important events even before the Communists came to power.

The May 4th Movement of 1919 established a tradition of Chinese students and intellectuals at the forefront of dissent, drawing hordes to the Gate of Heavenly Peace to protest concessions made to Japan after World War I.

The original square was built in 1651, in the early Qing Dynasty. The Communist government quadrupled its size to one hundred acres in 1958.

In the middle of the square is an obelisk known as the Monument to the Heroes of the Revolution.

At the south end are Mao's mausoleum and Qianmen, or the "front gate," which was the entrance to the road leading to the Forbidden City in earlier times.

The Great Hall of the People, the seat of government, is on the west side of the square. On the opposite side stands the Museum of Chinese

---

Thousands of workers, defying orders from their factories not to get involved in the demonstrations, helped students push through police lines and provided them with food and drink.

"My factory may fire me but I don't care," a bus plant foreman said as he walked near the front of the student procession. "These kids need help and I'm here to provide it."

A line of trucks with unarmed soldiers had circled the square to form a barricade, but the marchers swarmed onto the trucks, shouting, "Welcome 38th Army."

The central government continued to issue statements about the student-caused "turmoil," but also agreed to the student demands for a dialogue. However, the authorities said they would meet only representatives from official student organizations, not the new independent unions, an idea the students rejected.

Government spokesman Yuan Mu and State Education Commission Vice Minister He Dongchang on April 29 met forty-five selected students for a three-and-a-half hour dialogue in which students demanded that Li Peng meet them and that the press be allowed to report the truth. Yuan took a conciliatory stance, praising the students' "patriotic fervor," but urged the students to end their class boycott, which had spread to forty-one campuses in Beijing.

Wu'er Kaixi of Beijing Normal University, head of

A banner calling for freedom, democracy and enlightenment is carried in front of a giant portrait of Hu Yaobang.

A long view of Tiananmen Square, with the Chairman Mao Memorial Hall at the center, *between the Monument to the People's Heroes and Chengyangmen Gate.*

history and the Revolution.

A few hundred yards northwest of the square is Zhongnanhai, the compound where most of the nation's top leaders live. In earlier times, the area was a sanctuary for princes and mandarins.

Students calling for democratic reforms captured the world's attention from Tiananmen Square in 1989. Hundreds and perhaps thou-

sands died in the bloody clashes on June 3-4, but authorities said no one was killed on the venerable square.

The stone slabs of the square looked charred and scraped in places after Tiananmen was reopened following the military crackdown, but there was no other sign of violence.

the independent United Association of Beijing Universities, was invited to the meeting but then not allowed to attend after he refused to give up a plan to openly denounce the government's position that his group was illegal.

"We will by no means acknowledge that this meeting was a dialogue," Wu'er told reporters. "This is a plot to co-opt our movement. Our minimum condition is that they accept us as a legal organization."

More meetings were held over the next few days, with Beijing Communist Party Secretary and Mayor Li Ximing and Chen Xitong among the participants. But representatives from the United Association did not attend, and the government showed no signs of agreeing to their demands that the independent student group be given legal status.

Student leaders said they were also under pressure from teachers and other officials to stop their protests, particularly before the May 4th anniversary of China's first democratic movement. The students, however, were adamant about continuing their boycott, which had now spread to Tianjin and other cities, and forcing the government to meet some of their demands.

"Mother, I am not wrong," Wu'er Kaixi wrote in an open letter to his mother broadcast on a student-run loudspeaker at Beijing Normal University. "But perhaps for the sake of many more mothers and fathers in the future, you might have to lose your son. You always taught me to be courageous and speak out for my beliefs. That is what I am doing."

On Tuesday, May 2, sixty-five student leaders from thirty-three universities bicycled seven miles to deliver an ultimatum to the National People's Congress. The twelve-article, handwritten letter demanded that the government recognize the United Association of Beijing Universities and guarantee a free press, freedom of assembly and publication and an end to official corruption. If the demands were not met, they said they would march on Thursday, the anniversary of the May 4th Movement.

Police closed the square Thursday morning in an attempt to keep students away during the opening session at the Great Hall of the Asian Development Bank, meeting in China for the first time. Students at Beijing Normal also ran up against a wall of several hundred police who tried to push them back onto their campus. But the students broke through, and by early afternoon, after hours of trudging through the hot and dusty streets, descended on the square.

"Rise ye who refuse to be slaves," one group called out, singing the Chinese national anthem, as they passed the Communist Party headquarters at

A Chinese student reads a poem in front of a huge portrait of former Communist Party chief Hu Yaobang in Tiananmen Square in April 1989.

Zhongnanhai. Dozens of red and white banners calling for a free press and opposing corruption fluttered in the wind. Bystanders lined the streets by the thousaands, applauding and cheering the marchers and providing them with food, drinks and even money. Unlike the previous week's march, when students were angered by the *People's Daily* editorial, there was a festive, holiday atmosphere, a mood of defiant celebration.

At least fifty-five schools were represented in the march, including about ten from outside the city. They were joined by thousands of workers defying government warnings they would be fired if they attended the march. "This is the first time in forty years such a big movement for democracy has occurred," said one government employee. "I'll just show up at work tomorrow and see what happens."

A funeral wreath, banner and red flags make their way through a sea of people toward Martyrs Monument in Tiananmen Square, where thousands gathered to eulogize Hu Yaobang.

A group of three hundred journalists from the state-run press also held an unprecedented protest outside the gates of the Xinhua news agency. A group of journalists later joined the student march, calling for press freedom and supporting Qin Benli, the editor of a liberal Shanghai newspaper, the *World Economic Herald*, who was fired a week before after his paper published articles critical of the government.

The unarmed police could put up little resistance as the demonstrators, about one hundred thousand in all, streamed onto the square. Shortly before 4 p.m., student leaders ended the protest and announced that the two-week-old class boycott would end the next day. An hour later students left the square. Demonstrations were also held that day in Shanghai, Nanjing, Changsha and a number of other cities, but it appeared, for a brief moment, that May 4th might be the climax, and the student movement, lacking a next move after the triumphant street marches, might begin to taper off.

Zhao, in talks with Asian Development Bank officials on May 4, also gave impetus to the conciliatory mood by calling for "broad consultations and dialogue" with students, workers and intellectuals. Some students began drifting back to class the next day. The new independent student union at People's University said it chose to end the boycott "to seek a form of dialogue that is reasonable and practical and acceptable to both sides."

Students at Beijing University on Saturday, May 6, voted to continue their class strike, but with the start of the new week most Beijing students were

The two major student leaders, Wu'er Kaixi (r.) and Wang Dan talk to reporters in April 1989, after rejecting government-student dialogue as "a plot to co-opt our movement."

Chinese police try in vain to contain a crowd of student marchers during a May demonstration in Beijing.

back in class. Zhao, meeting a Turkish delegation, stressed that economic and political reform must go together and that many of the demands voiced by the students "represent problems that the party and government are trying to solve." He said the student movement had not gotten out of hand because of the tolerance of authorities and the "increasing reason" of the students.

But the students were merely catching their breaths and searching for new ways to express their demands for reforms. On May 9, a petition signed by more than one thousand journalists calling for a dialogue on press censorship was presented to the government. A group of five thousand students on bicycles responded to their appeal for press freedom the next day by riding to the offices of the *People's Daily* and the *Beijing Daily.* "People's reporters, speak for the people," the students chanted as

about two thousand local residents cheered them on.

The student bicyclists were joined by a band of fifty writers, poets and novelists. The students "should not be allowed to stand alone," said Su Xiaokang, the leading writer of the TV documentary "River Elegy" that had caused such a political stir the previous summer.

Government spokesman Yuan Mu on May 12 raised a growing government concern by appealing to students not to demonstrate during Soviet leader Mikhail Gorbachev's May 15-18 visit to China. "I'm sure that the overwhelming majority of the students will proceed from the standpoint of maintaining the

A Beijing policeman adds his victory sign to those of university students demonstrating in Tiananmen Square in May 1989.

political and social stability in China and act to protect the international prestige of China," Yuan said in a news conference.

But on Saturday, May 13, after failing to reach agreement on conditions for government-proposed talks, students were back on Tiananmen Square, this time with more deadly purpose.

More than three thousand students, most wearing white headbands, vowed to stop eating until their demands for a free press, human rights and an end to corruption were met.

"We love truth more than rice," the fasters chanted.

"Dialogue now, don't delay."

They were surrounded by thousands of non-fasting students providing a buffer against the crowds of curious people and the cold spring wind sweeping across the square.

Zhao appealed to the students not to jeopardize

Beijing University students on the fourth day of their hunger strike in Tiananmen Square.

the Sino-Soviet summit and Beijing Mayor Chen Xitong visited the square early Sunday morning to talk to the demonstrators. He left in fifteen minutes after being shouted down by the crowd.

The next day a combative crowd of thirty thousand, including citizens' and workers' groups, marched to Tiananmen to show their support for the hunger strikers. Protest flags waved from all the flagpoles on the square and several students paraded around with portraits of Gorbachev. "We Need Glasnost," one poster read.

An 8:30 a.m. deadline to evacuate the square came and went with no police attempt to clear out the defiant students. The students, in a sign of respect to Gorbachev, moved to the east side of the square, away from the plaza in front of the Great

square, away from the plaza in front of the Great Hall of the People where the official welcoming ceremony for the Soviet leader was to be held. But the government, obviously reluctant to have Gorbachev see Tiananmen Square strewn with protest banners, hastily changed plans and held the welcoming ceremony at the airport.

Talks continued between government officials and the students, with party Central Committee Secretariat member Yan Mingfu saying the month-old movement was "good and patriotic" but was having some "negative impact on the dignity of the country." The officials, however, refused to give ground on the key issue of recognizing the independent student unions.

The crowds, meanwhile, were rapidly swelling, with some one hundred and fifty thousand students, sympathizers and gawkers filling the square by that evening. They included several thousand marching intellectuals, led by Beijing University teachers come to show support for the fasters.

"Long live the teachers," the students yelled. "You give us infinite strength."

"We think the students have raised reasonable requests and we think the government should have a dialogue with them as equals. I really sympathize with the students and I worry about their health," said one teacher.

Several hundred thousand people roamed through the square on May 16 and the government was looking increasingly incapable of dealing with a situation approaching total anarchy. The authorities were humiliated by having to bring Gorbachev to Great Hall meetings through back roads and back doors to avoid the huge crowds occupying the main street and surrounding most of the Great Hall.

The protesters were demanding with rising intensity the resignation of Li Peng and the retirement of

Chinese leader Deng Xiaoping is flanked by Soviet leader Mikhail Gorbachev and his wife, Raisa, during a visit to Beijing in May 1989.

Deng, although Zhao, in his meeting with Gorbachev, stressed that the party still needed Deng's "wisdom and experience." Deng also told Gorbachev, in a statement that was later to be used against him, that the party in a closed-door decision had entrusted Deng with the ultimate authority for setting policy. Gorbachev earlier in the day had met Deng in the Great Hall, where the eighty-four-year-old Chinese patriarch had formally announced that the thirty-year schism between the two socialist powers had been brought to an end.

Outside on Tiananmen, ambulances with flashing blue lights and wailing sirens made their rounds, carrying collapsed hunger strikers to hospitals. First aid teams said more than three hundred and fifty of the some three thousand fasters had been hospitalized since the strike began on the 13th, although some later returned to the square. Twelve fasting

Chinese Premier Li Peng and Soviet General Secretary Mikhail Gorbachev raise a toast during a state banquet in the Great Hall of the People in Beijing in May 1989.

Soviet General Secretary Mikhail Gorbachev is greeted by Chinese Communist Party General Secretary Zhao Ziyang in Beijing in 1989. (Interpreter is at center.)

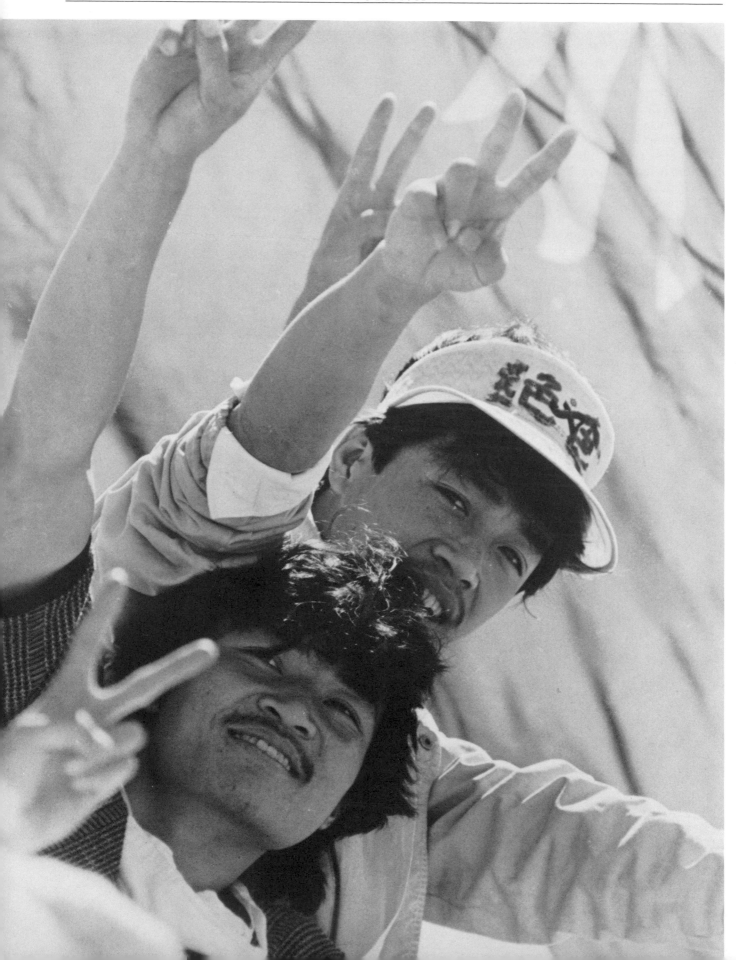

students also stopped drinking on the 16th, and by that evening three had been hospitalized.

Student leaders organized trucks to bring in water barrels and take out garbage and installed loudspeakers on lampposts to send their speeches and messages throughout the square. A headquarters, including a mimeograph machine, was set up on the steps of the martyr's monument in the center of the

Student demonstrators in Tiananmen Square flash victory sign.

Cadets of the People's Revolutionary Army were among thousands who joined students seeking political reform.

square.

The protest was now far more than just a student affair. Marchers that day included employees of the official media, hospitals, the state-run labor federation, local artists and filmmakers. There were groups marching under the banner of the "Beijing Citizens Support Group" and "Unemployed Youth

Support Group." Xinhua and the national television news carried unusually full and objective reports of the demonstrations, and it appeared the state was losing control even of its tightly controlled media.

After midnight, Zhao sent a message to the students on behalf of the party Politburo Standing Committee, affirming the students' patriotic spirit in calling for greater democracy and promising to "work out concrete measures to enhance democracy and law, oppose corruption, build an honest and clean government and expand openness." He did not concede to their demand for a debate with officials, to be broadcast live, but pledged that leaders would talk "with students and other people at various levels through multiple channels after the students return to campuses."

Zhao's call for restraint was answered with the biggest protest in Communist China's forty-year history.

Setting off from Tiananmen Square to the peal of firecrackers, crowds that grew to more than one million people, including many government workers, marched during the day through the streets of Beijing. For the first time students played a secondary role as factory workers, farmers and even police and soldiers filed through the streets, chanting pro-democracy slogans. Rallies were reported in more than twenty other provincial capitals, with twenty thousand gathering in front of city hall in Shanghai to demand the resignation of the city's Communist Party chief Jiang Zemin.

In one last embarrassment, journalists who had gathered at the Great Hall for a Gorbachev news conference were told that the venue had been changed, to the secure state guest house where he was staying. The streets around the hall were now completely under student control, and there was no way Chinese police could ensure a safe passage for their important visitor.

As nearly a million people once again flocked to the square on May 18 to bolster the spirits of the weakening hunger strikers, Li Peng met student leaders in an encounter at the Great Hall that probably closed the door to any hope of compromise between the two sides. Hunger striker Wu'er Kaixi, dressed in pajamas from his latest trip to the hospital, openly confronted the premier before fainting away. Li, his voice strident, said Beijing had fallen into anarchy and the students were leading China toward chaos even worse than that of the Cultural Revolution.

Farmers rally in Fangtai in support of the government's action against students holding Tiananmen Square.

*Students pass the time with a lively dance on the
ninth day of their occupation of Tiananmen Square.*

"We must protect factories and the socialist system," Li said, obviously mindful of the truckloads of workers, many wearing factory uniforms and banging their hard hats against the sideboards, that were streaming through Tiananmen Square carrying banners reading "Support the Students." Most startling of all was about two hundred Communist Party members marching behind a banner calling for the resignation of Deng. "Comrade Deng Xiaoping, the party members want you to take a rest," it read.

Gorbachev was spending the final day of his China visit in Shanghai, where nearly a quarter of a million students and supporters crammed along the waterfront where about two hundred students were staging a hunger strike in front of the city hall.

The official press, meanwhile, was offering comprehensive and sympathetic coverage of the protests, with the *People's Daily* reporting that more than a thousand reporters and workers from its staff had joined the previous day's march. The *Guangming Daily* wrote: "the condition of the students and the future of the country touched the heart of every Chinese who has a conscience."

During the pre-dawn hours of May 19, both Zhao and Li visited the hunger strikers on Tiananmen in their makeshift shelters in buses provided by the Chinese Red Cross. Li's visit was short and perfunctory, while Zhao was obviously moved by the plight of the students.

"We've come too late," he said, with tears in his eyes.

Amid reports that troops were mobilizing around the city in preparation for a move on the square, the student leaders on May 19 resolved to end their hunger strike the next day but continue their occupation of the square. More than twenty-four hundred student fasters had been hospitalized, although many had later returned to the square. The health situation on Tiananmen was deplorable because of lack of adequate water and sanitation facili-

University students on a hunger strike in Tiananmen Square in May 1989.

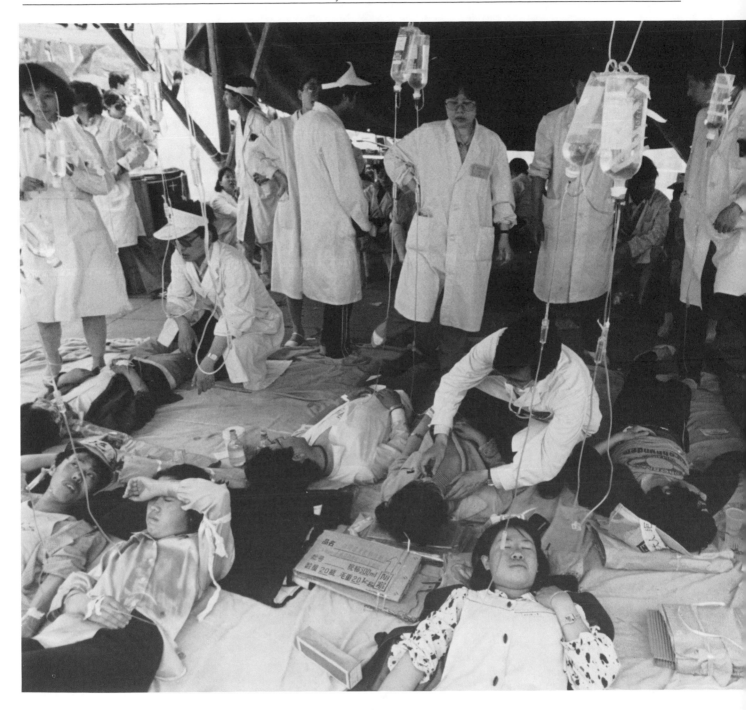

*Hunger strikers are tended to in Tiananmen
Square, where Beijing University students went on
strike for democracy.*

ties. Cases of hepatitis and other infectious diseases
were reported and living conditions in the hastily
erected tents were squalid.

That night, Li Peng and President Yang Shangkun
went on national television and announced they
were calling in the military. "We must adopt firm
and resolute measures to end the turmoil swiftly,
and maintain the leadership of the party as well as
the socialist system," Li said, adding that a "handful" of people were seeking to "negate the leader-

ship of the Communist Party of China and the socialist system."

Martial law went into effect at 10 a.m. on May 20
in eight central districts of Beijing, including Tiananmen. Regulations included a ban on marches,
strikes, class boycotts, giving speeches, spreading

rumors and attacks on party, government or military organs and "any other destructive actions." Foreign reporters were barred from conducting interviews or making tapes or videos on the streets. Troop convoys from the 27th and 28th Armies—the 38th Army responsible for security and order in Beijing had reportedly balked at taking military action against the city—took up positions on the outskirts of the city and rumors spread that troops were about to attack the square from the closed-off subway system or the railway station.

The people of Beijing, however, in a spontaneous act of rebellion against authority, took to the streets to block the military advance. Elderly men and women, bespectacled office workers, mothers with babies, and factory workers stood in the paths of the army trucks and pleaded with them to retreat. "The People's Liberation Army belongs to the people," the crowds chanted. "Patriotism is no crime."

By early Sunday morning, the 21st, all major roads into the city had been blocked with cement pipes, road dividers, trucks and buses.

Citizens climbed on troop trucks and lectured the young soldiers, many from the countryside who knew nothing of the democratic movement that had been sweeping Beijing and other cities.

"Who are you going to hit?" an elderly woman yelled at the soldiers. "Are you going to shoot students or the people? I think you should go home to your families."

The government, having failed to frighten the protesters into submission, was paralyzed by indecision. Zhao had lost power after calling for compromise and opposing the imposition of martial law, but the men who brought martial law to Beijing, Li Peng and President Yang, appeared to lack either the will or authority to give the attack orders. Up to two hundred thousand students and their supporters congregated on the square that Sunday night to hear Wang Dan say, "We will not retreat from the

Communist Party Chief Zhao Ziyang visited students hospitalized during a hunger strike in May 1989.

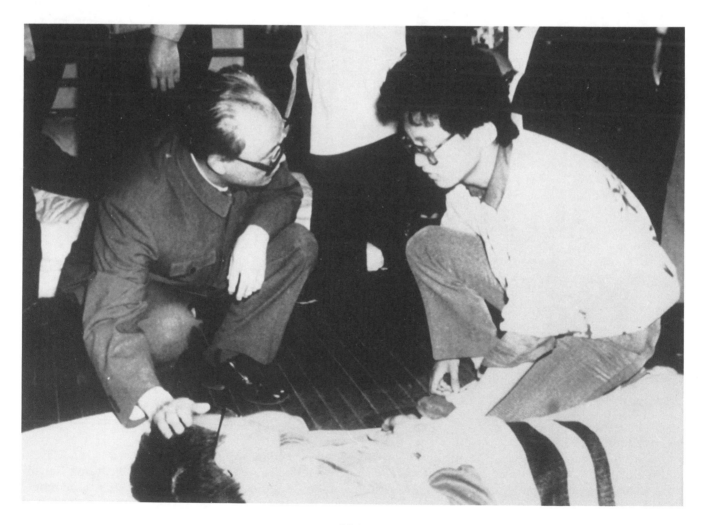

People's Liberation Army

When thousands of rookie Chinese People's Liberation Army troops surged across the Vietnamese frontier in February 1979, many did not recognize their commanding officers.

It wasn't because they didn't know the names of their superiors. But ever since the Cultural Revolution, each Chinese soldier had worn exactly the same uniform, with no insignias to differentiate rank. Under fire, the chain of command collapsed.

This was only one problem in China's ill-fated military venture into Vietnam. The others included unskilled officers, faulty 1940s vintage radio gear, jammed guns and stalled tanks. The enormous losses suffered by the Chinese side in the span of less than three weeks privately stunned military leaders back in Beijing. They had assumed the army would live up to the reputation it had gained in communist-led revolution and the Korean conflict decades earlier.

Although there had been a few border spats with India and the Soviet Union since then, as well as some shelling exchanges with the rival Chinese nationalists based on Taiwan, the People's Liberation Army had not been battle-tested for awhile. China's faulty performance in the Vietnamese fight, like other problems besetting the country at the time, were blamed on the disastrous "ten years of turmoil," formerly called the Great Proletarian Cultural Revolution launched by Mao Tse-tung. This led Mao's successor Deng Xiaoping to call for a fundamental reassessment and restructuring of the world's largest standing army, which totaled at least 4.2 million soldiers.

As Deng saw it, the army was plagued by swollen size, inefficiency, lack of technical training, generals in their seventies and eighties, hopelessly outdated equipment and poorly paid recruits.

As chairman of the Central Military Commission in both the government and the Communist Party, which made him commander in chief, Deng reversed some longstanding practices in an army that had evolved from a band of ragtag peasant guerrillas in the 1920s.

One of Deng's first priorities was to restore the rank system, scrapped during the Cultural Revolution by the discredited Marshal Lin Biao as a relic of "warlord feudalism." Lin had required all soldiers to wear identical shapeless fatigues and workers caps. The policy had never been rescinded, even after Lin plotted a coup and died fleeing the country in 1971.

Deng also replaced regional commanders who rose to prominence during Lin's time, opened officer academies and ordered rigorous military training for conscripts, who had once been schooled in battle tactics by memorizing the quotations of Chairman Mao.

He also ordered a large-scale demobilization because of the enormous cost to the government of feeding, clothing and housing so many soldiers. In addition, Deng told the armed forces to surrender some of their vast facilities for civilian use.

Over the years, the army had expanded into almost a separate country within China, with farms, airfields, ports and factories. The army also controlled enormous tracts of land that were off limits to foreigners and Chinese civilians alike.

In the years since the Vietnam episode, China's army has done much to modernize its weaponry and has expressed interest in buying high-tech defense gear from the United States that range from anti-missile systems to laser-guided torpedoes.

China's military also has become a significant weapons exporter itself, mostly in peddling automatic rifles and ammunition to small Third World nations. It reportedly was a major supplier of weapons to both sides in the Iran-Iraq war.

square, we won't give up until we reach our goals."

The *Science and Technology Daily* reported Monday that twenty-four members of the National People's Congress had signed a letter seeking the convening of an emergency session to discuss the leadership crisis in a "democratic and legal manner." *People's Daily* sources said the paper had received a letter from senior military figures, including former Defense Minister Zhang Aiping, calling for martial law to be lifted and stressing that the army could never open fire on the Chinese people. On the square, the students, having finally abandoned the hunger strike on Saturday, swept the mountains of trash and prepared for a military strike they prayed would not come.

"If the government suppresses the students, then there is no hope for China," said one student. "The only solution is for the government to take the initiative, and that can only be Li Peng stepping down."

Zhao Ziyang spoke to student hunger strikers in May 1989.

Pro-democracy students lie in front of a tank to prevent troops from entering central Beijing on May 21, 1989.

That is absolutely clear to everyone."

Up to a million people paraded through the streets of Beijing on Tuesday, May 23, to demand Li's resignation. Intellectuals from China's most famous think-tank, the Chinese Academy of Sciences, led the way, accusing Li of staging a military coup against Zhao. The Hong Kong press and the local rumor mills reported that Li was being stripped of his posts, and Zhao was on his way to a political comeback.

Meanwhile, the complexion of the movement was undergoing critical changes. Thousands of students from Beijing universities were leaving the square and returning to their campuses, exhausted by days of poor sleep, poor food and filthy living conditions. Their places were being filled by thousands of students arriving daily by train from around the country who had come to be part of the nation's greatest

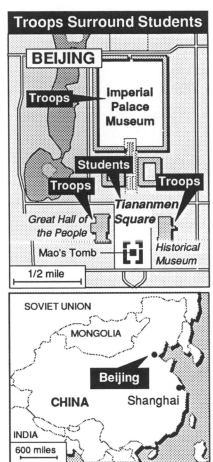

Trucks of demonstrators fill Tiananmen Square in a May 1989 rally for democracy.

protest movement. Many of the Beijing leaders were ready to quit the square, avoiding a confrontation with the military and focusing the movement on new directions.

The newcomers from outside, however, refused to budge. "We just couldn't leave," said a student from Lanzhou, a western city seven hundred and fifty miles from Beijing. "Tiananmen Square is the center of our student movement. If it died, the movement in Lanzhou and all around China would die too."

The movement had affected almost every major city across the country. Up to half-a-million people had marched to the Bund, Shanghai's waterfront business district, stopping all traffic in that overcrowded city. About one hundred thousand had taken to the streets in the normally apolitical city of Canton in the south, and in Lanzhou, workers were ignoring orders from their superiors and leaving their jobs to join student activists.

All major universities in the northeast cities of Harbin, Shenyang, Changchun and Dalian were shut down by strikes, and class boycotts were also continuing in Nanjing, scene of street marches by twenty thousand a night since martial law was declared in Beijing.

In Wuhan, students stopped train and vehicle traffic across a Yangtze River bridge, and in Ningbo, students broke into a city government compound. Even such remote places as Hohhot in Inner Mongolia and Urumqi in Xinjiang were rocked by prodemocracy unrest.

In Beijing, action was shifting behind the scenes. The top military command published a letter in the military newspaper expressing solid support for Li's hardline position against the students, and Foreign Minister Qian Qichen said the Politburo was about to hold a special meeting, apparently to thrash out differences between rival camps. NPC Chairman Wan Li, regarded as a reformist, also cut short a visit to the United States and flew home for what he said were "health reasons." Many thought he would call a special session of the NPC to oust Li, but he was stopped at Shanghai airport and disappeared from sight, seemingly put under house arrest.

By the end of the week it was apparent that Zhao was also under house arrest, stripped of power and being made a scapegoat for the political crisis. President Yang, the jovial ex-general who had become the chief proponent for tough action against the students, said in an unpublished speech on May 25 that Zhao's behavior "had a very bad effect" on the nation. Chinese and diplomatic sources said a document was circulated to lower-level party officials on May 26 revealing that Zhao was no longer general secretary of the party. He was blamed for heading an anti-party clique, splitting the party, instigating disturbances, revealing party secrets, corruption and taking credit for Deng's achievements over the past decade.

On May 27, student leaders Wu'er Kaixi, Wang Dan and Chai Ling held a news conference at the base of the martyr's monument and called for an end to the Tiananmen occupation following one last rally to "celebrate our great victory."

People on the square, although fluctuating during the day, had dwindled to one hundred thousand and many were now going home. Long lines of students formed at the Beijing railway station waiting for trains to the provinces. The government was giving students priority in obtaining tickets to get them out of the city. With Zhao apparently gone and all avenues of compromise closed for the moment, the Tiananmen sit-in no longer served as a vehicle to force the authorities to the negotiating table. Hopes that NPC Chairman Wan Li would return from the United States to lead the campaign against Li and the conservatives were dashed when Wan published a letter from Shanghai saying: "After I had time to study the situation, I realized that a small minority was behind a plot to cause turmoil in society."

About eighty thousand students from three hundred schools marched through the old quarters of Beijing on May 28, chanting for the downfall of Li. A new group of student leaders, mostly from outside Beijing, emerged and said they would refuse to leave the square. Some said they would stay until at least June 20, when the NPC was slated to meet.

"If we stay, troops won't dare enter the square or the city," one student said in a speech, encouraging others to stay. "If we leave, they most certainly will come."

But the pressure was beginning to tell. There were few non-students in Sunday's march, in sharp contrast to the rallies of a million people just a week before, as factories increased threats against workers who joined the demonstrations. The presence of up to 200,000 troops ringing the city had ended the relaxed, carnival-like atmosphere of previous marches.

The confrontation with the government had become a serious affair.

The students made a last dramatic gesture on May

Students carry giant V-for-victory signs in a march for democracy.

30 when they unveiled their "Goddess of Democracy," a thirty-three-foot high Styrofoam monument, at the north end of the square. The statue, built by the Central Fine Arts Academy, was modeled after the American Statue of Liberty, with both depicting a woman in classical robes holding aloft a torch of freedom.

"America represents democracy and freedom," said one Beijing Science and Technology University student. "I think most of the students received the idea of democracy and freedom from America and other Western countries." The statue brought up to 100,000 people back to the square and lifted the flagging spirits of the demonstrators.

Xinhua, however, said the statue was "an insult to the national dignity and image" and demanded it be removed.

Meanwhile about a thousand students demonstrated in front of police headquarters, just east of the square, demanding the release of three members of an independent trade union that was formed May 19 in defiance of a government ban on all but the official All China Federation of Trade Unions. The government was appalled by the establishment in Beijing and other cities of independent labor unions, a direct challenge to the concept that the Communist Party represents the interests of workers, obviating the rationale for Western-style trade unions.

The government, in a clumsy attempt to discredit the students, on May 31 organized the first of several pro-government rallies in rural areas of Beijing. About four thousand farmers, workers and students, many wearing new straw hats provided by their work units, joined one rally at Daxing County south of Beijing, listlessly chanting, "Long Live the Communist Party" and "Down with Fang Lizhi." Fang was burned in effigy. "They told me to come, so I've come," said one peasant. "To tell you the truth, we were forced to come," said a high school student.

Military intimidation was on the increase with the start of June.

Motorcyle convoys roared noisily through the city and large contingents of troops stationed inside the railway station occasionally came out to make their presence felt. About three hundred army troops marched within a block of the square early in the morning of June 1. More troops appeared on the streets on Friday, June 2, as several hundred thousand gathered on the square to hear Ho Dejian, a

An estimated half-million people joined this pro-democracy demonstration in Canton in May 1989.

pop-singer who defected from Taiwan in 1983, and three others announce plans for a hunger strike.

That night, fifteen military trucks advanced from the west but were halted by crowds about two miles from the square at about 2 a.m. Ten truckloads of soldiers entered the Great Hall.

Early on the morning of June 3, in one of the more bizarre episodes of the confrontation, tens of thousands of unarmed, exhausted soldiers began appearing on Changan Avenue after completing a twelve-mile jog into the city. They were stopped in front of the Beijing Hotel, several hundred yards east of the square, by thousands of people who blocked the street with four trucks. The troops, after

Huge crowd gathered to watch student protestors burn copies of the Beijing Daily *in retaliation for anti-student articles (June 2, 1989).*

a half-hearted effort to break through, gave up, with some straggling back toward the east, others sitting forlornly on the side of the road, some with tears in their eyes.

One soldier said as he retreated, "I was told to come to the city for exercises. I didn't know the people didn't want me here."

Another said, "If I'm going to die, I want to die on the battlefield, not on Changan Avenue."

The People's Army Attacks the People

As troops were breaking ranks and retreating to the east, students were entering a captured supply bus to the west of the square and brandishing assault

rifles out the window, to the delight of thousands of onlookers. The moment of triumph, however, was short-lived.

At 2:10 p.m., riot police burst out of the Communist Party headquarters of Zhongnanhai, and for the

On the thirteenth day of their strike for reform, students mill around Tiananmen Square.

first time in forty years of Communist rule, fired tear gas at Beijing residents. Dozens of people were beaten as the police battled their way to the supply bus at the Liubu intersection and recaptured the weapons.

China's prominent student leader Chai Ling spoke to reporters during a pro-democracy rally at Tiananmen Square on June 1, 1989.

Simultaneously, about five thousand unarmed soldiers marched out of the west, or back, side of the Great Hall, but they were immediately surrounded by throngs of people and unable to advance toward the square.

One elderly woman wearing pajamas lay down in front of the troops and yelled: "If you want to shoot, shoot me. Just don't shoot the students." The massive confrontation was largely peaceful with the crowd applauding at one point when the troops sang a military song. But late in the afternoon tempers flared, with rocks, tree branches and beer bottles flying between the two sides. A few soldiers lashed out at people with their belts.

The soldiers retreated into the Great Hall at about 8 p.m., and the action shifted to the Muxidi intersection of Changan Avenue about two-and-a-half miles west of the square. The battle began shortly thereafter as crowds moved buses onto a bridge to block the advancing troops. The first wave of troops from the 27th Army attacked at about 10 p.m., firing tear gas and beating people with clubs.

The crowds retaliated by setting fire to the buses and hurling rocks and bottles at the the troops.

Several gas tanks exploded, sending orange flames soaring into the sky.

Two tank crewmen were pulled from their vehicle and beaten senseless by the crowds. The tank was set ablaze, with red flags reading "Democracy" and

"Freedom" flapping from its turrets.

Around 11 p.m., the troops opened fire, shooting low into the crowd, which scattered at each volley but quickly regrouped with reckless bravado. Blood covered the street and bicycle pedicabs pedalled furiously back and forth, carrying out the dead and wounded.

About fifty military trucks plowed through the smashed roadblock, with troops firing into the air, killing several people watching from apartment balconies.

A single armored personnel carrier, meanwhile, was stopped on the north end of Tiananmen and its driver dragged out and beaten to death. Another APC appearing on the west side of the Great Hall was stopped by people hurling chunks of concrete.

More troops advanced from the south. Thousands of people massed at the Tianqiao intersection, blocking it with carts, cars and furniture, but the troops smashed their way through, firing as they went.

The main military contingent advanced slowly from the west, and at 1 a.m. reached a barricade of four burning buses at the Xidan intersection. A command jeep was attacked and overturned and an officer emerged from the jeep and shot four people. He was seized by the crowd, which beat him to death, disemboweled him and set him on fire, hanging his body on a burning bus. The killing continued all along the western route into the square as the troops shot their way through the crowds and barricades at each intersection.

A column of several thousand troops was at the same time entering the square from the southeast, taking up positions along the history museum after students with sticks and bars raced forward to do battle.

Most of the students, numbering in the thousands, huddled around the martyr's monument, but some moved up to Changan Avenue, at the north end, to confront other troops. The soldiers opened fire, and many students were hit in the back as they fled.

The square was lit up with tracer bullets whistling above Mao Tse-tung's mausoleum and the flames of burning buses and military vehicles.

At 2:45 a.m., a tank appeared near the Kentucky Fried Chicken restaurant in the southwest corner and began clearing debris on the west side of the square to open the way for the military advance.

A man tries to pull a Chinese soldier away from his comrades as thousands of Beijing citizens turned out to block troops on their way to Tiananmen Square on the weekend of June 3-4, 1989.

A student demonstrator shows victory sign as People's Liberation Army troops withdraw on the west side of the Great Hall of the People near Tiananmen Square.

By 4 a.m., the square was surrounded by troops, and suddenly the lampposts along the edges were turned off, throwing Tiananmen into darkness. Strains from the Internationale, the socialist anthem, could be heard from the student loudspeakers.

Ho Dejian, the Taiwanese singer, after holding quick negotiations with military officers, took the microphone and told the students they had no choice but to leave. "We've achieved a big victory, . . . We're not afraid to die, but we've already lost too much blood."

Some students were still reluctant to go, but when the lights went back on at 4:30 a.m. and the troops began moving into the square, the two thousand students around the monument filed out of the southeast corner of the square, holding hands and singing the Internationale. Some wept, some defiantly raised a V-for-Victory sign and promised they

A pro-democracy demonstrator is caught between soldiers and students outside Tiananmen Square.

would be back.

Tanks rumbled onto the square, one destroying the "Goddess of Democracy." Hundreds of troops, their rifles raised, took up positions on the monument.

The three-week occupation of Tiananmen Square, and the seven-week drive to bring democratic reform to China had ended, crushed by brute military force.

The violence and bloodshed, however, were far from ended. As the students retreated toward their universities to the north, an armored personnel carrier sped up from the back, crushing seven students to death and seriously injuring four others. Students trying to help their fallen classmates were driven back by tear gas and bullets.

*A Chinese student displays an assault rifle out the
window of a troop bus taken over from soldiers
early in the morning of June 3.*

Students built a display of arms captured from troops attempting to march toward Tiananmen Square the morning of June 3.

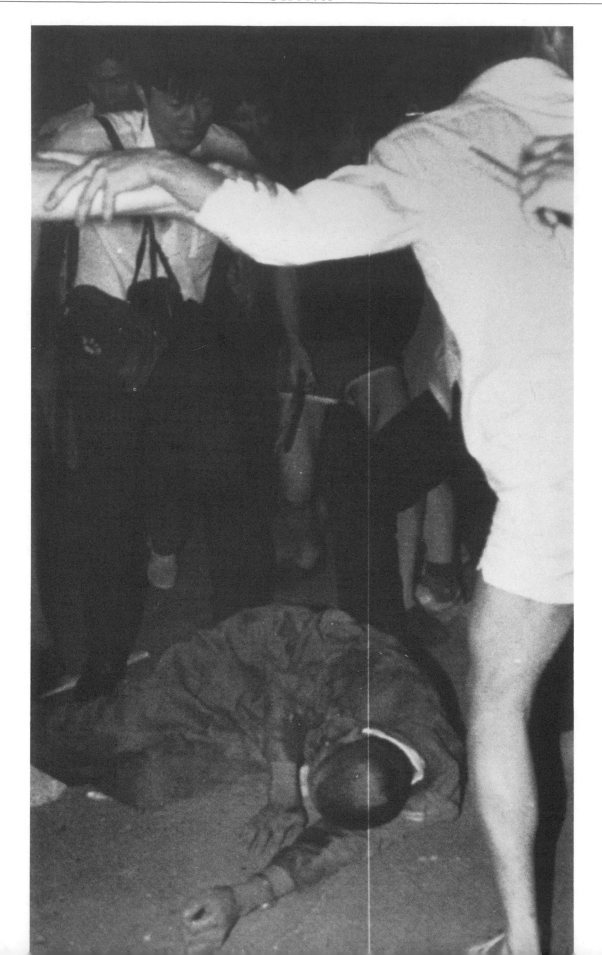

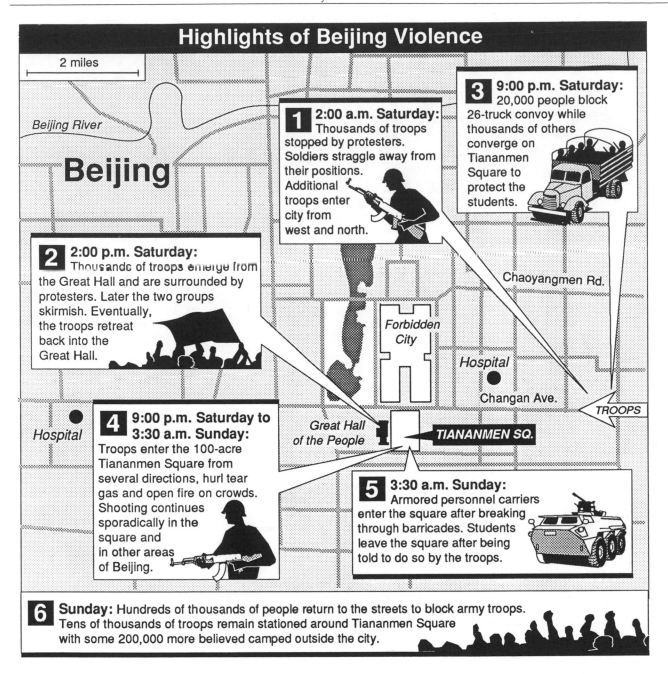

Highlights of Beijing Violence

2 miles

Beijing River

Beijing

1 **2:00 a.m. Saturday:** Thousands of troops stopped by protesters. Soldiers straggle away from their positions. Additional troops enter city from west and north.

2 **2:00 p.m. Saturday:** Thousands of troops emerge from the Great Hall and are surrounded by protesters. Later the two groups skirmish. Eventually, the troops retreat back into the Great Hall.

3 **9:00 p.m. Saturday:** 20,000 people block 26-truck convoy while thousands of others converge on Tiananmen Square to protect the students.

Chaoyangmen Rd.

Forbidden City

Hospital

Changan Ave.

TROOPS

4 **9:00 p.m. Saturday to 3:30 a.m. Sunday:** Troops enter the 100-acre Tiananmen Square from several directions, hurl tear gas and open fire on crowds. Shooting continues sporadically in the square and in other areas of Beijing.

Hospital

Great Hall of the People

TIANANMEN SQ.

5 **3:30 a.m. Sunday:** Armored personnel carriers enter the square after breaking through barricades. Students leave the square after being told to do so by the troops.

6 **Sunday:** Hundreds of thousands of people return to the streets to block army troops. Tens of thousands of troops remain stationed around Tiananmen Square with some 200,000 more believed camped outside the city.

The driver of an armored personnel carrier that rammed through student lines, injuring many, lies dead after being beaten by students who set his vehicle afire during the army attack on Tiananmen Square on June 4.

Armored personnel carriers and military vehicles roared up and down Changan Avenue and other main streets, which were littered with smashed bricks, uprooted trees, overturned street signs and the shells of burned-out buses. The corpse of a soldier, beaten to death, lay on Changan Avenue.

At about 10 a.m., a convoy of seventy trucks, vans and armored personnel carriers was stopped by crowds and barricades at Muxidi, scene of the previous night's worst bloodshed. The soldiers abandoned their vehicles, which then were torched.

Killings also continued near the square as troops sporadically and indiscriminately opened fire on unarmed crowds of people. Numerous people were shot in the back as they fled from automatic rifle fire in front of the Beijing Hotel and other spots around the square.

"My government has gone crazy," said one doctor who put the number of dead at about five hundred. He held up his bloody gown and said, "This is the blood of China."

"We have people shot in the head, chest, stomach, legs, even the eyes," said a nurse at another hospital. "The government is so rotten," said a student, his leg shattered by a bullet. "They don't care how many people die."

The government, meanwhile, was celebrating its victory. National television, in repeated announcements, said the troops had "suppressed a counter-revolutionary riot" and "achieved a great victory in the struggle to end turmoil in the capital."

The Beijing municipal government said soldiers and police had "strictly observed discipline" and said "their heroic acts and glorious exploits have won fervent praise and strong support from the masses of students and citizens."

An announcer for the English-language Radio Beijing, monitored in Washington, said thousands of people were killed, but he was quickly yanked off the air and replaced with a broadcaster repeating the government line.

By evening, hundreds of thousands of people were back out on the streets. Their anger was palpable. "Even Hitler and the Japanese troops during World War II didn't act like that," said one outraged citizen. People blocked some roads with large trucks, others with foodstalls or whatever else was available. Soldiers with AK-47 automatic rifles, taunted by the insults of crowds, ran up one narrow

Beijing citizens shout in anger as they gather around the body of a man killed when an armored personnel carrier, on its way to Tiananmen Square, crashed through a troop convoy.

residential lane just off Tiananmen, firing randomly.

Shooting continued throughout the day Monday. Soldiers opened fire on a crowd of nearly three thousand near the Beijing Hotel, with one man laced with machine gun bullets from his chin to his stomach. Three others were shot down when seventeen truckloads of troops attacked a crowd west of Tiananmen Square. Beijing citizens, showing astonishing bravery, returned after each fusillade to face the troops. "I don't care anymore whether I live or die," said one man who was shot as he tried to defend his alleyway from an army charge. "Living under these fascists is misery."

In what came to be a symbol of the popular resistance, a single student Monday stepped out in the path of oncoming tanks on Changan, refusing to let them pass. "Why are you here?" he cried, climbing up on the lead tank. "You have done nothing but create misery. My city is in chaos because of you." He was finally pulled to safety by onlookers.

The city was in a state of near collapse. Most factories and offices were closed because people couldn't, or wouldn't, go to work. With roads into the city blocked by the military, food suppliers couldn't get through, and long lines were forming to buy milk, oil, salt, soy sauce and coal gas for cooking. Prices for meat, fruit and vegetables were up 40-50 percent.

By Tuesday the army was moving inexorably to take over strategic bridges and key intersections throughout the city. But there were also persistent rumors of serious divisions within the army, with armed clashes between rival army groups. Chinese military sources and foreign diplomats said there was solid evidence of fighting between army groups, and Chinese witnesses reported isolated incidents of skirmishing among the troops.

People saw the clashes as pitting the hated 27th Army, which was responsible for most of the carnage of June 3-4, against other armies opposing the use of military violence against Chinese civilians. In particular the 38th Army, which was responsible for the security of the Beijing area and which reportedly had balked at entering Beijing when martial law was declared, was seen as playing the role of saviors. Later it was to become evident that the People's Liberation Army was generally united and the possibility of civil war was very slim. But when a few hundred soldiers claiming to be from the 38th Army appeared near the Muxidi bridge Tuesday, they were hailed as heroes come to rescue the city.

"Exterminate the 27th Army. Avenge blood with blood," the crowd chanted, handing out eggs and cigarettes to the troops.

Government spokesman Yuan Mu on Tuesday announced that nearly three hundred people, including soldiers, "thugs," bystanders and twenty-three students, had been killed since Saturday night. Yuan said seven thousand others, including five thousand soldiers, had been wounded.

The real death toll, thought to be considerably higher, may never be known. Hundreds of bodies were taken to hospitals along Changan Avenue and to the south of the square where most of the shooting took place. But many others took their fallen relatives home and the bodies were later quietly disposed of at state crematories. Many Chinese put the number of killed in the thousands. That hundreds died is certain; that thousands lost their lives is a real possibility.

Despite the state's restored lock on the official media, news of the bloodshed in Beijing reached other cities and caused major disruptions. The most serious outbreak of violence was in Chengdu, the provincial capital of Sichuan. Trouble began when police broke up a small group of students camped out around a Mao statue in the center of the city.

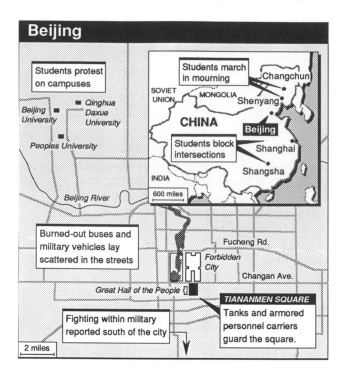

A rickshaw flatbed carries the wounded to the hospital after the Tiananmen shooting on June 4.

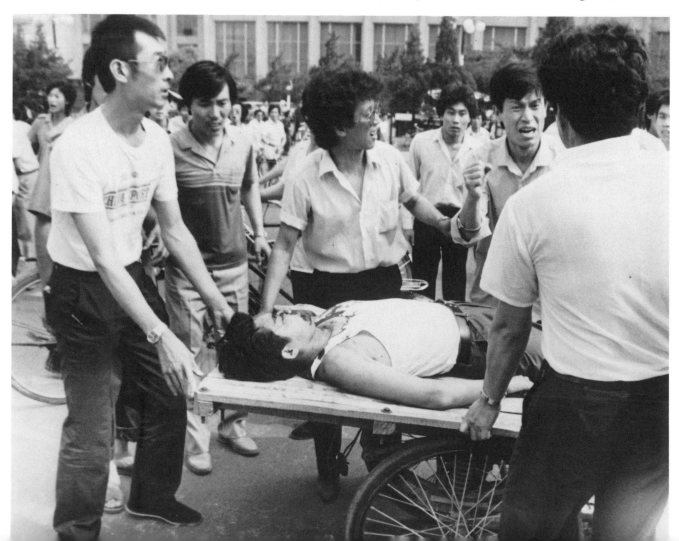

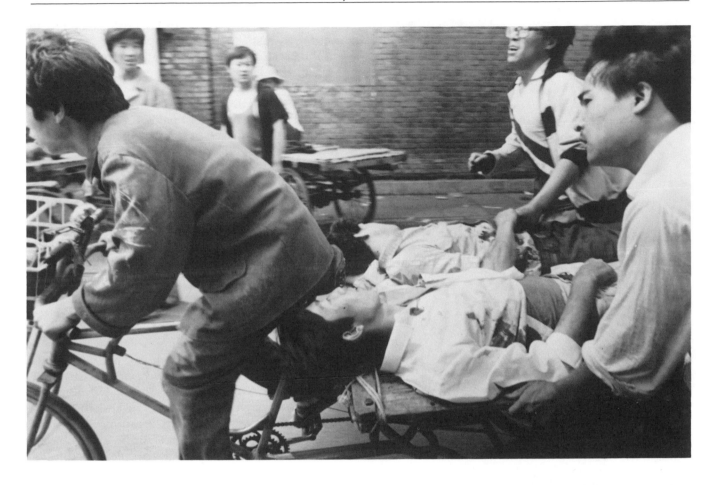

A rickshaw carries wounded to a nearby hospital after troops fired on crowds gathered outside Tiananmen Square.

Large crowds gathered to confront the police, and a pitched battle ensued, with hand-to-hand combat. Riots continued for two more days, with mobs burning down a marketlace covering an entire city block. City officials said eight people died in the melee. Residents estimated the death toll at about thirty, and claimed police bayoneted some victims.

In Shanghai, all public transportation in the city of twelve million was stopped Monday as people set up blockades at major intersections. The next night six people were killed when a train plowed through a barricade set up by protesters. The enraged crowd then set the train on fire, and, according to official reports, injured twenty-one railway security officers. Three days later, on June 9, about fifty thousand Shanghai residents marched peacefully to mourn the six victims, although by that time many of the barricades were down and arrests had begun.

In all, more than eighty cities were hit by demonstrations and rioting before and after June 4.

In Xian, the provincial radio reported on June 7 that crowds "wrecked communications facilities, blocked buses, trolley buses, and cars, and forced passing vehicles to halt." In the northeast city of Changchun, where ten thousand staged a funeral march for the victims in Beijing, the local radio warned that "if this situation continues, the city's economy will be paralyzed." Officials in the western city of Lanzhou held an emergency meeting and decided to "resolutely crack down on those elements beating up people, smashing and looting." In the southern city of Guiyang police arrested twenty-four "lawless elements," some armed with knives, daggers and iron clubs, who went on a rampage through city streets. Buses were burned in Wuhan and trains were stopped in Changsha.

The exodus of foreigners from Beijing, which began with the June 3-4 invasion, accelerated after June 7 when troops opened fire on one of the main compounds for diplomats and other foreign residents.

The troops stationed on a bridge outside the compound, claiming they had been attacked by sniper fire, strafed surrounding buildings with automatic fire, with dozens of bullets striking windows facing the street. Troops sealed off the compound, and

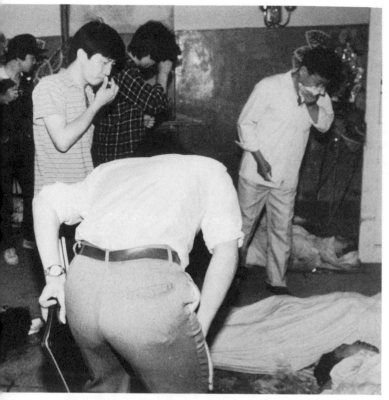

Relatives and friends trying to identify the dead at Fuxing Hospital after bloody June 1989 night at Tiananmen Square.

Students died near their collapsed bicycles after PLA troops and tanks stormed Tiananmen Square in a pre-dawn raid.

plainclothes security officials later dragged off a Chinese man suspected of the sniper attack.

The U.S. Embassy, which later accused the army of deliberately attacking the compound, ordered the mandatory evacuation of dependents of diplomatic personnel and many other countries took similar steps. Foreign students, business people and tourists scrambled to get past troop contingents along the road to reach the airport, where many countries had special planes waiting.

Foreign reaction to the violence in Beijing, which much of the world followed through the dramatic footage of Western TV crews, was intense and almost universally critical. British Prime Minister Margaret Thatcher expressed "utter revulsion." U.S. President George Bush said: "I deeply deplore the decision to use force against peaceful demonstrators." Australian Prime Minister Bob Hawke broke down in tears of anger. France froze relations "at all levels" and Canada recalled its ambassador. Mass rallies condemning the killing in Beijing were held throughout the world, even in the Communist states of Poland and Hungary. Soviet parliamentarians called on Chinese leaders to use "wisdom, reason and a weighted approach" to end the bloody clashes. Chinese communities around the world were deeply shaken, particularly Hong Kong, where two hundred thousand people rallied to denounce the killings.

The United States gave shelter to dissident astrophysicist Fang Lizhi, who fled to the U.S. Embassy with his wife Li Shuxian after the military attack.

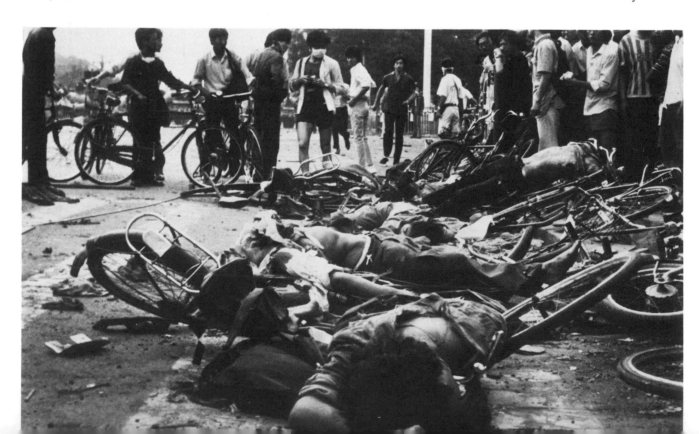

Within days, the Public Security Department issued a warrant for the couples' arrest, accusing them of "committing crimes of counter-revolutionary propaganda and instigation." The government also accused the United States of breaking international law by refusing to hand over Fang and his wife.

Eventually, most Western countries and Japan agreed on a general policy of curtailing high-level official contacts and stopping arms sales to China to show their outrage over the violent suppression of the demonstrators. The West also agreed that international lending institutes such as the World Bank should suspend negotiations for new loans to the Chinese government.

Premier Li Peng made his first post-attack appearance on June 8, telling cheering troops in the Great Hall, "You've done well, comrades." The government also showed lengthy videotapes of demonstrators attacking military trucks and armored personnel carriers and grisly shots of three soldiers' charred bodies, one of whom had been disemboweled.

State-run television and radio urged people to

Photo by Shinh Chia-fu shows civilians fleeing from tear gas in front of a statue of Mao Tse-tung in Chengdu, central China, on June 7, 1989.

turn in those who took part in "hooliganism and destruction" and broadcast telephone numbers informers could use in Beijing's main districts.

On June 9, Deng Xiaoping appeared in public for the first time since his May 16 meeting with Gorbachev. In what came to be regarded as the definitive line on the turmoil, Deng told a gathering of military officers and party hardliners that "this storm was bound to happen sooner or later." The protesters, he said, were trying to "overthrow the Communist Party, topple the socialist system and establish a bourgeois republic entirely dependent on the West." The PLA, he said, "is truly a Great Wall of iron and steel of the party and the country . . ." and they are "the most beloved of the people." For the enemy, Deng said, "we should not have an iota of forgiveness." The reforms will go on, he said, but more stress must be given to educating people in socialist values.

Chinese jounalist Liu Binyan in exile in Hong Kong in June 1989.

Beijing was taking on a semblance of normality, with the roads cleared, markets re-stocked and bicyclists allowed to pedal past the military encampment on Tiananmen. But at night teams of club-wielding police roamed the streets, soldiers stopped cars and pointed guns at drivers and the roundup of protesters intensified.

The state-run news on June 10 said six hundred people had been arrested, including leaders of the student protests in Beijing and officials of the independent labor unions in Beijing and Shanghai. Television news broadcasts showed dozens of people being arrested and questioned by police at gunpoint in various cities. On June 12 the government formally banned all independent student and worker associations and gave police and soldiers nationwide the right to shoot "rioters and counter-revolutionaries."

The police on June 13 published a wanted list of twenty-one top student leaders who now were being branded as instigators of a "counter-revolutionary rebellion." Of the twenty-one, at least two, Wu'er Kaixi and Nanjing University's Li Lu, smuggled themselves out of the country and sought refuge in the West. The government in the coming days confirmed the arrest of eight others, including Wang Dan.

On June 14 the police expelled two foreign journalists, John Pomfret of The Associated Press and Alan Pessin of the Voice of America, accusing them of violating martial law regulations in their reporting on the political turmoil and giving them seventy-two hours to leave China. VOA had a listening audience of millions in China and, along with BBC, provided Chinese with information about events in their own country that was either not reported in the official press or presented according to the sanctioned government line.

The crackdown continued the next day, June 15, when three men in Shanghai were sentenced to death, and executed six days later, for setting train carriages on fire in the June 6 incident in which the train killed six protesters. Ignoring international appeals for clemency, Beijing executioners put to death seven people on June 22 and two more were executed in Chengdu for rioting. Human rights organizations abroad expressed fears that many more were receiving harsh sentences, including death, for participating in the protests, but as June drew to a close the official media stopped reporting arrests and trials, and the true extent of the crackdown could only be guessed at.

At least four thousand are known to have been arrested in connection with the political turmoil, but the actual number of people detained was probably far higher.

Memorials sprang up around Beijing to soldiers killed in the fighting and their relatives, mostly peasants from the countryside, became TV fixtures as they were paraded from one top leader to another. But while the fallen soldiers were being hailed as martyrs, the hundreds or perhaps thousands of civilians killed were ignored. Instead the government insisted that no shots were fired at protesters in Tiananmen Square and not one person was killed on the square.

The national television news on June 22 announced the arrest of thirteen Chinese nationals on charges of spying for Taiwan and fomenting unrest during the student protests. The report, accompanied by film clips of the men mingling with Tiananmen crowds, appeared to be meant to back up Chinese allegations that the students were being manipulated by outside forces. A Taiwanese journalist was detained on July 3 and expelled several days later for making contact with fugitive student activist Wang Dan. Police surveillance of the reporter also led to Wang's arrest.

The long-expected announcement of Zhao Ziyang's demise came on June 24, when the party Central Committee stripped him of all his party

Deng Xiaoping congratulated officers of the People's Liberation Army in Beijing after the bloody suppression of the pro-democracy movement in June.

posts after accusing him of "unshirkable responsibilities" in supporting the turmoil and "splitting the party." Hu Qili, another moderate said to have opposed the hardline stance toward the students, also was fired from his post on the seventeen-member Politburo and its five-man Standing Committee.

The party acknowledged that the sixty-nine-year-old Zhao, who had not been seen in public since his emotional meeting with student hunger strikers on May 19, "did something beneficial to the reform, the opening of China to the outside world and economic work." But it said the party would "look further into his case," indicating it was still possible that Zhao would face criminal charges for aiding the "counter-revolutionary rebellion."

What did come as a minor surprise was the naming of Jiang Zemin, the sixty-two-year-old party secretary of Shanghai, as the new general secretary of the party. Many Chinese and foreign observers had focused on Qiao Shi, a member of the Standing Committee and the party's legal affairs chief, as most likely to get the job. Jiang, however, appeared to possess the qualities Deng was looking for as new party boss—a man who as mayor and party head in Shanghai had been deeply involved in promoting China's open-door policy but who at the same time was willing to go along with the crackdown on political dissent and other forms of "bourgeois liberalization."

Joining incumbents Li Peng, Yao Yilin and Qiao on the reconstructed Standing Committee were Jiang, Tianjin Mayor Li Ruihuan, fifty-four, and Song Ping, seventy-two, an economic planner and head of the party Organization Department.

With the new party hierarchy now in order, the ideological education campaign began in earnest. Deng's June 9 speech praising the PLA for crushing the "counter-revolutionary rebellion" became compulsory reading in all Chinese schools, offices and factories.

Jiang Zemin, in his first public statement since taking office, on June 28 called for resolute actions in putting an end to the turmoil. "We should thoroughly expose and mete out according to law timely and severe punishments to the plotters, organizers and behind-the-scenes commanders who staged the turmoil and rebellion, the backbone elements of illegal organizations and the criminals who took part in beating, smashing, looting, burning and killing."

The NPC Standing Committee, in a special session to endorse the party decisions on Zhao, fired Deng's former protege from his last remaining government post, as vice chairman of the state Central Military Commission headed by Deng. The NPC, which students had once hoped would meet to oust Li Peng from office, hailed the violent suppression of the democracy movement as "legal, correct and necessary."

The party's theoretical journal *Seeking Truth (Qiushi)*, in an edition to mark the Communist Party's sixty-eighth birthday on July 1, delivered the message that was to be repeated in countless editorials over the coming months—that only socialism can save China and there is no alternative to rule by the Communist Party. "We cannot deviate from the leadership of the party while adhering to the socialist road," it emphasized.

The recent turmoil had taught some lessons, it said, "but the most important is that we must consistently adhere to the four cardinal principles and fight against bourgeois liberalization." The four principles, first enunciated by Deng in 1979, were adherence to socialism, the dictatorship of the proletariat, the leadership of the Communist Party and Marxist-Leninist-Mao Tse-tung thought.

The party also marked its anniversary by announcing an internal investigation of its members, many who supported or even joined the pro-democracy marches. Some party branches, the *People's Daily* said, were "weak and lax, and did not carry out their roles as fortresses in battle. . . . It is necessary to strictly check on the performance of every party member in the struggle."

XI

Aftermath

Among the main targets of the conservative leadership that summer and fall of 1989 were corruption, pornography and the United States.

The NPC, China's legislature, as it tried to restore order to the stricken nation, expressed "strong indignation" over U.S. sanctions imposed after June 4 and the *People's Daily* railed against "those people in the American Congress who deliberately distort the facts and interfere with China's internal affairs." The daily added that "they never talk about the suppression of the black human rights movement or student protests against the Vietnam War in their country, but sanctimoniously claim to be guardians of 'human rights.'"

The newspaper *Economic Reference* said the Voice of America, "clearly reflecting the American government's policy, started the most disgusting rumors, fanning the flames, and even acted as a contact between reactionary forces in China and the United States."

The rhetoric had cooled off by the end of 1989 and Chinese officials stressed they wanted to restore their badly strained relations with the United States. But they insisted that they were the wronged party and Washington must take the initiative in improving ties. Deng, in a meeting with former President Richard Nixon, accused the United States of becoming "involved too deeply" in the seven-week democracy movement. He said China was the "real victim" of the spring events and "it is unjust to reprove China."

The vitriolic against the United States seemed excessive in that the Bush Administration sought a measured response to the June violence so as not to

Officers of the People's Revolutionary Army carry a wreath to honor their comrades killed and wounded during the assault on students in Tiananmen Square.

seriously disrupt economic relations and generally had acted in concert with other Western countries in suspending high-level contacts and imposing sanctions. But human rights issues had always been a sore point in Sino-U.S. relations, with China bristling with outrage every time American leaders, particularly Congress, brought up such questions as Tibet and political prisoners.

The war on corruption was an attempt to show that this issue, a dominant theme during the student-led protests, had not been buried when the students were crushed. Anti-corruption campaigns had been played out again and again in China's history and had invariably failed. The system, with its one-party rule devoid of checks and balances, its chronic shortages of goods and, more recently, its two-track pricing system, was a natural breeding ground for the corrupt. The practice of officials cornering scarce materials at low state-set prices and then selling them for big profits on the free markets and black markets was rampant.

The government in mid-August gave state employees involved in embezzling, bribery or speculation until October 31 to turn themselves in and receive lenient treatment. Those who fail to confess, it said, "will be punished severely."

The most graphic example of the government's approach to economic criminals came in mid-September when a group of allegedly corrupt officials was herded before an audience of twenty-four hundred in a city gymnasium. Television clips of the sentencing showed two men being given the death sentence and led off for immediate execution. Four others who had committed similar crimes but had turned themselves in to police and confessed their guilt were allowed to go free. The prosecutors' office said thirty-six thousand people, including nine thousand, three hundred Party members, surrendered to police over the ten-week period to avail

311

themselves of lenient treatment.

State-level leaders, trying to shake off the general impression that they were mired in luxury and privilege, were told to drive Chinese-made cars rather than Mercedes, forego their special supplies of food and rounds of banqueting, cut back on travel abroad and, along with other state employees, give up their summer vacations. Two state-owned conglomerates, including one linked to Deng's son, Deng Pufang, were shut down after being accused of involvement in speculation. The children and spouses of Politburo members and top officials in the State Council were ordered to quit their jobs in trading companies and other commercial ventures.

The government promised the anti-corruption campaign would capture some "tigers," or senior cadres, and a few were entrapped. The vice chairman of Xinjiang province in the far west was stripped of his post for speculating in raw materials together with a woman member of a Beijing drama troupe with whom he had an illicit relationship. The top trade official in Guangdong province was sacked after being accused of using $57,500 in public funds to buy an imported car and portable telephones for his private use.

In September, Liang Xiang, reformist governor of the island of Hainan in the south, was dismissed from his posts for helping his wife and son amass personal wealth and arranging for his son's illegal residence in Hong Kong. The government insisted

A teacher and her schoolchildren are directed by a martial law officer in Tiananmen Square during the October 1989 celebration marking the founding of the Communist youth organization Young Pioneers forty years earlier.

there were no political overtones in Liang's purge, although Liang was closely associated with Zhao Ziyang's reforms and, like Zhao, had urged restraint in dealing with the pro-democracy student movement in Hainan. The Beijing government was also moving to assert more controls over Hainan, which was given wide latitude over economic matters under Zhao's coastal development policy.

The anti-pornography drive also took on a decidedly political flavor, with new Politburo Standing Committee member Li Ruihuan, who headed the campaign, linking the spread of literature and videos devoted to sex and violence to the bourgeois liberal tendencies of the pro-Zhao camp. Among the banned books were political works by Zhao, Fang Lizhi and his wife Li Shuxian, journalist Liu Binyan, dissident political scientist Yan Jiaqi, economist Chen Yizi, private entrepreneur Wan Runnan and documentary writer Su Xiaokang. Liu was living in the United States and the others—Yan, Chen, Wan and Su—fled the country after June 4 and were instrumental in the founding in Paris in late September of the anti-government Federation for Democracy in China.

At the end of August, the *China Daily* reported that three million copies of "reactionary and pornographic" books and magazines had been confiscated and nine million copies of books and more than ninety thousand videotapes had been taken off the market in the clean-up campaign.

In Lanzhou, authorities burned pornographic and illegal publications and tapes in the square in front of the railway station. Authorities in Shanghai said thirty thousand books were reduced to five tons of pulp. "The point of eliminating poisonous weeds is to raise fragrant flowers," the *Guangming Daily* said in a commentary. "Without cleaning out the 'cultural garbage' which has flooded the country, socialist culture cannot develop."

Although official reports of arrests and trials abruptly stopped in July, the government made clear the crackdown was continuing by revealing several particularly harsh prison terms given to dissenters. On July 13 a court in Dalian sentenced Xiao Bin, a

Workers spruce up Beijing's Gate of Heavenly Peace in preparation for the celebrations of the fortieth anniversary of the People's Republic of China on October 1. The area in front of the gate, and Tiananmen Square which it faces, was still guarded by troops under martial law in August 1989.

forty-two-year-old office worker, to ten years in prison for telling an ABC television crew that twenty thousand people were killed in the military assault to recapture Tiananmen Square. China Central Television apparently had intercepted the unedited tape of the streetside interview with Xiao as ABC was sending it by satellite to its New York headquarters. Two women who led police to the man on the tape were commended and given cash rewards.

A high school teacher who splashed paint on a portrait of Mao Tse-tung during the student demonstrations was sentenced to life in prison. A student at a Hangzhou university was imprisoned for nine years for allegedly spreading rumors to the Voice of America. Police in Chengdu executed six people who had joined the June 4-6 riots in that provincial capital, bringing to at least eighteen, and probably many more, the number put to death for participating in anti-government demonstrations.

The government was also driving home its line on the "counter-revolutionary rebellion" with a hard-hitting propaganda campaign.

Books and carefully edited television documentaries and videotapes were produced depicting crowds attacking soldiers and burning military vehicles. Deleted were the sounds of troops opening fire, and demonstration scenes of students calling for an end to official corruption or expressing their patriotic feelings.

Military officers were dispatched around the country to give lectures to children and other groups about the heroic efforts of the PLA against the anti-government rabble. A major exhibition on the quelling of the rebellion opened at the military museum in Beijing. Hundreds of thousands of schoolchildren and workers were bused to the museum for a look at burned-out tanks, student documents and artifacts advocating democracy and hundreds of photographs critical of the demonstrators and favorable to the military.

The big ideological crunch came on universities, with most campuses ordering students to return from summer vacations early for a month of political education classes. Students spent long hours reciting the June 9 speech of Deng Xiaoping and Jiang Zemin's National Day speech and reading *People's Daily* editorials describing how students were manipulated by "a small handful" of people trying to overthrow the socialist system and the Communist Party.

"We must not allow the lecture platforms of socialist universities to be used for the wanton dissemination of bourgeois liberal views," Education Minister Li Tieying said in a speech to educators. "It

would mean a total failure for our education system if students have good professional knowledge but are opposed to socialism and alien from the people," Premier Li added at the meeting.

The hardest hit was Beijing University, where the freshman class was cut from twenty-one hundred to only eight hundred and all first-year students were sent for a year of study at a military school southwest of Beijing. The president of the university, Ding Shisun, was relieved of his post, although officials denied he was being punished for tolerating student dissent.

The government also denied any political overtones in the decision to remove Wang Meng, a freethinking novelist, from his post as Culture Minister. However, the replacement of Wang, who had been hailed as a bridge between artists seeking freedom of expression and the government demanding cultural discipline, with He Jingzhi, the conservative deputy chief of the party Propaganda Department, sent out unmistakable signals.

The campaign against bourgeois liberalism was also marked by a government decision that all state-level employees who had graduated university in 1985 or later would have to spend a year or two working at the "grassroots"—rural or provincial—level to give them a better grounding in China's realities and help them resist the temptations of Western liberal thought.

Although the government insisted it would continue to dispatch students abroad, scholarships for undergraduates dried up and foreign study was generally limited to short-term trips by scholars and researchers. Only "politically and professionally mature" people should participate in foreign study programs, said Premier Li.

The conservative leaders who consolidated power in the months after June 4 made clear that the open door policy remained intact in so far as China still needed foreign money and technology. But they also showed a xenophobic mistrust of the outside world, particularly the West, which they accused of abetting forces to overthrow the government in China.

Vice Minister of Education He Dongchang, in a variation of Deng's saying that a few flies will inevitably enter an open window, urged that China erect a "wire screen" across its open window to the outside world to prevent "flies and worms" from getting in.

Attacks on countries that had opposed its harsh crackdown on dissent were frequent and bitter. When the seven leading industrialized nations urged China to cease actions against those claiming their legitimate rights to democracy and liberty, China retorted that they had made "groundless charges, which only represent gross interference in China's internal affairs." Foreign Minister Qian Qichen said in New York in October that China wanted good relations with the United States, but the U.S. government "took the lead in imposing sanctions and exerting pressure on China" and it was now up to the United States to take steps to end the hostility.

Some of the most strident criticism, reminiscent of Cultural Revolution rhetoric, came after France allowed Chinese pro-democracy delegates from fifteen countries to gather in Paris in late September to form the Federation of Democracy in China. The dissident group was led by pro-democracy activists who had managed to escape to the West after the June crackdown, including student leader Wu'er Kaixi, political scientist Yan Jiaqi, economist Chen Yizi and computer company entrepreneur Wan Runnan.

France, the Foreign Ministry said in a statement, was guilty of a "brutal trample" of the principles of mutual respect. "It is indeed a rare case in international relations that the government of a country brazenly supports activities on its territory by a handful of foreigners aimed at opposing and subverting the government of a foreign country."

Foreign businessmen who fled the country in June drifted back through the summer months, but it was hardly business as usual. The majority returned to fulfill contracts and carry out administrative matters, but there was little talk of expansion or new investment in the foreseeable future. There was a strong reluctance to do business with a government that, despite its protestations that the open door policy lived on, was accusing foreigners of subverting the country and was purging those who had been in the forefront of economic reform.

Most businessmen said that of greater concern than the political turmoil was the economic retrenchment that had begun in the fall of 1988. Foreign economists agreed that China needed austerity measures to hold down excessive growth and rein in inflation, but feared that the government, by failing to adequately deal with price and supply problems, was leading the nation into a protacted period of stagflation.

Under the austerity measures, factories were unable to obtain the credit needed to buy raw materials or equipment, and many small factories were failing to fulfill export contracts or supply foreign joint ventures with needed parts and goods. Foreigners also worried that Beijing, in reasserting central controls over industry and trade, was depriving officials at the local level of the authority needed to do business in timely and rational ways.

The government acknowledged that about one million of the nation's eighteen million rural enterprises had gone out of business and that the number of private businessmen had dropped from fourteen million at the beginning of the year to twelve million. Government officials said such contraction was inevitable because of the proliferation of inefficient and illegal businesses, but little was said about how the government would cope with the millions of people losing jobs because of the economic slowdown.

The Communist Party Central Committee, meeting in November 1989, committed the nation to at least two more years of belt-tightening. There was no mention of new reform initiatives, and a clear message that reforms would take a back seat to "rectification," the drive to reassert state controls and restore large state enterprises to their rightful place as the engine of China's socialist economy.

The ideologues in Beijing were putting the squeeze on small township enterprises and private entrepreneurs, the most vital sectors of the economy. Premier Li said private entrepreneurs would continue to play a supplemental role in the economy, but there must be no challenge to the supremacy of public ownership. It's all right to learn the advanced management systems of capitalism, the *Economic Daily* said, but private ownership must not be allowed to spread in China because it causes class confrontation, profiteering and exploitation of workers.

Meanwhile the government continued to spend billions of dollars to subsidize money-losing, inefficient state-run industries. The nation's budget deficit was becoming increasingly hard to handle, and the slow growth in exports raised the possibility that the government would run out of foreign exchange reserves and have difficulty repaying its foreign debt, which by late 1989 stood at $44 billion, more than double the amount of 1986.

China was also losing needed foreign exchange because of the collapse of its tourist industry after the military attack on Beijing. Chinese tourism officials said that revenues for 1989 would be only about $1.3 billion, half the target of $2.6 billion and compared to $2.2 billion in 1988. Armed police replaced soldiers on Tiananmen Square at the end of October and the visible military presence in the city was sharply reduced.

Li Peng told a visiting Japanese delegation that hundreds of weapons had been stolen from troops during the June battles, and anti-government forces still pose a threat to the city's security.

Most China watchers, however, believed that the most serious threat to the Party and government was not a few citizens with guns hidden away but the precarious health of Deng Xiaoping, the paramount leader. There were widespread reports that Deng, who turned eighty-five on August 22, was suffering from prostate cancer and did not have long to live. As the summer months passed and Deng failed to appear, Hong Kong and Taiwan news organizations reported that Deng had slipped into a coma, or was already dead.

But on September 16, Deng appeared, looking tanned and fit, at a meeting with Chinese-American T.D. Lee, a Nobel Prize-winning physicist from Columbia University. Deng said: "The recent turmoil has taught us a major lesson. After the turmoil, all of us have become sober-minded." The octogenarian appeared frequently in the coming weeks, reinforcing the impression that he was in good physical shape and remained in political control.

But the jockeying for post-Deng power had already begun, with the focus on the Central Military Commission. The November Central Committee meeting, the first since the June session that purged Zhao, accepted the resignation of Deng as chairman of the powerful commission, his last official party post. Deng, certain to continue as paramount leader as long as he is in good health, managed to craft a compromise whereby Jiang Zemin succeeded him as chairman while the ambitious eighty-two-year-old President Yang Shangkun was named first vice chairman, the post formerly held by Zhao Ziyang. Yang's younger brother, PLA General Political Department chief Yang Baibing, also won promotion to secretary general of the military commission.

Yang, a main mover in the decision to bring troops into Beijing, was likely to be a key player in any future power struggle following Deng's death. His hardline views on political dissent made him an ally with Premier Li, and he headed a powerful faction in the military.

Deng, Li Peng and others, meanwhile, were referring to party boss Jiang Zemin as the "core" of the new leadership. Jiang's position as heir apparent, however, was a tenuous one at best. A technocrat who had spent his past four years in Shanghai, Jiang had no power base in Beijing and lacked contacts with the military, always a crucial factor in Chinese politics. Despite his apparent anointment by Deng, many Chinese and foreign observers saw Jiang as an interim leader, similar to Mao's designated successor Hua Guofeng, who would be shuffled

to the side when the next power struggle took place.

Jiang's chosen role, as of the fall of 1989, was as spokesman for the hardline stance emphasizing ideological orthodoxy and economic retrenchment. At a rare news conference for Chinese and foreign reporters, Jiang eschewed an opportunity to soften the harsh line on dissent. Asked if the "Tiananmen tragedy" could have been averted, Jiang answered: "We believe it was not a tragedy. Tiananmen was a counter-revolutionary rebellion opposing the Communist Party leaders and seeking to overthrow the socialist system." He refused to rule out the possibility that student leaders arrested for their pro-democracy activities would be executed.

Jiang's, and the party's, policy was defined more precisely three days later when Jiang delivered an eighty-minute speech at the Great Hall of the People to celebrate forty years of Communist rule.

China, Jiang said, is involved in "a serious class struggle that concerns the life and death of our party, state and nation." He called for constant vigilance, saying, "we must carry the struggle through to the end, educate and unite with the overwhelming majority, isolate and attack the handful of hostile elements, make a thorough investigation into all counter-revolutionary scheming, remove hidden perils and draw profound lessons."

"Only socialism can save China," Jiang said, adding that a return to capitalism would "give rise to a capitalist class by fattening it with the sweat and toil of the laboring people" and reduce most Chinese to "extreme poverty." Calls for a multi-party system are "extremely destructive to our cause and liable to be exploited by a small handful of reactionaries," he said.

The speech became mandatory reading for all Chinese, with factories, offices, schools and research institutes requiring people to spend hours in political education classes reciting passages and praising Jiang's "penetrating analysis" of the situation in China.

The stultifying political atmosphere continued through October 1, National Day and the fortieth anniversary of the day Mao Tse-tung stood on the rostrum of Tiananmen Gate and declared the founding of the People's Republic of China.

There were no military parades, as on the thirty-fifth anniversary in 1984, because memories of the military's bloody takeover of the city were still too fresh. But troops and police maintained a heavy presence, spotchecking people's IDs, detaining and expelling from the city non-Beijing residents and keeping a close watch for acts of protest or sabotage. A large section of central Beijing was closed off on the evening of October 1 to keep all but invited guests away from Tiananmen, scene of a massive dance and fireworks show. While Deng and other top leaders watched from the same rostrum where Mao once stood, several hundred thousand dancers, many of whom were factory and office workers chosen for their political reliability, went through the motions against the backdrop of a spectacular fireworks display. In a pointed jibe at the crushed student movement, the authorities erected a temporary statue, depicting a worker, farmer, intellectual and soldier, on the same spot where the "Goddess of Democracy" had once stood. The show was boycotted by Western ambassadors because of the continuing strain in post-June relations.

The well-scrubbed city was adorned with one million potted flowers, and red flags and red banners draped from hundreds of buildings. Most of the banners were strongly political, calling on people to love the motherland, to support socialism and the great Communist Party, and to celebrate the quelling of the "counter-revolutionary rebellion." Volumes of paper and hours of TV time were spent every day detailing the achievements of the past forty years in industry and agriculture and reminding the people that it was all due to the socialist system and the Communist Party.

Official celebrations of the past, however, could not hide the gnawing uncertainties about the future. The much-acclaimed triumph over the counter-revolutionary rebellion had been a hollow one at best. The students were back on campus, obediently shuffling off to political education classes. But their hatred of the government, and their despair over their own futures and the future of the nation, were deep. The chances that students would take to the streets again appeared slim, but soon there were fears that the next time the students and their supporters, having seen the government's capacity for brutal repression, would abandon their peaceful tactics for more violent confrontation.

China also cannot ignore the radical changes taking place in the Soviet Union and other socialist nations of East Europe. Its own people's aspirations for a more open and free society are bound to be stimulated by the events in the Soviet Union, Poland, Hungary and East Germany. The Communist Party, in accusing the Tiananmen advocates of democratic reform of treason, insist that one-party rule is undisputable and multiparty elections will never take place in China. But the Chinese, always sensitive to the lessons of history, know that no dynasty lasts forever.

The first decade of Deng Xiaoping's reforms has been a heady one for China. Farmers who at the end of the Cultural Revolution had barely enough to eat now own color TVs and motorcycles. In the cities the newly-rich—taxi drivers, private vendors and traders—show off their designer clothes at the discos and luxurious joint venture hotels that didn't exist ten years before. Hundreds of thousands of Chinese have traveled overseas as students, businessmen, athletes and even tourists, an idea inconceivable a decade before when travel even outside one's village was rare. Regardless of the cycles of economic confusion and political repression, the vast majority of Chinese have more money, lead more diversified lives and have more freedom of movement than they've ever had before.

The decade of the 1990s, however, will provide far more challenges and difficulties for the Chinese people and their leaders. The first aspects of reform—returning the land to the family farmer and making wages better reflect work performance—were largely uncontroversial and produced quick results. The next stage, making the land more productive, eliminating price subsidies and revamping doddering state-owned industry without disturbing the socialist sensibilities of old guard ideologues, will be far more of a struggle. Rising consumer expectations will be nearly impossible to meet as the nation strains to overcome its serious lack of energy and raw materials and poor transportation and communication systems.

The population, now 1.1 billion, will be 1.3 billion by the end of the century and it is far from certain that the nation's farmers have the ability to feed that many people. The education system is in shambles because of lack of money, unemployment is growing by the millions as the government tries to rationalize the economy and health and welfare services are deteriorating as more people slip outside the umbrella of state protection.

As the leaders in Beijing constantly point out, China needs stability and unity to face the daunting tasks ahead. The vast majority of Chinese, a patriotic, loyal and hard-working people, are eager to cooperate. But the days of blind obedience to a political party, an infallible leader or an ideology, appear to be over.

Photo by AP photographer Jeff Widener is of a lone young man, later identified as Wang Weilin, defying a column of army tanks on Changan Avenue in front of the Beijing Hotel. The prize-winning photograph has been called the "symbolic photo of the year."

Widener watched from his perch high above the street in Beijing as tanks clanked across the concrete. It was just after the Chinese troops shot and killed demonstrating students in the Chinese capital. As four tanks rolled down the street, a single young man stepped out in front of them.

Because of the distance, Widener could not hear what the man shouted at the soldiers who drove the tanks. But the tanks stopped. Within minutes, several other people ran in from the side. They talked to the man and then ran off with him. The tanks' engines revved up and they continued down the street.

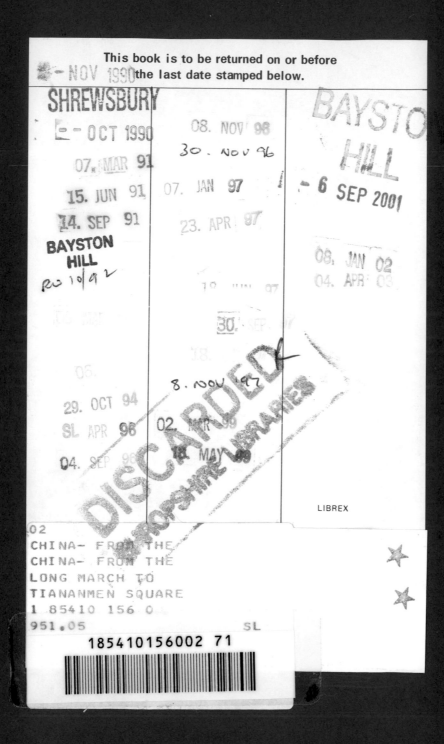